Some Unsung Black Revolutionary Voices & Visions from Pre-Colony to Post-Independence & Beyond

Edited by

Bill F. Ndi

Langaa Research & Publishing CIG
Mankon, Bamenda

Publisher

Langaa RPCIG
Langaa Research & Publishing Common Initiative Group
P.O. Box 902 Mankon
Bamenda
North West Region
Cameroon
Langaagrp@gmail.com
www.langaa-rpcig.net

Distributed in and outside N. America by African Books Collective
orders@africanbookscollective.com
www.africanbookscollective.com

ISBN-10: 9956-551-11-2

ISBN-13: 978-9956-551-11-8

© Bill F. Ndi 2021

About the Authors

Editor

Bill F. Ndi, Professor of Modern Languages, Communication and Philosophy at Tuskegee University, Tuskegee, Alabama, USA, earned his Dual Doctorate from the University of Cergy-Pontoise in 2001. He is a poet, playwright, storyteller, literary critic, translator, historian of ideas and mentalities as well as an academic who has held teaching positions in several universities in Australia, France and elsewhere. His areas of teaching and research comprise among others English Languages and literatures, French, Professional, Technical and Creative Writing, World Literatures, Applied/ Historical Linguistics, Literary History, Media and Communication Studies, Peace/Quaker Studies and Conflict Resolution, History of Internationalism, History of Ideas and Mentalities, Translation & Translatology, 17th Century and Contemporary Cultural Studies. He has published extensively in these areas. His publications include numerous scholarly works on Early Quakerism and translation of Early Quaker writings. He has also published poetry and plays in both the French and the English languages. Professor Bill F. Ndi has 25 published volumes of poetry of which six (6) are in French, a play and 4 works in translation. He is co-editor of *Outward Evil, Inward Battle: Human Memory in Literature* with Adaku T. Ankumah, Benjamin Hart Fishkin, and Festus Fru Ndeh as well as co-editor of *Fears, Doubts, and Joys of not Belonging, The Repressed Expressed,* and *Living (In)Dependence: Critical Perspectives on Global Interdependence* with Adaku T. Ankumah and Benjamin Hart Fishkin. His most recent edited work is *Secret, Silences, and Betrayals.* Also, he has served as a National Endowment for the Humanities' scholar.

Contributors

Adaku T. Ankumah, Department Chair and Professor of English at Tuskegee University, received her PhD in Comparative Literature from the University of Wisconsin-Madison with a minor in drama. Her dissertation and initial research interests focused on revolutionary playwrights from the African Diaspora, such as Kenyan Ngugi wa Thiong'o, Martiniquais writer

Aimé Césaire, and African American Amiri Baraka, who use their creative efforts to work for the destruction of what they consider to be the colonial/capitalist foundation of post-colonial Africa. Ngugi's play *The Trial of Dedan Kimathi*, a play that examines the arrest and trial of one of the famous leaders of the Mau Mau revolt against the British in Kenya in the 1950's, has been the subject of her published research. She has also done research on the role of women in revolutionary theatre, voicelessness of African women, and gender and politics in the works of African women authors like Mariama Bâ, Ama Ata Aidoo and Tsitsi Dangarembga. Professor Ankumah's recent research interest includes the writings of women in the African diaspora. This includes research on memory in literature and its role in helping those dealing with painful, fragmented pasts forge a wholesome future in Edwidge Danticat's *The Dew Breaker*. She has also examined memory and resistance in the poetry of South African performer and writer Gcina Mhlophe. Her notable edited work is *Nomenclatural Poetization and Globalization*. Also, she co-edited, with Bill F. Ndi, Benjamin Hart Fishkin and Festus Fru Ndeh, *Outward Evil Inward Battle: Human Memory in Literature,* and with Bill F Ndi and Benjamin Hart Fiskin: *Fears, Doubts, and Joys of not Belonging, The Repressed Expressed,* and *Living (In)Dependence: Critical Perspectives on Global Interdependence.*

Andrew T. Ngeh is Associate Professor of written African Literature. He has been teaching African Poetry, the African Novel, Critical Theory and Scientific Writing in the University of Buea for the past nineteen years. He has published quite extensively in peer-reviewed journals nationally and internationally. Andrew T. Ngeh has more than thirty-seven articles published in peer-reviewed journals, nationally and internationally. In addition to that, he has four books to his credit: *Power Dialectics in Anglophone Cameroonian Poetry* (2014), *Critical Issues in Anglophone Cameroonian Poetry,* (2017), *Drama and Commitment: Degendered Bodies and Re-gendered Minds,* (2019), and *Writing a Critical Essay: A Practical Guide for Students,* (2020). In 2019, he co-edited a book entitled, *Rethinking Language and Literature in a Changing World* published by Cambridge Scholars Publishing. His recent academic outing was in July 2020 with the publication of *Writing a Critical Essay: A Practical Guide for Students* published by Generis Publishing.

Benjamin Hart Fishkin, Associate Professor of English at Tuskegee University specializes in teaching Nineteenth Century British Literature. He holds a Ph.D. from the University of Alabama where he served as a Junior Fellow in The Blount Undergraduate Initiative. Prior to earning his Doctorate from the University of Alabama in May of 2009, he obtained a BA in English and Film from the University of Michigan, Ann Arbor, and an MA from Miami University, Oxford, Ohio where he examined the interest of Charles Dickens in the theatre and how the stage influenced his novel writing. He has published *The Undependable Bonds of Blood: The Unanticipated Problems of Parenthood in the Novels of Henry James.* He co-edited *Outward Evil Inward Battle: Human Memory in Literature* with Adaku T. Ankumah, Bill F. Ndi, and Festus Fru Ndeh, and *Fears, Doubts and Joys of not Belonging The Repressed Expressed,* and *Living (In)Dependence: Critical Perspectives on Global Interdependence* with Bill F. Ndi and Adaku T. Ankumah. Benjamin Hart Fishkin is presently working on the concept of chaos, upheaval, and tragedy in a comprehensive study of the novels of the Southern Cameroonian author, Emmanuel Fru Doh. Besides this growing interest in Anglophone Cameroon or British Southern Cameroons literature, his recent research interests include the problems of marriage, family, and relationships in the age globalization.

Bill F. Ndi teaches at Tuskegee University. He has numerous scholarly publications on Early Quakerism and translation of Early Quaker writings. He has also published extensively in both the French and the English languages. These publications include scholarly articles and book chapters, poetry, and plays. Professor Bill F. Ndi has 25 volumes of poetry of which six (6) are in French, a play and 4 works in translation as well as 1 edited volume of critical essays.

Derick Hendricks hails from St. Thomas, United States Virgin Islands. He received his Ph.D. in History from Morgan State University, his Master Arts in History from Texas Southern University, and his Bachelor of Arts in Social Sciences with a concentration in History and Political Science from the University of the Virgin Islands. He has been a Lecturer in the Department of History, Geography, and Museum Studies at Morgan State University for the past 14 years. His research interest includes African Diaspora History, the Black Power Movement in the United States and in the Caribbean, and the Vietnam War.

Elisabeth N. M Ayuk-Etang is an academic, a scholar, a gender advocate and an ecofeminist critic. She teaches at the University of Buea, Cameroon. She holds a PhD in Black Women's Writings from the University of Yaoundé 1, Cameroon. She has published extensively in peer-reviewed journals and authored book chapters on the status of the Black woman in Africa. Her research interest is on Black Women Studies, Women and Development in Africa, Ecofeminism and Sustainable Development in Black Communities. Her notable publications appeared in Bill F. Ndi, Benjamin Hart Fishkin, and Adaku T. Ankumah *Living (In)Dependence: Critical Perspectives on Global Interdependence* (2019). They include the following: "Women, Dependence, Independence, and Land Usage in The Cameroons: An Ecofeminist Reading of Bole Butake's *Lake God* and *And Palm Wine Will Flow*" (2019); "Migration, Dependence, Freedom, and Independence in Ifeoma Chinwuba's *Merchant of Flesh*" (2019). She is currently working on "The Place of the Woman in Higher Education Institutions (HEIs) in Africa." She is a recipient of many prestigious awards including the University of Michigan African Presidential Scholars (UMAPS), fellowship.

John Tilghman is an Associate Professor of History at Tuskegee University. He is a native of Baltimore, Maryland who holds a Bachelor's degree in U.S. history from Coppin State University and a Master's of Arts degree and Ph. D in U.S. history from Howard University. His publications and research center on U.S. urban history, postwar black freedom struggles in the U.S., social movements in the African Diaspora, and the writings of Walter Rodney.

Mark Henderson is an Associate Professor of English currently working at Tuskegee University. He earned his Ph.D. at Auburn University with concentrations in American literature and psychoanalytic theory. Research and publication-wise, his interests include the American Gothic, American modernism, American film, and Afrofuturism. The concentration for the M.A. that he earned from the University of Louisiana at Monroe is creative writing.

Thomas Jing, novelist, scholar, and researcher was born in Ndop in the Cameroons. He attended Sacred Heart College Mankon-Bamenda and CCAS Kumba before enrolling at the University of Yaoundé where he obtained a B.A. in History. After a stint as a History and French language teacher at Government Secondary School Nyasoso, he left for Canada to study Translation at the University of Montreal. Equipped with an M.A. in translation, he returned to Cameroon and worked at the Ministry of Livestock, Fisheries and Animal Industries as senior translator and service head for documentation and archives. During this time, he wrote articles for a number of local newspapers and magazines, notably *Cameroon Post and Cameroon Life*. Amid growing political tension in Cameroon, he left for South Africa where he worked with the Jesuit Refugee Services as spokesperson for refugees and asylum seekers and Editor of Kwanza, the organization's English-French bilingual newsletter. He later left for Canada where he did a PhD at the University of Regina in Saskatchewan. His PhD dissertation focused on using African folkdances for community organization and educational promotion in North American diaspora black community. He has published two novels, one in English (Tale of an African woman) and the other in French (Testament d'un patriote exécuté). He has also contributed articles for scholarly reviews. His main research interest is African folkdances and education among diaspora blacks.

Dedication

Some Unsung Black Revolutionary Voices and Visions is a collection of academic essays entirely dedicated to Dr. Mami Rubber aka Dr. Mrs. Hannah Kah Ndi née Fokum, an unsung revolutionary whose voice and vision raised number ones in all walks of life before she rested in the Lord on 3 January 2021 at the Adventist Hospital in Silver Spring, Maryland USA.

Victory is won

The day we accepted to be born
Was the same day we our victory won
Over death who would she marked an end
To this life we now savor and trend
Knowing we'll need to go and roost home
Not before we have the crannies combed
Elsewhere, we have laughed and should laugh
For death is nothing but a riffraff
Gloating with sole joy to still our joy
A thing that should not make us coy.
With our quintessence immaterial,
To her we give all the material
Laughingly as we know our essence
Present with our material absence.

Table of Contents

Section II: North America & The Caribbean

Introduction

Bill F. Ndi (Editor)

Throughout history, revolutionary thinkers and leaders in Africa and the African Diaspora have voiced their discontent and rejection of the exploitative and most often dehumanizing conditions to which Africans and their descendants in the Diaspora have been subjected. These visionaries almost always end up being assassinated because they advocate a revolutionary transformation of their respective countries. They understand that while political decolonization has its appeal and importance, of equal importance is the question of economic and social decolonization as well as inclusivity that warrants participation from all stakeholders of their respective nation's wellbeing. Revolutionaries are not content with just political and diplomatic sloganizing. They involve themselves in the mobilization and education of the masses in their respective countries. They equally understand this necessity for at least two fundamental reasons: firstly, centuries of black extraction, enslavement, exploitation, and misrepresentation by European imperialism and later along with American capitalist collaboration have manipulated and exacerbated ethnic/class divisions in their societies and continue to do so; secondly, were these nefarious intrusions left unchecked, the countries will remain rife for further exploitation.

Therefore, for revolutionaries, their task was, is and will be to wage an unrelenting struggle against all the internal and external factors and barriers that stood, stand, or may stand in the way of emancipation of their respective countries. Moreover, their struggles focus on the complete liberation and emancipation of Africa and the African Diaspora in order to pave the way for meaningful autonomy with development. Concretely, they take colonialism, neo-colonialism, imperialism, tribalism, classism and other forms of separatism and exploitation as the main hindrances to the liberation struggle of all Africans. Determined to free their people from the yoke of imperialism, colonialism, and neo-colonialism, most of them utilize pedagogies, activism, writing vigor, artistry, etc. that stress revolutionary transformation. Their undertaking dwells in the best of Africana tradition and redefines greatly sought-after change as liberation that culminates in indisputable development of the people of Africa and her Diaspora.

Theirs is a call to the triumphant and the humiliated, the victors and the vanquished, the oppressors and the oppressed, to always look back into the past for pathways to freedom for all. A call much more pressing especially in the present globalizing dispensation of the 21st century world in order to make the world a biblical paradise devoid of oppression, subjugation, domination, enslavement, and any other form of coercion. Therefore, for the peoples of African descent, there is need for a worldview of liberation not only based upon their common history of subjugation, but also on the African origin and blackness of the oppressed. This treatise is a joint effort that endeavors to highlight the strength of a group in overcoming the bane of oppression heaped upon the black man. This endeavor finds its genesis in the fact that hegemons seem to be a well-coordinated in their effort to keep blacks ignorant of their own history and to pit them one against another; and they have had the black space chopped up into unrecognizable geographies—spheres of influences in diplomatic parlance—which turn the black man against himself. It is in these unrecognizable geographies that there have been and are individuals who distinguish themselves in their vision to overcome their oppressed stead. They live in such black spaces, and when they part this world, they leave a far-reaching impact on generations of

African yet unborn. The black world having had its share, not to say an overdose, of oppression has produced a good number of revolutionaries and visionaries whose voices could not, and can no longer, be silenced.

Of the revolutionaries who must be remembered for their significant contribution towards the liberation of the subjugated black man, are equally a significant number of them whose contributions and legacy through writing and activism have not been given their due credit; or in short, theirs have been left in the shadows and unsung. This collection of essays teases out of academics from different disciplinary areas, their take on such unsung revolutionaries. Finding out who they are and bringing them to light; in short, who are they? What were or are their contributions? How far-reaching are the effects of their contributions? Or, why were or have their contributions not been given their due attention? Is this as a result of the conscious cultivation of ignorance that has birthed agnotology? In the current global dispensation, do governments operate as they should? Does their visionary stance on liberation as the fundamental basis for development still belong or fit satisfactorily in the post-colonial world of the twenty first century? Or, again, has it already been achieved with Africans and Diasporic Africans now swimming in the pool of development with liberation? The various scholars draw from historical, sociological, psychological, anthropological, literary, political, economic, scientific, international, and other perspectives of the revolutionary voices and visions from pre-colonial to post independent Africa and its Diaspora to address the questions.

The object of this book is to revisit how these voices and visions, or the lack thereof, have positioned Africa and its Diaspora on the global map especially in the 21st century globalized world. And also of note is what needs to be retained of their voices and visions. It would as such elucidate the authors' assumption of the role of scholars as detectives and physicians in an attempt to make order out of the chaos/chaotic order that resulted/result from opposition to the visionary stance of the Pan-Africanist intellectuals, writers, community organizers, musicians, business magnate, religious, moral and spiritual leaders, and political and scientific giants. Exploring heralds covering the periods from pre-colony to post-independence and beyond, the respective chapters shed light on these questions and highlight why these heralds remain vital and topical to the black struggle to free black people from the shackles of subjugation, oppression, enslavement, and summary executions in the age of Black Lives Matter movement. It is worth noting that the revolutionaries and visionaries, here examined, all seem to concur there is no successful subjugation without expressed or implicit complicity of the oppressed or subjugated. Theirs is a call to lead a successful opposition to oppression and subjugation for the black world to breathe freedom; a God-given one for that matter.

Striving to give these revolutionary authors, activists, historians, pop icons and their works their proper and well-deserved place in the context of 21st century globalization and hegemonic rule of the dominant and domineering powers, this attempt to revisit and reframe such revolutionaries is a timely reminder that our past must not only inform our present but shape our future. The consequence of this neglect of the past may lead the formerly enslaved, colonized, and neo-colonized peoples heading towards a repeat of a disastrous history. Ignoring the endeavors and struggles of forebears to free themselves from the shackles of bondage in every shape and form is a challenge only to be overcome by a thorough knowledge of such a past. This publication therefore aims at filling such a lacuna that would push black people further into a complicit self-subjugating role if left unattended. It also bridges the rift in-between the hegemon and the dominated as it helps better the understanding of such a relationship.

The postulations herein all seem to hinge on the fact that in the relationship between the enslaver and the enslaved, the colonizer and the colonized, the dominating and the domineered, the controller and the controlled, those holding the shorter end of the leash are all everything but complicit. This is not to say there are no few bad apples willing to trade one of theirs for a plate of rice. In the cases here under study, these torchbearers have stood up and voiced not only the own discontent with the human propensity to reduce their fellow humans to objects of subjugation but have also done so for the discontent of their own people. They do such in hopes, aspirations, and expectations that even if they do not gain freedom for themselves or were killed in the process, future generations of theirs would continue the fight until freedom is the air for all and sundry to breathe. Amongst these freedom fighters are writers, activists, politicians, historians, musicians, community organizers, and moral and religious leaders whose strife is inextricably linked to black emancipation and freedom. In this treatise, special attention has been given to Martin Delany, Sutton E. Griggs, Gebreyessus Hailu, Zora Neale Hurston, Fela Anikulapo-Kuti, Fodeba Keïta, Walter Rodney, the Virgin Island youths of the 60s and 70s, and Francis B. Nyamnjoh. Their legacy, their aspirations, their hopes and expectations, their toils and travails, their strategies and tactics are all buried in their works but must not be buried with them just because they are dead or alive and unattended to.

Following the logic of the geographies of the prevailing cries against Black oppression and persecution and better still the areas of concentration of black populations, *Some Unsung Revolutionary Voices and Visions…* is split into two main sections; viz. Africa, North America and the Caribbean. This is not to say there aren't any black revolutionary voices and visions in other parts of the world not mentioned here. Though a platitude, it is worth mentioning that everywhere there is oppression, there are voices and visions rising and standing up against the oppressors. Through committed activism and unrelenting vocalization of general discontent and pervasive repressive malaise of their peoples, they push their role in the liberation struggle to a level that challenges moderate thinking so unwilling to embrace untainted egalitarianism. Having postulated in *The Repressed Expressed* that in the relationship between the dominant and the dominated, the dominant very often erects obstacles on the path of publishing truth. In the case of revolutionaries, their activism, their accomplishments, and life's works are either buried, (mis)represented, or distorted and drowned in the cacophony of colonial, imperial, neo-colonial, and globalization *mission civilisatrice*. It is against this backdrop that in the age of "fake news," alternative facts and alternate reality, it becomes more pressing to set the record of buried facts, capable of freeing the world from the yokes of oppression and exploitation, straight. Following the said logic, section one explores revolutionary voices and visions in continental Africa, opening with a chapter, as will be seen, reminiscent of a call which elicit responses on the continent. From thence, section 2 explores revolutionary voices and visions in North America and the Caribbean.

Through an elucidation of Gebreyesus Hailu's novel, *The Conscript,* Bill F. Ndi, in this opening chapter starts by challenging perceived misconceptions that make of subordinates accomplices of their own oppression or subjugation. These misconceptions deprive the oppressed of any sense of worth, especially vis-à-vis their own agency in the process of self-liberation, and self-determination. This chapter underlines the novel as being both the seed of rebellion and the embodiment of rebellion. Also, the far-reaching effects of this rebellion reclaim and recast the oppressed not just as participants who are well versed with the circumstances of their own subjugation but humans who know the vistas available to them to open and gain redemption, liberation and self-determination. In spite of its thinness, it is this chapter's contention that *The Conscript,* is a revolutionary artifact of knowledge recollection, redemption, and reproduction of conduct contrary to perceived complacencies, and ought to have a major impact on the reception, perception, and critical appraisal of African literature. Gebreyesus Hailu is hailed as an author whose imaginative pregnancy and collective consciousness, ought to be counted among African literary giants. The chapter arouses interest in one of the earliest novels written and published in an African language, viz. Tigrinya. The chapter challenges the reader to the often-cited prejudice of subaltern complicity of the African in supporting his/her own affliction. It is such prejudice that grants agency to the subaltern/oppressed only when it comes to the woes s/he suffers. Over and above, the chapter makes a case for Gebreyesus Hailu's *The Conscript* to take its rightful place in the pantheon of revolutionary literary fiction from an African calling for the mentalities of the colonized to be revolutionized.

Chapter two, "Okot p'Bitek's Pro-Feminist Response to the Masculinity Politics and Mythopoetic Action: Poetics of Degendering and Regendering" identifies isolation and acceptance of the social construct of gender and the coercive nature of gendered subjectivities as the kernel of feminist discourse which questions the oppression of the woman in African contemporary society. Ngeh and Ayuk-Etang bring to the fore representation of women in literature, the role of gender in both literary creation, literary criticism as studied in gynocriticism. They establish the connection between gender and various aspects of literary form. And, they demonstrate that in a literary genre, meter encompasses masculine values of heroism, war, and adventure. This androcentric stance compromises the rights of the woman and yields marginalization, alienation and exclusion from socio-cultural activities. Woman, the victim here, is maligned with a sense of inadequacy. The chapter leans on Okot p'Bitek's *Song of Lawino* (1966) and *Song of Ocol* (1970) to problematize and thematize this gender dialectics to extend it beyond the self-referential rhetorical coordinates that underpin postmodern accounts of textual variability. The authors unravel de-gendering and re-gendering as elements that sociologically and culturally contextualize this enshrined and problematic vocabulary of oppression and silence. Informed by both the postcolonial and feminist critical theories, this study argues that men's actions on women constitute a grave danger to a harmonious existence between the two genders. In this light, this chapter submits that it is important to undo gendering to be able to restructure gender relations along more egalitarian and inclusive lines.

In the third chapter "Fela Anikulapo-Kuti: Anticolonial and Postcolonial African Revolutionary, Visionary, and Musician," Thomas Jing explores the man, musician, and activist, Fela Anikulapo-Kuti as a household name in Africa. Also dealt with in this chapter are his origins, the sociopolitical and historical influences that inspired and shaped him, his struggles for the liberation of black people as well as his music and the message it conveyed. It examines his life mainly through an anti and postcolonial lens to show his evolution, from the time he started his career playing highlife music to the period he altered the message of his songs to speak for the voiceless in an increasingly violent and corrupt Nigeria, the African continent, and the world. The chapter also deals with his radical transformation and the heavy price tag that came with it: numerous arrests, imprisonment and the brutal treatment he suffered in the hands of successive Nigerian regimes determined to silence him.

Finally, the chapter also takes a critical look at some of the flaws of the crusade that he led especially by dealing with his views on women.

In this next chapter, "Fodéba Keïta and *Les Ballets Africains*: Dancing To Freedom," Thomas Jing sheds light to Fodéba Keïta, the little known Guinean poet and choreographer, one of Africa's finest whose cultural accomplishments in culture match what Nelson Mandela did in politics. From the founding to *Les Ballets Africains*, a dance ensemble which has been a source of tremendous cultural pride for Africans worldwide to taking the world stage by storm, Keita Fodéba revolutionized the obsolete thinking that ballet dancing was everything western with nothing African. This article captures the man and his journey in the creation of the dance which silenced many a mocking tongue deriding the existence of any such thing as African ballet. The author also spells out the impact Fodéba Keïta's *Les Ballets Africains* has had in the emancipation of black people everywhere black people find themselves. In effect, *Les Ballets Africains* distinguishes itself as the dance troupe that Fodéba Keïta started; and which took the world by storm and forever changing many westerners' perceptions of Africa. The author herein illustrates how in culture Keïta shines with exceptional luster, thanks to his creation of *Les Ballets Africains*, a dance ensemble whose impact and reach is global.

Benjamin Hart Fishkin, in this fifth chapter, highlights how characters in Mimboland live and experience wild sexual and social lives because they are so limited and constrained in their public ones. Again, the chapter emphasizes Francis B. Nyamnjoh's *Married But Available* as portraying people with so little control of their public affairs that they take unnecessary risks when they are in private. This chapter also brings out Nyamnjoh's extreme perceptiveness and shows how he notices that these fleeting and unsatisfying affairs and indiscriminate liaisons are symptomatic of a much bigger problem.

Exploring the novel, the chapter unveils how people are unfulfilled by a lack of liberty. The attempt to fill this gap wreaks havoc with family dynamics in the nation. Through character analysis, the chapter points to characters going from one stale party to another, all the while staring at each other as if to ask themselves if they are having fun yet. Nyamnjoh's biting humor exposes Mimbolanders' bad decisions, telling risqué stories, and revealing that there would be no need for such antics if the people had political and economic freedom.

The chapter further illustrates how in *Married But Available*, the author takes a swipe at colonialism. He does so by introducing a character from France who travels to the fictional Mimboland. This character, Lilly Loveless is a graduate student working on a dissertation entitled "Sex, Power and Consumerism in Africa". She does so with the colonial mindset of *mission civilisatrice*, hoping that she can help liberate people only to realize the reverse shall be true. Nyamnjoh ridicules her assumptions about how people in Africa make love. Her views, the author highlights as knowledge coming from what is presumed to be Paris with all of its plastic conveniences. This is another one of Nyamnjoh's novel ways of challenging prejudices as never was before done. This chapter shows *Married but Available* flipping the relationship between the colonizer and colonized and turning the ambassador into the recipient who must operate and survive in unfamiliar territory.

In the chapter "Language, Freedom, and the Revolutionary Visionary: The Writings of Zora Neale Hurston," authors Bill F. Ndi, Benjamin Hart Fishkin, and Adaku T. Ankumah, appraise Hurston's literary works, from novels, autobiographical material and short stories and show that she "deserves her place amongst heraldic revolutionary and visionary black voices" (1). Refusing to accept the assimilationist tendencies of the elite Black writers, Hurston believed that Black America's contribution to American culture is not in Africanisms in the language but in their use of language and imagery. She employs the language of ordinary Black folks unashamedly in her works, their use of metaphors, similes to adorn their prose, writing the dialect of Blacks in her own way, to the dismay of her critics. The result is literature that is unique in liberating the voice of ordinary Black people, mainly from the South, and touching on various issues from relationships, gender, sexuality, social issues from their perspective. This voice is not "polished" for the consumption of white society. In fact, the voice of the ordinary people reveals the infidelities in relationships, in both males and females; male domination; aspirations not just for economic freedom but for self-actualization. In other words, they want to express their full humanity as people from other races do. Language becomes the instrument for such liberation.

Mark Henderson in the next chapter, "Afrofuturism as Revolution in Martin Delany's *Blake; or, The Huts of America* and Sutton E. Griggs' *Imperium in Imperio,"* deals with the use of science fiction for the purposes of addressing issues pertinent to black people around the world. It hinges on Afrofuturism which has proven to be a useful, speculative tool. However, the author clarifies and spares the reader the erroneous conclusion that one might be tempted to make, thinking that "science fiction" refers to only the twentieth century and beyond. After all, what is "futuristic" is relative to a given time period. Furthermore, this chapter draws upon African-American science fiction author Samuel R. Delany and mentions two nineteenth-century novels—*Blake; or, The Huts of America* (1859) & *Imperium in Imperio* (1899)—by African-American authors Martin Delany and Sutton E. Griggs respectively, to demonstrate how black authors use the science fiction trope to instill a sense of alternative history that anticipates future civil rights activities and activism in the

United States. Both works speculate upon successful black-nationalist insurrection and separation, thus making them key fictional points of argument in the nineteenth-century portion of American civil rights history. The chapter therefore concludes that these two authors are worthy of further exploration as examples of how Afrofuturism has been key to the struggle for African-American freedom even since the mid-nineteenth century.

Elizabeth Ayuk-Etang, through a critical examination of the works of Zora Neale Hurston and Harriet Jacobs, posits that these two revolutionary heralds deserve their place among the unsung superstars of resistance and protest against the oppressive forces that have crushed and continue to crush blacks from slavery to post-independence and beyond. The chapter unveils the common characteristics of most slave and post slavery narratives from women in a masochistic society; i.e. rape, oppression, marginalization, and subjugation from the society as well as from loved ones. The chapter examines the commonalities that underlie the lives of slave women and most slaves, and the motives for their resistance against brute hegemony. It further analyzes the authors' sense of revolt as powerful weapons against the epoch and its dehumanizing activities. The chapter scrutinizes the texts under study with a radical feminist perspective and the Theory of Resistance from Philip Rickian's perspective. These two perspectives take precedence in acknowledging the presence of diverse opinions in the same society, the latitude to judgment and the acceptance of exposure of secrets as a tool for societal amelioration. An appraisal of both texts reveals that though each story is set in a different era with its unique realities, the fate of the woman remains that of permanent and special torture and oppression. Both writers therefore, well ahead of their time, decry the extreme subjugation of women. They expose their challenges as a means towards their emancipation and, as such, deserve their rightful place in any discussion centered on revolutionary voices and visions.

John Tighlman in "Dr. Walter Rodney: Historian and Voice for the Black Working Class" focuses on Walter Rodney's theories on capitalism, Black Power, and coalitions among working-class Guyanese people on behalf of working-class African descendant people. He examines three of Rodney's famous published books: *How Europe Underdeveloped Africa, Groundings with My Brothers*, and *A History of Working-Class Guyanese People, 1881-1905*. These books constitute those in which Rodney identifies how slavery and colonialism created black people's current conditions in supposedly independent African and Caribbean nations. Rodney used the books as an outlet to converse with the black working-class people about how to transform, alter, or change their conditions. Furthermore, it highlights Rodney as a scholar-activist committed to the working class struggles in the African Diaspora and one who uses history to explain the black working class's plight.

Derick Hendricks, in the final chapter, demonstrates how the young adult population of the U.S. Virgin Islands played a major role in dispersing ideas about Black Nationalism throughout the Virgin Islands in a key moment of the island's history, from 1968-1974. The young adults, comprised mainly of young college students on the St. Thomas campus of the College of the Virgin Islands coming under the banner of The Black Cultural Organization, were instrumental in conveying ideas about the self-help philosophical concept of Black Nationalism throughout the American territory. Their organization aimed at educating Virgin Islanders and at increasing the society's responsiveness to racism and its effect. Accordingly, from 1968 to 1974, the body organized public activities, sponsored historical and cultural programs, which emphasized the achievements of African peoples, and published a newsletter called *The Black Revolutionary* to educate Virgin Islanders and to develop greater community awareness of racism and its ramifications. In the opinion of Barbara Isaac, one of the founders of the organization, if the group was not sponsoring a lecture presentation in a particular week, then the members were marching in Main Street against the war in Vietnam or for some other social cause. In addition, the chapter illustrates how the Black Cultural Organization sponsored Black History Week programs on the St. Thomas college campus, and how it led to other educational self-help events in the St. Thomas community. It brings to life the opposition members of the organization faced from some residents in the community and faculty and staff on the campus. The members, who included both males and females, sought support from college instructors who could identify with students who were the descendants of Africans. In effect, this chapter discusses race relations at the College of the Virgin Islands during its early years and the significance and impact of the Black Cultural Organization as well as its repercussions within the wider U.S. Virgin Islands community.

Revolutionaries and visionaries come and go, yet their ideas endure in their sway and hold on the mentalities of both their generations and those yet unborn. This generational human reality between revolutionary visionaries and the rest of society has dramatic and far-reaching effects to the point where theirs become a life spring source for a world evolving around and embracing corruption. The scholars herein have engaged in an open conversation, bringing to the fore some unsung heralds of black revolutionary visions and voices who, through their writings, activism, artistry, natural and musical talents, scholarship, intellectualism, etc. have legated weapons with which to lead a ferocious fight to liberate the oppressed black man. By revisiting these heralds, the scholars explore at liberty contributions deemed worthy of extraordinary accomplishments by those who have not been sung or given their due recognition in their surgical-precision use of their God-given talents and faculties in, and towards, the eradication of societal ills. Also, scholars have had to draw their own conclusions from their disciplinary perspective as to why their chosen icon deserves a place among the unsung. In all, each contributor, in the spirit of committed writing *à la Sartre*, informed by his or her disciplinary theoretical underpinnings, unearths critical contributions to the black struggle which would otherwise be buried in the deeps of historical oblivion. Holding onto the concept of historical revalidation, the editor in the spirit of the Sankofa bird underscores the constant need to revisit and revaluate history, especially in an age when some quarters of the fourth estate would rather drum up the concept of alternate facts, virtual reality, and alternative truth. With all of the aforementioned bombarding human senses, retracing history and making the relevant and untainted facts survive, become a number one priority to straighten the record and leave the world with some sense of decency. This postulation also shares the view of history being in constant flux and reflux with happenings of the yesteryears informing and shaping the here and now as well as tomorrow.

This one-of-a-kind manual scrutinizes uncelebrated yet influential voices and visions with critical methodologies. These are black voices and visions whose passage on earth cultivated, cultivates and will continue to cultivate black critical awareness; a topical concern beckoning intellectual discourse for historical re-evaluation. Bringing together these anti-colonial historians, writers, musicians, dancers, artists, and advocates for egalitarianism, social and economic justice underscores the import and legacies of their seem-to-be-forgotten groundbreaking voices and visions. Their unrelenting pursuit of freedom for the oppressed, the enslaved, the subjugated, etc. makes of theirs, extraordinary legacies worthy of protection and preservation. This collection portrays a group of voices and visions with unequivocal and uncompromising stance and approach to the black liberation struggle. The Decolonization Movement and other contemporary liberation movements such as Black Lives Matter, Rhodes Must Fall, and EndSARS have all stood or are standing on the shoulders of the heralds studied in this volume; to air with the same fervor their discontent to the continued oppression their people suffer. It would not be erroneous to credit critical race studies to the endeavors of earlier revolutionary voices and visions such as those examined hereunder. Thus, the editor herein enjoins the readers to initiate the long overdue celebration of these unsung superstars of anti-colonialism, anti-enslavement, anti-oppression, anti-subjugation, anti-injustice, anti-racism, etc. Such a celebration would be a clarion call for a groundbreaking revolution of mentalities that would bulldoze the pathway to utter emancipation for humans who are victims of oppression wherever they may be.

Section I

Africa

Chapter 1

A Call to Revolutionize the Mentalities of the Colonized: Gebreyesus Hailu's *The Conscript*

Bill F. Ndi

Scholars of African literature, African literary history, and most especially those of literature on slavery and colonization have long held that colonization turned the enslaved and colonized into active participants of sorts to most of the epistemological prejudices that have long characterized and marked both the enslaved and colonized African in popular memory and culture. Against this background bell hooks in her magnum opus, *Yearning: race, gender, and cultural politics* highlights, under the chapter "Stylish Nihilism: Race, sex, and class in movies, that

> Colonization made of us the colonized—participants in daily rituals
> of power where we, in strict sado-masochistic institution, find pleasure
> in ways of being and thinking, ways of looking at the world that
> reinforce and maintain our positions as the dominated. Any coming to
> critical consciousness simply heightens the reality of contradictions. We
> are often silent about how we cope with those contradictions. To focus
> on them is to expose our complicity, to expose the reality that even the
> most politically aware among us are often compelled by circumstances
> we do not control to submit, to collude. (155)

The critical questions this chapter intends to address here is whether Gebreyesus Hailu adheres or subscribes to bell hooks' line of thinking in *The Conscript*. Or, again, does *The Conscript* stray from this firmly rooted observation? And if Gebreyesus Hailu does, is it just for the fun of it? Or does he pits the relation between the

1

dominant and subjugated to reflect a recollection, rebirth, travail, and tumultuousness of a journey to a kind of political conduct of which he has made a call to revolutionize the mentalities of the African that he considers to be misrepresented? The contention following these questions is that in order to have a clear understanding of Gebreyesus Hailu's thin novel, *The Conscript,* the reader must start by challenging perceived misconceptions that make of subordinates accomplices of their own oppression or subjugation. Such misconceptions deprive the oppressed of any sense of worth, especially vis-à-vis their own agency in the process of self-liberation, and self-determination. This novel is not only the seed of rebellion but the embodiment of rebellion and the far-reaching effects of one that reclaims and recasts the oppressed not just as participants who are well versed with the circumstances of their own subjugation but humans who know the vistas they can open to gain redemption, liberation and self-determination. *The Conscript,* as a revolutionary artifact of knowledge recollection, redemption, and reproduction of conduct contrary to perceived complacencies, ought to have a major impact on the reception, perception, and critical appraisal of African literature. Gebreyesus Hailu is an author whose imaginative pregnancy and collective consciousness ought to set him in the pantheon of African literary giants. In spite of this categorization, one may still question why this thin novel should be hauled in to the pantheon of black revolutionary voices and visions.

Literary memory and recollection of things past, present, and/or future have often opened new vistas to pave the way to swift and expedient changes with far reaching effects. Revolutions are never the result of some historical or chance accidents but the concurrence of amassed collective or individual memory that pushes to transformation. Hailu's *The Conscript* as one of the earliest and undisputable African novels written in an African language, Tigriyan, proves this point. It anchors on individual and collective memories of the ruthlessness of Italian Colonization of Eritrea to reveal how such memories can be agents of transformation of the colonized African to adopt a political conduct that leads to self-liberation and self-determination. This novel also anticipates and emphasizes the concerns of Post-colonial thinkers from Fanon to Homi Bhabha. It gives the colonized agency in his/her own evolution, revolution, and transformation.

The Conscript arouses interest, as it is one of the earliest novels written and published in an African language. Dating back to 1927, the author uses this medium viz. Tigrinya, to challenge the above-mentioned prejudice of subaltern complicity of the African in supporting his/her own affliction. Such a reductive view grants agency to the subaltern only when it comes to the woes s/he suffers. This novel further challenges the widely accepted notion that the publication of Achebe's *Things Fall Apart* foreshadowed African literature. It is true one would be rather naïve to discard the import of Achebe's *Things Fall Apart* in its role in bringing the African novel in the English expression to the limelight. Achebe's novel will fit perfectly well with wa Thiong'o's assertion that "Africa has given her human beings, her resources, and even her spiritual products through African writing in European languages" (*Something* 127). However, *The Conscript* predates Achebe's by about 30 years and did not give anything African to the world in a European language. Besides, the acclaim of Achebe's, one is tempted to contend, stems from the fact that it uses the tool that the oppressor treasures in employing to bewitch the black soul. In talking about Hamidou Kane's *Ambiguous Adventure,* Ngugi points out that Kane seems to borrow from Spencer in crediting the colonial school as a better tool for conquest than the canon because it made conquest permanent. He goes on to postulate that while "[t]he canon compels the body [,] the school bewitches the soul" (*Something* 21). Notwithstanding, both Gebreyesus Hailu and Chinua Achebe share the commonality that they "… recognized the importance of speech, presence, and literary representation in sustaining colonial power" (Newell 87).

3

Over and above, Gebreyesus Hailu's *The Conscript* also explores interesting themes in African literature which had not been made relevant by prior research in African studies: knowledge production and agnotology i.e. the making and unmaking of ignorance. The experiences of the conscripts at sea as well as their views of life at sea are portrayed as instances of knowledge production and agnotology, and of beauty and spirituality. Also, the vivid description of Egyptians, Ferdinand de Lesseps' statue and the response of the *Habesha* to what they view as marvels make the Narrator wonder the import of sightseeing without deep knowledge of history and historical correctness. This aspect makes of *The Conscript* an insightful work that, in the age of globalization, could help address contemporary issues of remembrances, renaissance, and revolution as far as the transformation of black world is concerned.

Moreover, social injustices meted on black people around the world have been the hot topic of discussion in academic circles. However, such discussions have been limited to social injustices while ignoring those infringements meted on knowledge production, display, and insights. Gebreyesus Hailu articulates and centers his work on exposing colonial injustices do redeem and reproduce episteme that socially self-appropriated elitist/high culture would rather spite than embrace. He commits to the idea of the incompleteness of human appearances and makes it his warhorse. The French philosopher and literary theorist Jean Paul Sartre, in his seminal work *What is Literature?* points out what moves writers like Gebreyesus Hailu to committed writing, i.e. writing aimed at sensitizing to such injustices. He writes: "I [the author] am [is] given this world with its injustices, it is not so that I [he] might contemplate them coldly, but that I [he] might animate them with my [his] indignation" (62). Thus, fleshing out these injustices, marked by misrepresentation of African/African Diasporic knowledge production, redemption, and reception would reveal how blacks, in the globalizing world marked by restrain and political correctness can deal with problems of authentic identity that are shaped by pain and rejection.

There is need to clarify and shed light to Gebreyesus Hailu's endeavor, heretofore considered as estheticized revolutionary voice and vision through remembrances, renaissance, and rebellion as well as through knowledge production. Bearing in mind that colonialism, as Ngugi upholds, had the real aim of destroying the African, his values, and ways forever, special attention must be paid to hearken to revolutionary voices and visions as his. Pointing to the real aim of colonialism, Ngugi has this to say:

> The real aim of colonialism was to control the people's wealth: what they produced, how they produced it, and how it was distributed; to control, in other words, the entire realm of language of real life. Colonialism imposed its control of the social production of wealth through military conquest and subsequent political dictatorship. But its most important area of domination was the mental universe of colonised [sic], the control, through culture, of how people perceived themselves and their relationship to the world. [...] To control a people's culture is to control their tools of self-determination in relationship to others. (*Decolonising* 16)

From Ngugi's assertion here above, it is evident that black revolutionary voices and visions have not simply been victims of historical accidents and / or deformation, but those of a concerted effort to undermine and leave the black populace in a position that facilitates control and domination. This makes it even more compelling to embrace *The Conscript* for the literary bravura it heralds, even though marginalized, i.e. the novel has not been the subject of much discussion in academic or literary circles. However, lest one forgets, there cannot be domination without resistance, no matter how modest the resistance. In the face of such aberration, Gebreyesus Hailu takes center stage to put up a model for awakening awareness to future generations of young Africans who might be tempted to make the same mistake their *Habesha* brothers made in the past. Gebreyesus Hailu seems to explore discipline in the 21st century anthropological ramification of the word; against which background Noel Dyck underlines discipline as entailing "not technical means for exercising power over self and/or others but also an essential symbolic medium for defining and articulating preferred social practices, objectives, and ways of being" (12). It is in this light that it is worthwhile to briefly explore *The Conscript,* a novel written by this towering theologian and historical figure in Tigrinyan literature specifically and African literature as well as literature on colonization in general. To shed light hereunto, aspects such as plot, structure, setting, characterization, style, themes, time and space management, message, and more will constitute the object of any such exploration. Is it not true as Eustace Palmer would have it that "a well-made novel" as *The Conscript* "is a composite of message and technique"? (Palmer x).

However, before delving into the book analysis proper, for clarification, a brief journey along the author's biographical path would help situate the novel in the context of its birth. This historical background provides the narrator the ingredients for the exploration of his concern with the exploitation of the African under the guise of what the French subverted as a *Mission Civilisatrice.* The same went further to inculcate in young colonized African kids in school to claim the Gauls as their ancestors while, as Ngugi points out, "consigning their African ancestors to dark oblivion" (*Something* 26). The repercussions of this on the African elite are far reaching as "the African elite's continued self-identification with Franco-Anglo- and Lusophonism attests to the burial of the Afro under layers of Europhonism" (Ngugi *Something* 26). When it comes to the context of Gebreyesus Hailu, one needs to recall the failed Italian adventure to capture and colonize Ethiopia in the 1890s. This culminated in the Italian-Ethiopian war of 1895-1896. The causes of this war, as well as its consequences, are not in discussion here. But, one needs to retell that the crushing defeat suffered by the Italian reemphasizes V.Y. Mudimbe's notion of "colonialism as a confrontation of two types of societies, each with its own memory" (qtd. In Ngugi *Something* 26). Or again, the scene in *The Conscript* where the Italian commander is (mis)instructing /(mis)educating the *Habesha* about the Arabs. He claims the Arabs might look white, but they are not like the Italians: "we alone are the brave whites; we, Italians, your master" (*Something* 27). The conscripts come to understand that the stereotypes about the Arabs are fabrications and reflect nothing close to what or who the Arabs really are. It is evident that this peddling of stereotypes produces ignorance, which goes a long way to aggrandize the colonialist at the expense of the dominated and colonized. However, the 1896 Ethiopian victory at Adowa was the first crushing defeat of a European power by African forces during the colonial era. The historian Denis Richards, commenting on the significance of this victory, has this to say: "the results of this battle was that Abyssinia [Ethiopia] continued to be ruled by Abyssinians [Ethiopians]—a state of affairs so outrageous to the Italian dignity that revenge had to be sought, and obtained, in 1935" (252). Thus this victory offers and imposes the appeal of its memory as well as it promises a vision of revolutionary challenges to be taken up by the colonized, not only Ethiopians but blacks wherever they were despoiled. It is in this context that Gebreyesus Hailu derives his rooted belief in a revolutionary voice and vision to embed the educated African into the social ideology of self-assertion and self-liberation. Who is Gebreyesus Hailu?

The Tigrinyan-English translator of *The Conscript* notes that the life of this author is fascinating. Gebreyesus Hailu was born in Eritrea under Italian colonization in the early 20th century, specifically 1906, in Afelba, in the southern region of Eritrea. Our translator points out that he "was born in a small village in Eritrea…" He learned to read and write at an early age. He attended San Michele School in

Segeneyti and in 1923 began his education at the Catholic Seminary of Keren. In 1924, he moved to the Ethiopian College in the Vatican, where he earned his licenza ginnasiale in 1927, finishing the program in three years rather than in the standard five. Needless to reproduce here all the biographical details one can read in the translator's note. At the age of 18, he travelled to Italy. While on this trip, he met with *ascari* recruits travelling overseas. This experience as well as his encounter with another former *ascari* while on his way to get his education in Rome are undoubtedly the seeds from which sprouts his thought-provoking classic novel written in Tigrinya in 1927 and published in 1950. This also holds sway to the choices he makes about the narrative. The protagonist's name and age come to mind. The combination of events calls for thanks to God for enabling him to express the concerns and feelings of his people at a young age. *The Conscript,* as one of the earliest novels written in an African language, is the first in the literary history of Eritrea. However, the translator's note states that prose fiction and nonfiction in Eritrean language predate *The Conscript.* Besides his acclaim as the author of *The Conscript,* Gebreyesus Hailu was a prominent and influential figure in the cultural and intellectual life of Eritrea during the Italian colonial period and in the post-Italian era in Africa who served as a Cultural Attaché of the Ethiopian Government and the Holy See (Vatican) after the World War II. He earned a PhD in theology and was vicar general of the Catholic Church in Eritrea and played several important roles in the Ethiopian government, member of the national academy of language, and advisor to the Ministry of Information of the Ethiopian government—until his retirement in 1974. He died in 1993.

The Conscript adopts an oppositional stance to that of embracing what Eustace Palmer dubs a "sociological bias" (ix). Palmer asserts that such a bias stems from the fact that the earliest African novelists derived their inspiration from traditional lore, indigenous customs, and oral tradition. While the reader might find some of these elements in Gebreyesus Hailu's work, he only uses them as esthetic elements of style or again as narrative techniques to shape, explore, define, and evaluate his central thematic concerns of bringing and instilling order that his protagonist wishes were brought to bear upon the chaos that colonization wrought on his people. Eustace Palmer, the grandfather of African literary criticism, will agree that Gebreyesus Hailu is "a good novelist" who, "apart from his preoccupation with his message, […] should have some concern for the appropriate style and show signs of technical competence" (xi). *The Conscript* is a cogent expression of strength and exquisiteness of African life in style. It is a work that conjures Ben Okri's *The Famished Road* in which he laments how "we've looked too much in that direction [of repression and victimization of the colonized subject] and have forgotten about our own aesthetic frames" (86). This work has been given life thanks to Gebreyesus Hailu's ingenuity in managing what James C. Scott calls "elementary forms of disguise" (138). Scott also gives the example of how "[i]n Europe from the fifteenth through the seventeenth centuries, both secular and religious authorities understood the dangers that autonomous sites of dissident folk culture could pose" (124-125). This comparison is made in the light of *The Conscript*—an anti-colonial war literature—in a bid to substantiate the 23 years lapse between the writing and the publication of the work. Even if by his own admission, the author advances pecuniary reasons for not having the work in print before 1950 one is tempted to question whether his work would have had to wait 23 years to find a sponsor, had it addressed a narrative favorable to colonial exploitation of Eritreans in particular and Africans in general. In short, the novel needed Gebreyesus's "experimental spirit and capacity to test and exploit all the loopholes, ambiguities, silences, and lapses available …" (Scott 138) before proceeding with the publication.

Everything Tuquabo, the protagonist is and does is modified by learning and experience on the war front and how he perceives his relationship vis-à-vis his white commander. Gebreyesus Hailu thus anticipates Edward T. Hall, who in *Beyond Culture,* emphasizes man and action as malleable. Hall further points out that: "… once learned, these behavior patterns, these habitual responses, these ways of interacting gradually sink below the surface of the mind and […] control from the depths (42). By capturing Tuquabo's learning and experiences in Tigrinya, Gebreyesus Hailu is heralding a stance that writers such as Ngugi wa Thiong'o would champion in the later part of the 20th century. It is explicitly spelled out in the eponym of his masterpiece, *Decolinising the Mind.* In this work, Ngugi asserts that "Language as communication and as culture are the product of each other. Communication creates culture: Culture is a means of communication" (15-16). He goes a step further to say, "Language carries culture and culture carries, particularly through orature and literature, the entire body of values by which we come to perceive ourselves and our place in the world" (*Decolonising* 16). This is exactly what Gebreyesus Hailu legates to younger generations of Africans and posterity: how we perceive ourselves as Africans and what our place would be in the world if we choose not to come to the realization that we as a people need to, and must call to a halt the abuses and impositions of colonialism and crypto colonialism. Such a halt would start with the use of our own languages to denounce the excesses of colonialism and crypto-colonialism. He further paints a picture of the colonizer seizing our land as well as our future, i.e. the youths they drag to die in senseless wars of conquest and aggrandizement that they wage for their own benefit.

What does seem to be a constant is that colonization brought with it more than a handful of unpleasant surprises. In the eyes of Gebreyesus Hailu, Italian colonization brought in its train, new set of problems that traditional Tigrinyan society did not easily recognize. Increasingly people (especially young people) found themselves unconnected and unacquainted with the world in a way that their parents, their grandparents, their great-uncles, and their great-aunts would never have been. This portrayal echoes Edward T. Hall's claim that:

> ... man automatically treats what is most characteristically his own (the culture of his youth) as though it were innate. He is forced into a position of thinking and feeling that anyone whose behavior is not predictable or is peculiar in any way is slightly out of his mind, improperly brought up, irresponsible, psychopathic, politically motivated to a point beyond redemption, or just plain inferior. (43)

The above claim captures the dynamic of the relationship between Eritrean youths and their parents in the chaotic environment of colonization. The way they behaved with their peers was totally different; their conception of being and becoming was thwarted, their views on their conscription unauthenticated, and their performance as soldiers fighting another man's war turned into an epiphany of resting authenticity in the face of foreign value systems. Initially every youth had forgotten how to be contemplative or introspective and, in their haste, they overlooked the relationships that were truly important, not until the harsh realities of the war—chaos pure and simple—had been thrown at them while they were protecting the comfort of their Italian colonizers. The realities in the battlefield unveil the heartlessness of the colonizer when in the end "the Italian who led them to this and made this happen was going to have a good night's sleep in his homeland. Nothing was going to happen to him. Everything worked well for him" (48). Sending the cruel monster to his home safely reminds of James C. Scott's contention on "Elementary Forms of Disguise" that,

> Like prudent opposition newspaper editors under strict censorship, subordinate groups must find ways of getting their message across, while staying somehow within the law. This requires an experimental spirit and a capacity to test and exploit all the loopholes, ambiguities,

silences, and lapses available to them. (138).

Starting with authenticity, therefore, there is a possibility for restoring order in a globalized world through the estheticization of remembrances, rebirth and revolution brought to bear upon the disorderly climate colonization created. What Tuquabo starts as a difficult task turns out to be deeply and personally significant beyond imagination. His return journey from the war has transformed him and his comrades into anti war campaigners "grieving their comrades who fell in battle and died," as they "mournfully sang, 'Let no one go to Tripoli, lest they be cut with long knife and sword.'" (48). Gebreyesus Hailu takes exactly the kind of cognizance Newell attributes to Achebe's writing of *Things Fall Apart*. She underscores that "in recognition of the role played by narrative in the construction of the 'native' as Other and in the erasure of his own African *Presence,* Achebe wrote *Things Fall Apart*" (87).

The Conscript opens with a dramatic scene in which Tuquabo, the protagonist is shown putting down his guns beside him and going down on his knees to solicit blessings from his father and mother. He raises the audience's expectations in a Dickensian twist by suggesting he knows not what his fate in Tripoli will be. This literary suspense is a subtle foreshadow of the troubles, tumultuousness, and uncertainties colonization brought upon the colonized African. Nonetheless, Gebreyesus Hailu seems to intimate this very dramatic act is not the beginning of things to come but where things should end. That is to say, the gun which is a foreign weapon used to fight people who have not provoked the Tigrinyan should be placed on the side in order to embrace the core traditional value of living in honor of one's parents. The narrator points out on several occasions how young *ascari* i.e. Eritrean soldiers recruited to fight for their oppressors, have embraced value systems so foreign to theirs. This act is tantamount to the proverbial chicken coming home to roost. Young Eritreans/Africans in this predicament must come back full circle and start honoring their fathers and mothers. This implied prescription is a clever use of biblical allusion to one of the Ten Commandments. Is it not written in the scriptures that children should obey their fathers and mothers for their days to be longer? Is the act of going to war not the quickest way to shorten one's life? In all, this dramatic opening is an invitation to young Africans in general and young Eritreans in particular, to constantly be mindful of their provenance. Gebreyesus Hailu carefully exploits that which is a constant in African mythology. This constant has been clearly captured in the symbol of the Sankofa bird looking back to know where it is going. This makes the act of going and coming to complete a circle. No doubt the cyclical structure of the novel.

The Conscript is a call for African writers, African keepers of memories and national discourses to make use of their national languages i.e. the languages of their communities. This brings to mind another revolutionary voice coupled with vision, Booker T. Washington, in a class of his own. In his *The Atlanta Compromise Speech,* he implored the South to do what he had instigated on his race: "Cast down your bucket where you are." (Atlanta Speech). These visions seem to echo the opposite of the proverbial grass which is always greener on the other side. Gebreyesus Hailu captures the essence of a visionary striving to liberate his people and in a language which they understand. This endeavor readily brings to mind Darwin Turner's discussion of the status of humanists and humanities in which he posits that "in Arnold's time, the college teacher of literature was expected to know the classical languages so that he might teach the truths of Greece and Rome" (qtd. In CLA Journal, V 57 n° 1. September 2013). In the case of *The Conscript*, Gebreyesus Hailu's revolutionary vision spells out the truth to fellow Tigrinyan speakers, and brothers and sisters about the harsh realities of teaming up with a foreign enemy against one's own. Tuquabo makes known that his preferences, upon experiencing an illegitimate war of conquest against his African brothers in Libya, are predicated upon the total liberation of Africa for the benefit of all Africans. *The Conscript* is thus a novel no African should do himself/herself the disservice of not reading. Even if the reading has to be in a foreign language in the 21st century, we must espouse Achebe's feelings relative to the English language as a medium for conveying his Africanness. He points out that "the English language will be able to carry the weight of my African experience. But it will have to be in a new English, still in full communion with its ancestral home but altered to suit its new African surroundings" (qtd. *in* Larson 26).

The Conscript is a tale of collective fear, tragedy, youthful pride and exuberance, narrowed down through the pain and suffering of Tuquabo's parents. The narrator highlights that "[t]his is not just one story, but the story of many parents…" (49). The story follows Tuquabo from when he runs away from home and then later on comes back after his military training to bid his parents farewell, as he would soon be leaving for Tripoli to his journey to Libya as well as his engagement in battles. He survives the war only to come back home to his old father, who would soon die, and the sad memory of his late mother; unfortunately, this memory is one he would have to bear for a long time. The individual's storyline itself is not the colonnade holding or making this narrative one worthy of discussion of black revolutionary voices or visions. However, within the above-mentioned collective fear, tragedy and youthful exuberance is the fate of a people, the *Habesha* in particular and Africans in general. It tackles the great problems brought and left by colonization in its wake on the African continent and her psyche. It also addresses a conscientization effort for Africa to break away from the chain of subjugation and to stop fighting senseless wars that only go to benefit foreign interests. Gebreyesus Hailu, demonstrates an understanding that

> to do the right job, [… man] needs to understand psychology, sociology, and enough other social sciences to get under the skin of the

14

public and client, to know what makes them act the way they do and how they can be enticed differently. (Tye 91)

Also of note is the fact that the tale is told with courage and verve in an era when the brutality of the colonial administration, ruling with fear and intimidation, would have spelled doom for the writer. Is it not true, as Larry Tye would have it that "we are dominated by the relatively small number of persons—a trifling fraction [...]—who understand the mental processes and social patterns of the masses..." (92)? This was exactly the case in Eritrea in the 1920s or as the given example in *The Conscript* illustrates. We have a few Italian commanders manipulating a bunch of *ascari* to their doom. This storyline is revolutionary in its denunciation of a context in which the euphoria of fighting and killing for the expansionist interest of a colonial power overshadows every aspect of daily life of the ordinary African youth; from politics, business, social conduct and ethical thinking. It is an early appeal for Africa to reprioritize her relations with colonial powers or foreign interests that do nothing but swindle the best Africa has to offer. *The Conscript* culminates in a singular and universal act of rebellion made more significant in its anticipating African writing that emerged in the 50s and 60s, circling back to the author's decision to write in the language of the oppressed, an endeavor Ngugi wa Thiong'o attempted. It is for this same reason amongst others that the blurb writer highlights this novel as

Anticipating midcentury thinkers Frantz Fanon and Aimé Césaire, [...] paint[ing] a devastating portrait of Italian colonialism. Some of the most poignant passages of the novel include the awakening of the novel's hero, Tuquabo, to his ironic predicament of being both under colonial rule and the instrument of suppressing the colonized Libyans. (Blurb)

It should be remembered that this tale of subjugation and

15

liberation falls within the purview of that which Ngugi, in his discussion of the politics of language in African literature, made clear to be about "national, democratic and human liberation" (*Decolonising* 108). He further underlines that his crusade to have writing in African languages should be viewed as an attempt to reconnect with millions of revolutionary tongues in Africa and around the world thirsting after liberation. In short, an endeavor like Hailu's, "is a call for the rediscovery of the real language of humankind: the language of struggle" (ibid. 108). And indeed Hailu's language is in itself, a struggle. His language flips from the domain of literature to make history in sowing the seeds of Africans' drive "to become part of those millions whom Martin Carter once saw sleeping not to dream but dreaming to change the world" (ibid 108).

When Habte-Mikael and Tek'a decide to see off their son to war, the narrator hints that: "his parents decided to see their son for the last time" (8). This is a kind of ominous foreshadow that the son might never come back to meet them or might never survive the war. However, the parents give Tuquabo their blessing. They draw his attention to what he represented to them until this point: "you were our light and joy…" (8) And they further reveal their feelings: "we feel orphaned" (8). Their additional remarks to their son turn out to be a series of heavily loaded rhetorical questions: "Why do you wish to fight for a foreigner? What use is it to you and your people to arm yourselves and fight overseas? You have all you want, why?" (8). These admonishments will keep churning in Tuquabo's mind all the while in the battlefield. This episode evokes a 20th century work based on the Vietnam War by Tim O'brien, *The Things They Carried* (1990). These admonishments still ring true in the 21st century. When Africa sends off one of her children into the Diaspora, she bears at heart identical questions and curiosities as those of Habte-Mikael and Tek'a's. It is also noteworthy to emphasize the way the guards snatched off their son. This scene, though at a different time in Africa's tumultuous experiences, echoes yet another situation in

Africa's history when the cream of her society was hacked off from her and forced into slavery. The parents are not allowed even a second to give their children the warmest affection they can give to a son they will not be seeing for a long time to come. As they attempt to kiss their son goodbye very well, "the guards snatched him from their embrace" (8). The resultant reaction from Tuquabo, and the subsequent fainting of his mother, that very last minute, hint at the trauma that would mark both mother and son for a very long time. Besides, Tuquabo leaving behind his parents in sadness and distress does not leave onlookers indifferent. Their collective questioning/cursing "what a cruel son! How could he leave his old parents behind?" fell in Tuquabo's ears as he "kept looking at his mother and heard the curses of the crowd..." (8). Habte-Mikael gestures in request to the crowd to stop cursing their son. He would rather they bless him. Habte-Mikael and Tek'a return to the village and "were overtaken by suffering, driven by sorrow. Darkness fell upon the house. It was like returning home after the funeral of a beloved one" (9). The suffering, the sorrow, the darkness, and the baneful atmosphere they come back home to set a tone for Tuqabo's going into war.

When Tuquabo comes home to bid his parents goodbye, the narrator uses this opportunity to revisit through flashbacks, Habte-Mikael's family history, lifestyle in his community, and Tuquabo's parents' concerns—most especially Tek'a's, his mother, who worries that her son's valor, bravery, and ability would take him to a war in which he might die. While she takes pride in her son's bravery, the narrator plunges the reader into her tortured psyche: "Her mind was haunted by concerns that her son would die in war one day, and where would he go to fight? Would he ever come back once he left for war? Unable to quiet her mind, she would try to appeal to her husband, but to no avail" (6). Tek'a's worries are in stark contrast with Habte-Mikael's to whom such worries border upon silliness. For him such valor and bravery are a thing of joy to be celebrated as he says, "it should give us joy to see such bravery of our son ... not sadness" (6). With this situation of despair and a dismissive husband to whom worrying about a lone child Tek'a defied protocol to take to church to pray for God to preserve him for her, she has no choice but total reliance on God for the protection of "her son from every calamity or disaster" (6). Tek'a shows a lot of courage in taking Tuquabo into a church, especially at a time she was forbidden from doing so. The centrality of the trope of God and His role in human life is always present. Habte-Mikael and Tek'a are a peace loving couple as demonstrated by their distress at the fact that the son escapes and joins the army as a conscript bound for Tripoli. The reader is allowed to have a glimpse at the kind of grooming young Tuquabo had. The narrator follows him on his mule back ride with his father on the way to their Saho Moslem friends. Gebreyesus Hailu draws on the religious ideal of peaceful co-existence with neighbors to set an example of good neighborliness. During these trips, the father would be telling him stories and singing. As they rode along, they would encounter birds and baboons. At their destination, they are treated with milk and porridge under a full moon while listening to the surrounding cattle chewing. However, while absorbing and taking in everything, Tuquabo preserves his impressions "in his clear and innocent heart for a later time in life when he would leave for another country so that his homeland might remain a treasure in his memory" (Hailu 7). With this mindset, there is no wonder that when peer-pressure is overwhelming, Tuquabo would easily succumb to it.

Tuquabo's grooming and growing up is in the backdrop of war in Tripoli and the narrator situates the reader as to the war of words traded by young men and children. Tuquabo, who has followed this very keenly, ends up making up his mind. When he does this, he starts by withdrawing, isolating himself, and speaking less. Amidst his mother's concerns and attempts to scrutinize him about his present behavior, Tuquabo becomes very evasive as any young person would. Having resolved to go to war for the vain reason of gaining fame and becoming a hero, he starts his evasiveness by talking less and isolating himself more. And when his mother senses "something in the air," she starts asking incessant questions which scrutiny he avoids, "fearing exposure of what was in his heart" (idem 7). This is reminiscent of Benjamin H. Fishkin's assertion that "[a] truly candid critic, if he values self-preservation, will keep his mental agility to himself and pretend that what has happened to his once solid and profitable country is a mirage" (qtd. in Fishkin, Ankumah, & Ndi 194).

He is a deep thinker: when at the seaside and getting ready to leave for Tripoli, the narrator captures others singing and dancing while Tuquabo is deep in his thoughts as he says, "Tuquabo was deep in thought... saw Massawa running away from him" (Hailu 14). This is an interesting ironic twist as Tuquabo in his thoughts seems to show Massawa which has never moved from creation to be the escapee. The narrator attempts to make the reader believe that it is all because, at nighttime, being on board a ship does not give the impression that the ship is sailing but of the land moving away. This optical illusion becomes a stir to Tuquabo's mind, pushing a lump up his throat. This causes him to lament the beautiful hills to which he says farewell and with a promise to "Go ahead, / Leave your family and country behind / For someone else's expanse / That you don't want. / Feel like a stranger / Until you're dead." (Hailu 15) This traditional song, the narrator tells us, pushes Tuquabo to the confines of regretting the day he was born. Nonetheless, he has only one choice left: assume responsibilities for making the wrong decision: "it was my choice that I came here, so let me suffer the consequences" (15), he said to himself with anger. Furthermore, the narrator describes the conscripts coming to consciousness, realizing they were leaving their own country behind. In a redemptive turn from an earlier mood of misrepresentation, he sinks all of the conscripts into deep thought, which initially seems to be Tuquabo's preserve. The sudden feeling of being forlorn had the conscripts stop singing without being aware.

This depressed feeling does not escape even some of the young men who appeared "not to be vulnerable to anything that distracted their happiness... They [even] struggled to sleep..." (Idem 15).

Gebreyesus Hailu also allows his revolutionary vision and voice to tread in the field of onomastics. He makes a conscious choice of telling a story of a young man as if addressing it to young men and above all chooses to keep the name he was given at birth. This retention of his name at birth is tantamount to the retention of childhood simplicity and purity. Hence, the protagonist, Tuquabo, has a name that carries with it meaning. This name is a statement in itself; the valuation of the pure and simple things in life. Estheticizing the protagonist's name captures his personality in time and space. This may account for Claire Culleton's assertion that

> Names prescribe and maintain our behavior, freezing in time and space our personalities; and because names can both order and stifle, codify and smother, characters in fiction often rebel against such nominal systematization (72).

From this assertion, it is evident that names come with negotiable qualities which reminds of the fictional character John Proctor in Arthur Miller's *The Crucible*. He states:

> Because it is my name! Because I cannot have another in my life! Because I lie and sign myself to lies! Because I am not worth the dust on the feet of them that hang! How may I live without my name? I have given you my soul; leave me my name! (qtd. in Ankumah 143).

One may wonder whether Tuquabo is really God's gift. His mother, whose joy he was, dies heartbroken while he is *en route* from war. As God's gift, he is to his people. He survives the war and lives to tell of the horrendousness of the war as a deterrent to the younger generation who might be tempted as he once was, thinking going to war would bring him fame and make him a hero. He is amongst those chanting, "Let no one go to Tripoli, lest they be cut with long knife and sword" (48). The reader follows Tuquabo in his journey to quest for what he sees as his ideal: heroism and fame. In the war front, when after an arduous day of battle, the narrator identifies him as standing "out as a hero on that day" (40), he is called to be one of the night guards. It is during his night guard duties that the narrator exposes his psyche as one engrossed in concerns not only for his family, but also for his parents, the Arabs, his country, the colonization of his country, and the resistance put up by the Arabs in defense of their barren land.

The Conscript is a modernist piece which springs from collective consciousness and ventures into the sphere of post colonialism long before any talk of post-colony. Tuquabo's position in relation to the Italian colonial policy of making use of the already colonized for further wars of colonial conquest marks a position open to the subjugated which however calls for deep reflection, self-confidence, and resolve to handle the potential conflict that could ensue from an act of insubordination. The trauma of colonization in Africa is/was not only felt by a cross-section but the entire African continent subjected to exploitation. The horrors of this exploitation, as well as those of the colonial wars, pushed for every assumption of the Italo-Eritrean relations to be reevaluated. Abraham Zere who, in his MA Thesis, highlights the nonresistance met by the Italian, reminds us in these terms:

> When Italians occupied the territory that would later become Eritrea, they faced very little resistance from the indigenous population. Rather, they seemed to have been welcomed or in any case faced little resistance from the local population. (13)

Gebreyesus Hailu seems to question the wisdom in continuing to follow these Italians blindly when all they do is lead younger

21

generations of Eritreans to their doom. This is a kind of collective "disciplinary request [to be] met … depending on individual motives, courage" and "a feel for the game" according to Pierre Bourdieu (64). In directing this request to Blacks/Africans, the novel evokes images and memories as well as reproduces songs and poems deeply embedded in Tigrinyan oral tradition chastising the ruthlessness of Italian colonization. This insistence on the importance of the local and particular dimensions of Eritrean culture strikingly resembles that which Stephanie Newell emphasizes in her discussion of West African writers of a later period (Newell 200). Local colors and engagement with oral tradition are made manifest through Tigrinya adages and proverbs, e.g. "the hyena that laughs at dawn is bound to cause havoc at dusk" (Hailu 25). Along these lines one would recall Harold Scheub who notes in "Review of African Oral traditions and Literature" that "There is an unbroken continuity in African verbal art, from interacting oral genres to such literary productions as the novel and poetry" (qtd. in *African Studies Review* 28, no.2/3: (1985) 1).

Furthermore, in terms of style, Gebreyesus Hailu demonstrates characteristics of a post-modernist writer, as he does not privilege one genre over the other. His novel is a blend of orature, poetry, drama, and prose fiction. This claim is in line with Bradford T Stull's postulation that in a post-modern world, "no genre is given primary place in the text, considered more valuable or worthy than any other" (14). This blend emerges as that which Lyotard qualifies as anamorphosis, i.e. "constituent and disruptive figure for language" (25). The lure to join the army comprises songs to mock young men who were not interested in going to fight in Libya. This made it fitting for people to desire to go to war upon listening to the peer pressure song, "He is a woman who refuses to go to Libya" (Hailu 7). But, when he takes Eritrean conscripts onto the Libyan soil to fight Libyan Nationalist forces who in turn are fighting for their freedom, the author does not spare a tinge of irony in his depiction of "The wretched *Habesha* whose lot is suffering" (Hailu 26). Upon arriving at the legendary town of Derna, the subtle and temporal irony of those who chose to be men and not women because they wanted to go to Libya becomes situational for, "[t]his was to be their final destination. Now they knew the moment had arrived when their masculinity would be tested and many of them would meet their deaths" (Hailu 20). The narrator here prepares the readers as well as the soldiers for that which awaits them in the days ahead. One could aptly borrow from Readings' *Introducing Lyotard: Art and Politics* that instances such as this "structure history in ways that upset the understanding of it as a procession of moments independent of acts of inscription" (58). The height of the irony is when, after the first battle, the narrator claims victory for the *Habesha* only to turn around and say, "No, I am wrong. It was for the Italians" (Hailu 40). The narrator here pulls a modernist feat in revising past knowledge in the light of present development. This moment becomes central to the trend of events in this novel as it is the moment of truth, epiphany, and caution for any who wishes to embark on a journey whose destination is unknown. Tuquabo's circular journey from home ends back home, where it all started. However, home is not what it was before he left for war. Even with his father's prompting that Tek'a has simply gone somewhere to be back the next day, "Tuquabo's heart could not rest" (55). One wonders, had Tuquabo not gone to the war in Libya, would it ever have occurred to him to assert agency? Is his uncompromising stance to quit the army and be done with war not the result of his frustration in seeing the suffering of his fellow African? What could the reader learn from Tuquabo's experience?

The Conscript highlights time and space culturally specific to Africa that renders it hard to generalize or universalize their application and interpretation. This situation reiterates Jean-François Lyotard's position on post-modernism as "an understanding of the historical event as composed of simultaneous and heterogeneous temporalities: a kind of temporal irony" (Readings 24). The novel is set on a continent constantly visited by disasters: both natural and manmade. Upon seeing the Libyan shepherds in their space, Tuquabo wonders why their peace should be perturbed. He feels they should have the right to their space, peace, and tranquility. He casts an approving gaze on the Arabs who are preparing to defend what is theirs. They do not let foreigners loot it without resistance: "they did their best to save their land from aliens" (Hailu 29). However, as Mary Douglas would point out in *How Institutions Work,* we have the Italian colonial institution preventing personal curiosity as it organizes public memory and heroically imposes its own certainty, the narrator shows how the Italian commander gives Tuquabo the treatment of a child. And this leaves Tuquabo with "a lump in [his] throat and shed sad tears" moved by a sense of shame as a *Habesha*. He, who had bowed down to the Italian like a dog when his own land was taken, was now "fighting for those who came to colonize and make others tools for colonizing African neighbors…" (Hailu 29). This confirms Mary Douglas's assertion that

> The instituted community blocks personal curiosity, organizes public memory, and heroically imposes certainty. In marking its own boundaries, it affects all lower level thinking so that persons realize their own identities and classify each other through community affiliation. (102)

The journey to and from the war becomes one of cultural and geographical awakening. It is a metaphor for a much-needed African renaissance after which the author aspires. Today, the need for this renaissance is even more than ever before. In the context of *The Conscript*, Eritreans display cowardice in not fighting to defend their land and this is a crime of which every single African nation may be guilty. Earlier mention has been made of knowledge production as well as agnotology. This is clearly evident that this is the kind of mentality that goads Tuquabo to go to war in the first place. The reader is informed that Tuquabo's ambition for fame and heroism "may also have been influenced by the *Habesha* chiefs who … hated to sit idle after a break from going to war," and begged the Lord not to leave them dormant saying, "please bring us war" (Hailu 7). This ignorant stance is amplified by their boastfulness and claim that the exercise would "help trim their fattened bodies" (Hailu 7). Their claim seems to suggest there is no other way to trim such fattened bodies. However, the narrator hints that "[i]t would have been good if you'd go for a trade or out to the field to hunt game or for something harmless of that order" (Hailu 49). The narrator simply neither understands the craze for war nor the ever less-appealing theater of the war. The narrator explicitly states that the choice to go to war "to a land of thirst and famine, death, and degradation is simply incomprehensible" (Hailu 49). So, the vivid description of the journey from start to finish leaves the reader with a picture of despair from which she learns lifelong lessons, for the transformation of the African continent.

The hot Libyan Desert is the theater of the war, and the time is a hot sunny afternoon, etc. The description of the Libyan Desert/wilderness contrasts the lush Ethiopian landscape and spells losses, futility, and hopelessness for the conscripts; those compare with nothing to what they had known hitherto. The narrator paints a vivid picture of contrasting African vegetation:

> Not even a single chirping bird was heard, nor was a bird in flight seen in the desert. With open cloudless sky, it was like a hot oven. The nausea created by the permanent blaze and the absence of breeze makes one wonder whether one is in the land of life or death. What a stark difference, when you think of the green, windy, fertile land of Ethiopia, where streams flow. (24)

This awe-inspiring contrast leads the conscripts, once in the wilderness, to realize they ended up with a devil's bargain. At that realization, they had no one else to blame and were all saying, "I deserve this for wanting to come here!" (Hailu 24). Here, the reader is brought face to face with the unmaking of ignorance which can only be achieved by practical experience. Gebreyesus Hailu has the youths who in their fancy had imagined fame and heroism as coming from fighting another man's war in a foreign land to realize the hopelessness of such a venture. The experience of fighting exposes the futility of losing one's life while protecting a coward interested in nothing but personal gain. In this whole venture, Gebreyesus Hailu portrays Africans or blacks as the duped. He, however, charts a course for the limitation of power of the imperialist through Tuquabo's characterization. Tuquabo exhibits capacities and abilities of the subjugated to craft, plan, and execute forms of resistance that leaders like Mandela would later exhibit.

In a way to echo the sentiment of the Italian, the narrator points out that "but for the Italian the *Habesha* was like a weak donkey, which you couldn't kill for meat or hide and therefore would leave behind to die in the field under God's hand" (Gebreyesus Hailu 47). This haunting image of a beast of burden—the author uses it repeatedly—and the Italian who goes unscathed and with pride is a depiction from a revolutionary conscious mind that would stand up against oppression and be willing to defend the freedom of the oppressed with whatever means necessary. This reminds one of Noel Dyck's reading of Foucault's portrayal of discipline which "inconspicuously assumes the posture of a complete and finished analytical undertaking that henceforth stands ready to serve as a reliable field manual for listing and spotting the indispensable features of disciplinary regimes" (4). The narrator qualifies the Italian's attitude as "cowardly" and emphasizes the truth about the source of his pride and fame: "he gained his pride and fame from the strong young *Habesha*... when he knew that they were weakened and dying of thirst" (47) and simply thinks it is fine to do so because they are paid mercenaries. Consequently, the young *Habesha* who, like Tuquabo, initially sought fame and heroism, end up forfeiting the same to their oppressor cum the origin of their misery. *The Conscript* is replete with this game of dupe and the duped. The colonizers/Italians are conscious of cheating the colonized of the best of the land. They show their pride and knowledge of their actions.

During the departure from Asmara, the narrator shows the Italian ruse at work. They created a big mess at the train station while showing their pride. Their military police intervened and beat people with whip like donkeys. This chaotic situation at the departure station in Asmara suggested that "they knew they were indeed taking the best sons of the land" (12). Also, they knew when "The metal doors closed, and …. [that] Many of them would not make it back" (12.) This is heightened by the symbolism characterizing time and space. *Habesha* women sang melancholy songs: "The train comes smoking and your mother's daughter is crying" (12). The black train transporting the conscript is depicted as a symbol of "an evil force driving some miserable creatures to hell" (Hailu 12-13). The train drops them off in Massawa at an ominous hour evocative of the dark hour that Tuquabo felt at home and the dark hours the conscripts would face in the battlefield.

Gebreyesus Hailu uses a common rhetorical device in a rare manner. As Tuquabo comes home to his parents for blessing just before going to war, the parents shower him with rhetorical questions which indeed are rhetorical admonitions. These admonitions reveal a heightened self-consciousness of the nefarious effects of colonialism and the steps needed to transition from a subjugated Africa to a liberated and free continent. Tuquabo, once in the Libyan wilderness, becomes convinced of the emptiness of his pursuit. He is compelled to this awakening by the bitter cold and noiselessness of the night during his duties at the night post. Forced by cold and the quiet, Tuquabo's mind wanders back home. This brings him an overwhelming feeling of loneliness, one comparing him to a chunk of wood. He starts by comparing this place to his country: "In our

27

country, one never feels lonely; even if it's scary to hear sounds of wild animals at night, listening to them eases your heart nonetheless. Here, Tuquabo was standing alone like a chunk of wood" (41). He is reminded of his homeland at the sight of "a vast area of empty land surrounding him on all sides" (41). This reminder of his homeland further pushes him to think of his parents. He says to himself:

> What would my parents be doing now? Maybe they are crying when they look at my unoccupied bed? And I am here alone in this desert in gloom. What a land is this? No single tree, no grass you could step on, no twinkles of light (or sign of cooking fire) to be seen from a distant village, no sound of animals. Everywhere you go is filled with sand, day or night, endless sand. And this they call a country! Ehmm. (41)

From the above experience of loneliness and stress, Tuquabo understands the benefits of companionship. He later requests to keep his comrade company during his comrade's night duty shift. During the stint with *Habesha* comrade,

> he cried lamenting that the *Habesha* with their heroic deeds and love among themselves would have been useful if all they did was for their land, not for the benefit of strangers for whom they worked as mercenaries in a strange land. The two were left alone for the rest of the night, and they chatted until morning. Befriended this way, Tuquabo and his companion marched together from place to place, as fellow soldiers. Beaten by the heat, the sun and dust, and without water, they trekked in the wilderness for days and days on end. (43)

Here, *The Conscript* operates a major shift presented as a matter of awakening to social, cultural, diplomatic, political history of subjugation the African suffers as crucial for development of the African people. Then Tuquabo continues:

The Arabs fight for this barren land. And us? A curse be upon us!

We didn't do anything when the Italians came to take our fertile land. Not only that, we led the Italians like the blind and carried them like children and allowed them to enter our homeland, and now we are supporting them to conquer this land. We let our country be taken, and now we are instruments to occupy someone else's country. We lost our country, and we are extending our hands to colonize other lands. How would the Arabs be fighting if they had as good a land as ours? When you think of it, the Arabs here are nomads, and they shouldn't have cared too much, as they could have moved easily, leaving this barren land to the Italians. But despite all this, they did not kneel down to Italian rule. (41-42)

Gebreyesus Hailu calls for mutual understanding from the African people. He brings the Sudanese people and the Ethiopians, both going to Libya to fight as mercenaries for the colonizing power. Through this encounter, he illustrates the misunderstanding Africans should set aside to forge ahead. The apogee of this folly is captured vividly:

> There, the two peoples, the Ethiopians and the Sudanese, came face to face. The latter were thinking, "These slaves! They are going to Tribuli for money!" while the former were thinking, "These black people! They could never be superior to us," both harshly judging each other. (16-17)

This distrust, which has continued to this very day on the African continent against Gebreyesus Hailu's call for a revolution in the mentalities, sounded a century ago, constitutes the shackle leaving Africa and the African subjugated and dominated. The author concludes his call belletristically. He has Tuquabo come to the realization that he has lost his mother. When this happens, Tuquabo comes face to face with the truth and wails out a dirge for her. The dirge unveils Tuquabo's revolutionized mentality as it gives hope that the bitter lessons learned would lay the foundation for the liberation of the black man. The African / black man, like Tuquabo, needs to journey from ignorance to experience in order to gain the requisite knowledge to be able to make a volte-face. The said belletristic quality is exemplified by the dirge that would help to stop the African from:

Going to a distant land
Not for the honor of my homeland
Leaving my family behind,
In agony and tears, for two years
And knowing I killed my mother, to follow my vanity
Here I return dragging my feet
To show my unworthiness
To those I upset, my people and beloved ones.
I deserve their curse

Lacking nothing, I had plenty to eat, drink
And clothing to cover
But left my homeland, oh, such rashness
Here I return to show my unworthiness
Let all who can speak,
Mouth their condemnation

I was one blessed with his grace and with riches
Why did I put myself through this?
Mother, I know it's because of me
My sweet mother, I have failed you,
Deep within the devil deceived me.
So be it, I accept your curse
To be denied of an eye, tooth, and hand
And be barren like a fiend
I deserve worse;
So be it, let all fall upon me.
Farewell to arms
I am done with Italy and its tribulations

That robbed me of my land and parents
I am done with conscription and Italian medals
Farewell to arms! (56-57)

Bringing in a poem that concludes Gebreyesus Hailu's *The Conscript* is a recognition of the ability of poetry to say a great deal in a short space as it supercharges words with their utmost meaning. This dirge is radically transparent in terms of openness, honesty, candor, and criticism. In sum, *The Conscript* comes across as consistent at each juncture, in its themes, characterization, plot, setting, time and space management, with the black struggle and the black need for liberation. The novel readily brings to mind Antoine Berman's perspective on translation. This Tigrinya novel turns out to be a project with an articulated purpose; one determined by the specific need of a revolution of black mentality. In Berman's specific terms, "Every consistent translation is carried out by a project, or an articulated purpose. The project or aspiration is determined both by the translating position and the specific demands of each work to be translated" (60). The outcome of the crisis, with Tuquabo breaking away from his past and resigning from the Italian/colonial army, while assuming his responsibility, is a call to how blacks should handle oppressive institutions: "be done with Italy [colonization] and its tribulations/ That robbed me of my land and parents/ done with conscription and Italian [colonial] medals" (56-57). Above all, Africans must steer clear of war and bid a "farewell to arms!" Gebreyesus Hailu brings to light, through *The Conscript,* ways of operating which the subjugated could use to counterbalance the weight of domination.

Works Cited

African Studies Review vol. 28, no.2/3, 1985, p1.

Ankumah, Adaku, T. *Nomenclatural Poetization and Globalization*. Langaa-RPCIG, 2014.

Berman, Antoine. *Toward a Translation Criticism: John Donne*. (Tans. & Ed. Françoise Massardier-Kenney), Kent State UP, 2009.

Bourdieu, Pierre. *In Other Words: Essays Towards a Reflexive Sociology*, Stanford UP, 1990.

Culleton, Claire A. *Names and Naming in Joyce*. The U of Wisconsin P, 1994.

Douglas, Mary. *How Institutions Work*. Syracuse UP, 1986.

Dyck, Noel. (Ed.) *Exploring Regimes of Discipline: The Dynamics of Restraint*. Berghahn. 2008.

Fishkin, Benjamin H., Adaku T. Ankumah, & Bill F. Ndi. *Fears, Doubts, and Joys of not Belonging*. Langaa-RPCIG, 2014.

Hailu, Gebreyesus. *The Conscript,* Trans. Ghirmai Negash, Ohio UP, 2012.

Hall, Edward T. *Beyond Culture*. Anchor, 1977.

Hooks, bell. *Yearning: Race, Gender, and Cultural Politics*. South End Press, 1990.

Larson, Charles. *The Ordeal of the African Writer* Zed, 2001.

Newell, Stephanie. *West African Literatures: Ways of Reading*. Oxford UP, 2006.

Okri, Ben. *The Famished Road*. Vintage, 1992.

Palmer, Eustace. *An Introduction to the African Novel*. APC, 1972.

Readings, Bill. *Introducing Lyotard: Art and Politics*. Routledge, 1991.

Richards, Denis. *An Illustrated History of Modern Europe 1789-1974* (6th ed.) Longman, 1977.

Sartre, Jean-Paul. *What is Literature?* Translated by Bernard Frechtman, Philosophical Library, 1949.

Scott, James, C. *Domination and the Art of Resistance: Hidden Transcripts*. Yale UP, 1990.

Stull, Bradford T. *Elements of Figurative Language*. Longman, 2001.

Tye, Larry. *The Father of Spin: Edward L. Bernays and the Birth of Public Relations*. Holt, 2002.

wa Thiong'o, Ngugi. *Something Torn and New: An African Renaissance.* Civitas, 2009.

_____ *Decolonising the Mind: The Politics of Language in African Literature.* Heinemann, 1997.

Zere, Abraham T. *Narration in Gebreyesus Hailu's The Conscript.* MA Thesis, The Center for International Studies of Ohio University, 2014.

Chapter 2

Okot p'Bitek's Pro-Feminist Response to Masculinity Politics and Mythopoetic Action: Poetics of Degendering and Regendering

Elizabeth N.M. Ayuk-Etang & Andrew T. Ngeh

Postcolonial literature shares what Roy Bhaskar outlines of philosophy since: "the activity may depend upon the powers of people as material objects or causal agents rather than merely thinkers or perceivers" (14). Within the context of p'Bitek's two collections, this paper considers the coordinates for a critical realist methodology for literary interpretation in the light of Bhaskar's observation and contention here above. The world is apparently a man's world wherein the woman is perceived as an object that has to be used and discarded. This study debunks this parochial, biased and patriarchal perception of the world, and proposes a more inclusive and harmonious coexistence between both genders.

Song of Lawino and *Song of Ocol* represent two different world-views, namely, the feminist and the anti-feminist perspectives respectively. It demonstrates the persisting dualisms such as micro/macro, structure/agency, center/margin, man/woman, society/individual, black/white, and colonizer/colonized which are common in postcolonial discourse. De-gendering and re-gendering overcome the persisting dualisms such as man/woman, structure /agency and center/margin. The orientation that this paper assumes is the effort of the authors at de-gendering and re-gendering which paves the way for the restructuring of gender relations and gender differences along more egalitarian and inclusive lines.

Literary representations of women come mostly from the pens of men, and are nearly always critiqued and maligned for their inadequacy. However, with the passage of time other representations of women have emerged. No longer silent or hidden, some female characters in literary works take on life and energy and are conceived as heroic, passionate, subversive, radical and vocal. Lawino's outspokenness bears promethean testimonies. This radical reorientation has inspired the potentialities of feminist inquiry in this study. Therefore, this chapter explores the voices and lives of women as symbolized by Lawino in *Song of Lawino* and *Song of Ocol* in order to bring out the construction of an ideal objectified woman, and the flawed misogynistic construction of women in a male dominant established tradition. Secondly, the chapter will examine the significance of degendering and regendering in the poetic vision of p'Bitek, and suggests the power of textual representations and deconstruction of women as both revolutionary and visionary in time and space.

As such, before delving into the core of this subject, there is a need to clarify any ambiguity and ambivalence by taking a close look at concepts such as "mythopoetic", "regendering, and "degendering". According to Bernard Fonlon in "The Idea of Literature", the first principle of any scientific discourse is the definition of one's terms or concepts to provide a sense of direction so the reader knows "clearly and precisely right from the start" what these terms or concepts mean (179).

According to the Online version of the Oxford dictionary, mythopoetic relates to the making of a myth or myths. Through experiences of community, rituals and teachings, make men and women to be conscious of their cultural realities. Mythopoetic relates or denotes a movement for men that use activities such as storytelling and poetry reading as a means of self-understanding.p'Bitek's Song of *Lawino and Song of Ocol* are exemplifications of African oral literary aesthetics. It is a story-telling occasion which brings out African oral traditions, history and culture. p'Bitek's poetic imagination is based on African cultural realities; in fact, it is the recreation of African cultural history based on history In this case, Ocol is being creative in his myth of men's supremacy over the women, a myth that is widely celebrated and valorized in patriarchal societies. On the contrary, degendering and regendering are means men use to exit from the practice of anti-sexist politics. Degendering and regendering are important because they address the fundamental basis of gender inequality. And by so doing, they problematize gender relations and create frictions in postcolonial relationships that ought to be harmonious, that is, man-woman relationship.

Women are not inferior in nature, but are inferiorized by African culture, tradition and patriarchy. Gendering in postcolonial discourse constitutes a grave danger to the collective and harmonious existence between the male folk and female folk. The process of gendering in which men and women are constituted as difference accounts for the absence of this harmonious existence. This difference serves as justification for unequal treatment in which men are cast as a category that is valued more highly than women are, and imbued with power over women as an inferior category. From this standpoint, the following questions arise: Are women inferior in nature or inferiorized by culture, tradition and patriarchy? What is the relationship between sex and gender in the postcolonial context? What is the place of degendering and re-gendering? What is the relationship between the cultural code and the message conveyed in the text? What is the place of masculinity and exit politics in the context of gendering?

Based on the questions above, this chapter contends that Okot p'Bitek in *Song of Lawino* and *Song of Ocol* uses Lawino and Ocol as allegorical figurations to comment on gender inequality caused by patriarchy. Lawino represents the oppressed and culturally and socially excluded and marginalized women. She tries to subvert both the social and cultural construct ascribed to the women by trying to undo gendering as a means of restructuring gender relations and gender difference along more egalitarian and inclusive lines. p'Bitek

37

in his two poetry collections writes with the consciousness and conviction that envision a non-hierarchical society. This study further contends that de-gendering and re-gendering are meant to create a stable and harmonious existence between the two genders. De-gendering and re-gendering become vital tools used to work out less hierarchical and dominating ways of being men in the world. In this light, if writing and thinking could demonstrably be seen to transcend the body, then there would be no argument for excluding women from the public sphere. p'Bitek's poetry speaks to the inclusion of women in public sphere and discourse and thus calls for a brief sociology of reception.

A socio-historical and literary investigation of the presentations and representations of women in African literary works revealed that women have been elbowed to the margin and the periphery of the society. They are not heard but are only seen serving men at home and in occasions; they are rendered voiceless because they are not given the opportunity by the men to express their views and opinions on pertinent societal and family issues. In p'Bitek's Song of *Lawino and Song of Ocol*, Lawino who is a symbol of the marginalized women is articulate, assertive, resilience and resourceful. P'Bitek attempts to restore the woman by giving her a voice.

In "Imaging the woman through Tanzanian Women's Maxims", Shani Omari and Fikeni E.M.K Senkoro basing their arguments on previous research works carried out by scholars like Matteru, 1982; Senkoro, 1988; Mbughuni, 1982; Kayoka, 2000; Momanyi, 2001; Omari, 2008; Lyatuu, 2011; Mkomwa, 2014) found that to a larger extent a woman is depicted as an inferior being compared to a man. For instance, Mbughuni (1982:15) concludes that one of the reasons for negative portrayal of women in literary works is due to the fact that "most authors are men; therefore women receive very little character development" (120). However, in the present study, although the author is a man, he tries to empower Lawino in spite of Ocol's confrontation and his use of violent language and diatribes on his beloved wife who is only trying to correct him.

Another scholar and critic, Stratton Florence in the blurb of her *Contemporary African Literature and the Politics of Gender* contends that, "The influence of colonialism and race on the development of African literature has been the subject of a number of studies but the effect of patriarchy and gender, and indeed the contributions of African women, have up until now been largely ignored by critics". This contention hinges on and traces the historicity of women's marginalization to the politics of colonialism and imperialism. Western education is synonymous with imperialism, and this is clearly demonstrated by Ocol's unpleasant behaviour and his uncritical acceptance of western values in spite of Lawino's cautionary note. His mission is to stifle Lawino and render her voiceless typical of patriarchy.

In "Unbending Gender Narratives in African Literature", Charles Fonchingong argues that,

> Male writers like Chinua Achebe, Elechi Amadi, Wole Soyinka, Ngugi wa Thiong'o, and Cyprian Ekwensi in their literary mass are accused of condoning patriarchy, are deeply entrenched in a macho conviviality and a one dimensional and minimalised presentation of women who are demoted and assume peripheral roles. Their penchant to portray an androcentric narrative is at variance with the female gender that are trivialized through practices like patriarchy, tradition, culture, gender socialization process, marriage and domestic enslavement. (135)

The paper concludes with some contemporary showcases and meta-narratives by both male and female writers like Buchi Emecheta, Mariama Bâ, Ama Ata Aidoo, Flora Nwapa, Sembène Ousmane and Léopold Sédar Senghor who attempt to bridge the gender rifts in the African literary landscape by both male and female writers like Buchi Emecheta, Mariama Bâ, Ama Ata Aidoo, Flora Nwapa, Sembene Ousmane and Leopold Sedar Senghor who attempt to bridge the gender rifts in the African literary landscape.

Another scholar on gender and feminist issues, Mary Moran, drawing her inspiration from the Liberian political experience that catapulted Johnson Sirleaf to the highest political position in Liberia in an article entitled, "Our Mothers Have Spoken: Synthesizing Old and New Forms of Women's Political Authority in Liberia", uses the case of Johnson Sirleaf to interrogate two common assumptions about Africa embedded in some of the scholarly literature as well as in much popular journalism and the discourses of humanitarian activism, specifically: 1) that highly unequal and even oppressive gender relations characterized the "traditional culture" of most if not all African societies prior to any particular period of upheaval and violence and, 2) that lack of democratic institutions and values are directly related to both these perceived gender inequities and the conflict which must be resolved by post-war reconstruction and democratic reform. (52) Moran's focus is on democratizing the patriarchal institutions in order to negotiate and navigate a place for the women in the political spheres. This is germane to our study in the sense that Ocol's dictatorship and autocracy is dangerous for the existence of the women. He is an embodiment of patriarchy.

In "Issues in Women's Liberation Struggles in Contemporary Nigeria: A Study of Ezeigbo's *Hands that Crush Stone* (2010), Osita C. Ezenwanebe underlines and highlights the pivotal contributions women made in the anti-colonial struggle for a complete decolonization process. Drawing his inspiration from Ezeigbo's play entitled, *Hands that Crush Stone,* Ezenwanebe's paper evaluates some contentious issues in women's liberation struggles in Nigeria as recreated in the play. He argues that,

> The particularities of gender are neglected in the anti-colonial struggle for Nigerian independence, and women's issues are subsumed within the nationalist literatures of cultural regeneration. With the influence of feminism, many Nigerian women embark on the

identification of women's personhood by controverting the representations of Nigerian women in male-centered works. (262)

Ezenwanebe is of the opinion that, African theatre, in particular, is very sceptical about the feminist ideology aimed at changing the status of women in society. Similarly, many people are suspicious of women's liberation struggle and its consequent effect on the society. Hence feminism in Nigeria is rent with many contentious issues. (262) His argument is that women in African societies deserve much more than the shabby treatment that they are accorded in a patriarchal set-up.

A gamut of critical reviews has been written on p'Bitek's *Song of Lawino* and *Song of Ocol,* but adequate attention has not been given to the concepts of regendering and degendering. In the introduction to *Song of Ocol,* G.A. Heron argues that, "If *Song of Ocol* is a reply to *Song of Lawino,* then it is a bad one. Okot p'Bitek raises controversial issues in his poems, but he only puts one point of view in the controversy... These two poems are not the thesis and antithesis of the argument from which the reader can deduce a synthesis." (20)

In his article entitled, "Poetic view Point: Okot p'Bitek and His *Song of Lawino, Song of Ocol and Song of a Prisoner*", Tanure Ojaide examines the three personae in these 'songs' and how they function thematically and stylistically, and proposes the poet's point of view. According to Ojaide, Lawino seems to be the most likable character of the three. She represents the indigenous authentic African way of life. Conversely, Ocol is a detestable character because he is presented as a cultural renegade. And the prisoner is presented as unstable and not reliable. (371)

Thus, the poet's viewpoint in Lawino is romantic and realistic, in Ocol ironic, and in Prisoner ambivalent and pessimistic. Lawino is the poet's voice in Lawino. The poem begins with "My Husband's Tongue is Bitter" in which Lawino recounts what her husband, Ocol, says about her people and black people in general.

41

Against this background, and as telli has suggested, Okot p'Bitek should give Ocol and Tina a chance to defend themselves in the light of Lawino's 'lawsuit' or complaint. Therefore, this chapter sets out to examine and excavate the ideological dialectics and masculinity politics in p'Bitek's poetic vision and his attempt to re-gender in order to degender. At the heart of this essay is masculinity politics where the meaning of masculine gender, politics, culture and race is in relations with gender. The study further submits that p'Bitek's poetic vision represents a more scholarly rendition of the ideas of marginal discourse that call for literary theoretical consideration.

Sustaining all critical effort is the whole matter of suasion, especially given that no writing is without intent. If writing is not an end in itself, reading cannot be. Reading is a quest both for pleasure and for persuasive material. Each text, upon completion, remains in the balance until it is tipped into oblivion or relevance by the studied verdict of readership – criticism. And that verdict is facilitated by a critical theory particular to each reader and each context. Texts therefore undergo a new birth each time they are (re)read against the backdrop of a critical theory. Tutuola's *The Palm-Wine Drinkard* (1952) owes its life in African letters to the critical act, in other words the aesthetic verdict, of a singular reader, Dylan Thomas. This study is informed by the postcolonial theory. Since the complex phenomenon of 'postcolonialism' is rooted in the history of imperialism, it is worth discussing this history. The word imperialism is derived from the Latin word, *imperium,* which has numerous meanings including power, authority, command, domination, realm and empire. Though imperialism is understood as a strategy whereby a state aims to extend its control forcibly beyond its own borders over other states and people, it should be remembered that such control is usually not just military but economic, social, and cultural or even linguistic. A ruling state will often impose not only its own terms of trade, but also its political ideals, its own cultural values, and often its own language, upon a subject state.

Three major phases have characterized imperialism. Between 1492 and the mid-eighteenth century, Spain and Portugal, England, France, and the Netherlands established colonies and empires in the Americas, the East Indies, and India. Then between the mid-nineteenth century and World War 1, there was an immense scramble for imperialistic power between Britain, France, Germany, Italy, and other nations. By the end of the nineteenth century, more than one fifth of the land area of the world and a quarter of its population had been brought under the British Empire: India, Canada, Australia, New Zealand, South Africa, Burma and the Sudan. The next largest colonial power was France, whose possessions included Algeria, French West Africa, Equatorial Africa and Indochina. Germany, Italy, and Japan also entered the race for colonies. In 1855 Belgium established the Belgian Congo in the heart of Africa, a colonization whose horrors are expressed in Conrad's *Heart of Darkness*. Colonization has adversely affected Africa's culture and the collective consciousness of its people because postcolonial literature and criticism arose both during and after the struggles of many nations in Africa, Asia and Latin America, now referred to as "tricontinent."

Postcolonial criticism has embraced a number of aims:

- To re-examine the history of colonialism from the perspective of the colonized;
- To determine the economic, political, and cultural impact of colonialism on both the colonized peoples and the colonizing powers
- To analyze the process of decolonization;
- To participate in the goals of political liberation which include equal access to material resources, the contestation of forms of domination, and the articulation of political and cultural identities.
- The need to develop or return to indigenous literary traditions so as to exorcize their cultural heritage of the specters of imperial domination.

Although some voices have advocated an adaptation of Western ideals towards their own political and cultural ends, the fundamental framework of postcolonial thought has been furnished by the Marxist critique of colonialism and imperialism, which has been adapted to their localized contexts by thinkers from Frantz Fanon to Gayatri Spivak.

Postcolonialism cuts across race, gender oppression, class division, culture, power and language, hence, postcolonial discourse potentially embraces and is intimately linked with a broad range of dialogues within the colonizing powers, addressing various forms of "internal colonization" as treated by minority studies of various kinds such as African-American, native American, Latin American, and women's studies. All of these discourses have challenged the main streams of Western philosophy, literature and ideology.

The nineteenth century witnessed the flowering of numerous major female literary figures in both Europe and America ranging from Mme de Stael, the Brontes, Jane Austen, George Elliot, and Elizabeth Barret Browning to Margaret Fuller and finally Emily Dickinson. The proliferation of these feminist voices was because for long, women were not only deprived of education and financial independence, they also had to struggle against a male ideology condemning them to virtual silence and obedience, as well as a male literary establishment that poured scorn and contempt on their literary endeavours.

The feminist literary criticism is the direct product of the women movement of the 1960s. This movement was, in important ways, literary from the start in the sense that it realized the significance of the images of women promulgated by literature, and saw it as vital to combat them and question their authority and their coherence. (Barry, 121) Thus, in feminist criticism in the 1970s the major effort went into exposing what might be called mechanisms of patriarchy, that is, the cultural mind-set in men and women which perpetuated sexual inequality. Particular attention was given to books written by male writers in which influential or typical images of women were constructed. By this, this study exposes the exclusivity of the dominant tradition and raises questions about the construction of literary history and the aesthetic values that have always seemed to find women's writing lacking. That explains why in this study the authors have chosen two texts written by one male poet expressing two different views, namely, the woman's perspective of life and the male's view as expressed in *Song of Lawino* and *Song of Ocol* respectively.

Pascal Newbourn E. Nwale (2002) clarifies the tenets of feminism thus:

> Feminist ideology purports to create its own better ideas, beliefs, or attitudes. In other words, feminist ideology creates its own counter-consciousness, and eventually its own counterculture. This counterculture comprises a new set of beliefs and a new style of life that is intended or hoped to challenge and eventually expose the inadequacy of the prevailing culture. Only when the ideological core of the prevailing culture is removed and replaced by a new ideological core can lasting and effective change occur, any change less than that involving the ideological core is superficial or transitory. In a nutshell, feminism challenges the prevailing *status quo* and develops a counter-ideology that questions the prevailing *status quo* and then attempts to modify it. Feminism advocates change rather than order. It criticizes the regime in power and existing social and economic arrangements. It advances schemes for restructuring and reordering society. It generates political movements in the form of women's movements in order to gain enough power and influence to effect the changes it advocates. Feminism is an ideology of action for it motivates people to demand changes in their lifestyles and to modify the existing social, religious, political, and economic relations. It also mobilizes its followers and adherents to preserve what they value. (114-137)

Feminist criticism undertakes a combative and polemical tone.

Again, it questions the patriarchal society that relegates women to the background and reduces them to objects and not subjects of the society with agency. This raises a question as to whether Lawino leans on a Counterculture and the De-gendering Agenda.

Lawino is a metaphor, a prototype of Mother Africa lamenting the corrosion and erosion of African cultural values by both colonialism and neocolonialism represented by the "Been-tos." Lawino who in this instance is the mouthpiece of p'Bitek clearly brings this out with realistic intensity. In the very first poem in *Song of Lawino* entitled "My Husband Tongue is Bitter", the harsh, violent and confrontational words of Ocol as recounted by Lawino is a clear demonstration of Ocol's hatred for the ways of the African people. Everything that Ocol stands against is seen in Lawino. Paradoxically, Ocol is the son of a chief, the guarantor and custodian of the people's culture; yet, he is the very antithesis of what he represents:

> Listen Ocol, you are the son of a Chief,
> Leave foolish behaviour to little children,
> It is not right that you should be laughed at in a song!
> Songs about you should be songs of praise! (14)

Lawino and Ocol represent two different worlds, namely the African and the West. While Lawino strives at negotiating and navigating a complex and painful past accentuated by colonialism, Ocol is there to frustrate such a move because of his separation from the cultural realities of Africa. The poet/persona reminds him that as the son of a Chief, he should not be mocked in songs; rather he should be praised and celebrated in such songs because he incarnates African values.

In *Anatomy of Female Power*, Chinweizu argues "...that a man comes of age at 60, and a woman at 15; which is why, in the eyes of women, men are babies or, at best, little boys"). When Nora Ephron, declares: "Men are little boys" (qtd in Chinweizu, 1990: 15) she was voicing a view held, and frequently articulated, by women all over the world. That men are babies or little boys is why a bride can fool her suitor, however much older than her he may be; and why a wife can rule her husband so readily. Although Chinweizu was writing against the backdrop of the anatomy of female power, we can as well relate the childish behaviour of Ocol with regard to the African ways. The rhythm and harmony of the collective existence of the African people have been disrupted by people like Ocol who are making everything possible to jettison and obliterate the African way of life.

The making of these childish statements demonstrates anger, rage and frustration which are contrasted with Lawino's self-confidence in the African way of life. The uncritical acceptance of Western values is itself a fall into childish rages, a return to the desire for an all-comforting protection. This is seen in lines like:

He says I am rubbish,
He no longer wants me!
In cruel jokes, he laughs at me,
He says I am primitive
Because I cannot play the guitar,
He says my eyes are dead
And I cannot read. (15)

While Lawino tries to negotiate and navigate the very complex past and the more complicated present situation because of the realities of physical, psychological, ideological, and cultural separations, the assimilated Ocol seems not to see its relevance. Lawino states:

Ocol says
The way his mother
Brings up children
Only leads

To ignorance, poverty and disease
He swears
He has no confidence
In the wisdom of the Acoli (152).

Lawino in p'Bitek's poetic vision is a dense symbol with metaphorical possibilities. She represents African cultural values. By rejecting her, Ocol rejects African cultural values. The venom of Ocol's resentment and hatred continues to smolder in his spirit, while a ruthless passion for power and dominance gnaws at the oppressed African woman symbolized by Lawino. Certain words and phrases in the poem like "play guitar", "cannot read", and "cannot count coins" are clear exemplifications of Ocol's loss of identity, and his passion for cultural imperialism. The richness of this poem resides in the various images and allusions to Western elements which deepen the thought and feeling of the poem:

He says Black People are primitive
And their ways are utterly harmful,
Their dances are mortal sins
They are ignorant, poor and disease. (17)

Ocol says he is a modern man,
A progressive and civilized man,
He says he has read extensively and widely
And he can no longer live with a thing like me
Who cannot distinguish between good and bad. (17)

"My Husband Tongue is Bitter" and "The Last Safari to Pagak" are two poems that treat the relationship of past to present; of that which one is made; of death; and especially, of the two sides of the self: the active and the self-observant, or the doer (in African thought, the female) and whether (the male). p'Bitek tends to clearly bring out

48

the ideological dialectics. These two poems are primarily satiric in drawing ironic comparisons between the African and Western ways of life symbolized by Lawino and Ocol respectively. Lawino in lamenting about Ocol's chastisement of Acoli's value is using the central concerns of African values.

Insulting one's wife and in-laws in Africa is unethical as it is unacceptable as Tanure Ojaide indicates: "…a modern man, a progressive and civilized man, who "has read extensively and widely" (17), and despises Lawino because she is antiquated, illiterate, pagan, and physically ugly ("the owl type"), and unintelligent. Consequently, she is said to be "blocking his progress" (17). He does not insult her alone but also insults her aunt, from whom he guesses Lawino inherited her stupidity Abusing one's aunt-in-law is unethical in the way of life which Lawino tries to affirm" (371).

Losing his cultural bearings, his past, he is dizzy, terrified, but pretentiously happy with his new found way of life while another part of him watches him coolly, an inversion of his desires. Poetry and life consist of making such webs filled with holes. Ocol's roots are in African culture, but he has westernized and modernized his ways by virtue of his imperial education which has not only eroded but corroded and blurred his vision and perspective. Ocol is an uprooted individual without anything to which he can return; he is without any society. To put it more bluntly, he is a cultural bastard.

In "The Woman with Whom I Share My Husband", p'Bitek clearly brings out Clementine as Ocol's 'partner in crime'. Since Ocol has imbibed both the Western ideology and philosophy, he must also align with Clementine whose vision is similar. All the things she does contrast sharply with the African way of life: her make-ups, her stature, her movements, etc.:

Brother, when you see Clementine!
The beautiful one aspires
To look like a white woman;

Her lips are red-hot
Like glowing charcoal,
She resembles the wild cat
That has dipped its mouth in blood,
Her mouth is like raw yaws
It looks like an open ulcer,
Like the mouth of a field!
Tina dusts powder on her face
And it looks so pale;
She resembles the wizard
Getting ready for the midnight dance. (22)

In this particular poem, the poet/persona who is a lady confronts another lady not because she is jealous, but because she does not fulfil the requirements of an African woman. The poet uses a plethora of similes with realistic intensity, exemplifying the ephemeral nature and artificiality of the western acquired culture: Clementine's red-hot lips that glow like charcoal and frightful looks that are compared to the wild cat are grotesque, nauseating and frightful images. All of these make her look pale, demonstrating the inanity and ephemeral and destructive nature of western culture.

The poet's diction in this particular poem creates a sense of despondency and disillusionment. In this poem there is a system of basic symbols in which phrases like "red-hot", "wild cat", "mouth blood", "raw yaws", "open ulcer" "so pale" "the wizard" can be the allegorical figurations of self-deception. "The Woman with Whom I share My Husband" is focused on the crisis that characterizes the meeting of two different cultures. The two cultures are symbolically and metaphorically presented in ironic, reflective and analytical manner, but also enclosing the emotions and channeling them towards thought, discipline, judgments, and decision- making. Within the context of thought, the underlying question is of what relevance is the western culture to the African way of life? Regarding discipline, if Africans are not disciplined, they will be carried away or misled by the value-less way of the west as highlighted in the following lines:

And she believes
That this is beautiful
Because it resembles the face of a white woman!
Her body resembles
The ugly coat of the hyena;
Her neck and arms
Have real human skins!
She looks as if she has been struck
By lightening
Or burnt like the kongoni
In a fire hunt (23)

In this stanza, the poet makes it abundantly clear that the imbibed western values which Tina incarnates adumbrate the disagreeable qualities of the west which are symbolic of the stress on the mind and body of those who consciously try to imitate as opposed to the easy, natural and pastoral way of the African people which suggests innocence and a clear perspective on life.

The persona's imagination deftly shifts between her life, the Acoli and its surroundings, the particular and the general, the local and the allegorical. Before the coming into their lives by Tina, Lawino and Ocol had experienced a peaceful co-existence:

Ocol rejects the old type,
He is in love with a modern woman,
He is in love with a beautiful girl
Who speaks English

But only recently
We would sit close together, touching each other!

51

Only recently I would play
On my bow-harp
Singing praises to my beloved.
Only recently he promised
That he trusted me completely.
I used to admire him speaking in English. (22-3)

Love in the context of the west is ephemeral because it is not natural; materialism is the hallmark of the concept of love in the setting of the West; physical and facial adornments and weight watching are the hallmarks of the western concept of love as opposed to the woman's pot in a typical African setting. Chinweizu in *Anatomy of Female Power* contends that:

> There is a joke which goes thus: 1st woman: The way to a man's heart is through his belly. 2nd woman: Aren't you aiming a few inches too high? This joke pays tribute to how the womb and the kitchen control the feelings of men. A man can be controlled by the hunger in his belly and by the other hunger which flares up just below his belly. (15)

This realistic philosophy which is rooted in African romance seems to be completely absent in the West. That is why Ocol goes in for the artificial adornments of Clementine. Again, that explains why Ocol who has imbibed Western values quickly discards Lawino and replaces her with Clementine. The impression created by the poet is that love in the western sense is deadening, dull and unspectacular; the mind hopes for miracles, but there is the ordinariness of most events in the love life of the African people.

p'Bitek in this poem records the confused mind of Ocol as he is caught between and betwixt conflicting values. A similar lack of ability and purpose to critically choose what is relevant, a similar self-satisfied confusion with the wrong values, and lack of will, the inability to master the modern world and make the right choices is behind the tragi-comedy of Ocol. That is why the speaker in the poem is very cautious with her diction; she is not jealous because she is sharing her husband given that sharing is an aspect of African socialism and communalism rooted in African epistemology and ontology:

Forgive me, brother,
Do not think I am insulting
The woman with whom I share my husband!
Do not think my tongue
Is being sharpened by jealousy.
It is the sight of Tina
That provokes sympathy from my heart. (24)

Sexual attraction, physical and artificial adornments seem to be Ocol's interest and not natural love. The poet/persona insinuates that along with whatever decisions Ocol makes in his love life, love should be at the centre. And that there is an increasing attraction to the artificial adornments of the modern woman, a need for some way to get beyond the self without giving up the self to modernism and the western vision and conceptualization of love. In other words, Lawino insinuates that her husband whom she now shares with Clementine can seize the world without being a vulture; he can give up his ego without losing interests in the world and in such basic pleasures like sex, love, and success. But she cautions as someone who is learned, he should choose wisely so that he does not plunge himself into crisis. It is clear that Ocol lives in the confusion of modern life rather than by way of African traditional life. This lack of critical mind will only accentuate the loss of his cultural bearings resulting in the stultification of both moral and cultural forces. This is deadening causing loss of cultural vitality and enthusiasm through man's gendering agenda and masculinity politics.

Having listened to the lament of the Mother Earth in Lawino,

Ocol, her husband has to be listened to as well. The charges and allegations leveled against him are too overwhelming to be ignored. As Taban Lo Liyong has suggested, Ocol needs to be listened to. This will allow for a comprehensive and panoramic view of the story. Although in *Song of Lawino*, Lawino cautions Ocol in a very gentle and soft tone, Ocol in *Song of Ocol* reacts violently to some of the concerns/charges raised by Lawino. This linguistic violence does not come as a surprise because it is common practice within the context of patriarchy. The fundamental concern within feminist discourse has always been how women should confront the task of being historically coerced into using a language dominated by male concepts and values. Some feminists have urged the need for a female language, while others have advocated appropriating and modifying the inherited language of the male oppressor. The patriarchal system has all that it takes to oppress, marginalize and subjugate the woman, and language is just one of the instruments of oppression. That explains Ocol's verbal assault, aggressiveness and confrontation. Lawino's cautionary note to Ocol is met with stiff resistance which is characterized by violence, diatribes, calumny and aggression.

According to M.A.R Habib in *Modern Literary Criticism and Theory*, the significance of language rests ultimately on its expression of male ways of thinking that go all the way to Aristotle: the laws of logic, beginning with the law of identity, as well as the Aristotelian categories which divide up the world into strictly demarcated entities. These binary oppositions, as many modern theorists have argued, are coercive: for example, according to Aristotle's laws, either one is a man or one is a woman; a person is either black or white, either master or slave. (668) However, feminists have often rejected these divisive ways of viewing the world, stressing that these are cultural and ideological constructions. They advocate unity rather than division. Ocol's violent and confrontation language on Lawino clearly explains the dominant tradition of patriarchy from a sociolinguistic perspective.

Michael Messner points out a variety of masculinity politics which have been created as men's movements have contended with issues such as: men's institutionalized privileges, the costs of masculinity for men, and differences and inequalities among men. (qtd. in Wing, 97)

The four different types of masculinity politics include the Gun Lobby, Masculinity therapy, Gay liberation and Exit politics. However, this section of this chapter shall preoccupy itself with Gun Lobby masculinity therapeutic politics and Exit Politics because they are relevant in p'Bitek's two collections under study.

The Gun Lobby masculinity politics borders on the institutionalization of gender inequality and the cultural ascendancy of hegemonic masculinity whose projects typically serve to render these configurations of practice as invisible and taken for granted. When an active defense of hegemonic projects becomes necessary though, it is possible to identify what Raewyn Connell has characterized as a "gun lobby" type of politics that is oriented toward maintaining competitive and dominance-oriented masculinity practices based on glorification of hyper-masculine violence; the production of exemplary masculinities that embody masculine heroism; physical prowess and athletic ability, and/or heterosexual conquest; and the legitimation of the continued (global) domination of ownership and management of corporations by men (qtd. in Wing 98).

Exit politics according to Raewyn Connell expresses explicit resistance to pressures to actively engage with and appropriate hegemonic masculinity projects. One is a personalized (or individualized) project of reconstructing the masculine self in which men may distance themselves from their fathers and other men and come to identify with their mothers and other women (the moment of distancing/negation) and come to renounce masculinity by attempting to become non-sexist individuals (the moment of separation). The other project favored by Connell is a collective project of social transformation that is directed at contesting the patriarchal gender order. Degendering and regendering are the hallmarks of Exit politics because they aim at minimizing gender inequality and gender differences.

In p'Bitek's poetics, especially in the context of *Song of Lawino* and *Song of Ocol,* hegemonic masculinity, gender inequality and cultural ascendancy take precedence. Furthermore, Lawino's stance on certain issues calls for regendering and degendering which are the benchmarks of Exit politics; that is men exiting from patriarchal politics.

Violence, diatribes, insolence, and calumny characterize the language of the very first poem, in *Song of Ocol.* This is a reflection of the cultural hegemony of patriarchy. To Ocol, Lawino has no point; her song is "A solo fragment/With no chorus/No accompaniment, / A strange melody/ Impossible to orchestrate" (121). Ocol's highly virulent statements are layered with many different tropes or kinds of material for interpretation. First, it demonstrates masculine politics where the men are at the center; secondly, it brings out the subjugation and oppression of the woman; thirdly, it expresses gender dialectics; finally, it questions the existence of the woman in a male dominated world:

Woman,
Shut up!
Pack your things
Go!
Take all the clothes
I bought you
The beads, necklaces
And the remains
Of the utensils,
I need no second-things. (121)

This reductionism marginalizes women in a conservative

framework by presenting women as the problem. It is evident from Ocol's insolent and abusive language that the problem is not inadequacies, but a "canon" which reifies and marginalizes particularly the female sex.

Lawino's crime is that she tries to caution her husband not to derail from the right path, but Ocol insults and abuses her. The way to live to avoid emptiness and extremes is Lawino's concern; considering the fact that Ocol, the son of a traditional chief is analogous to that pumpkin in a homestead which must not be uprooted; it must be protected and preserved for posterity. The pumpkin is perceived here as past, as memory, as tradition, as origin, of which different views are offered; it is a vegetable considered as a delicacy in Africa. Although p'Bitek's sympathy lies with Lawino, he is more concerned with his Acoli culture which is a microcosm of the macrocosmic African culture; he does not sentimentalize it, but brings out the reality and authenticity of such a culture. However, the path which Ocol has taken is characterized by loneliness, reclusion, and estrangement, and this can only foster despair and disillusionment. Lawino's counsel if heeded will bring about a new exhilaration and cultural stamina in Ocol's being, but he resorts to insults:

Song of the woman
Is the confused noise
Made by the ram
After the butcher's knife
Has sunk past
The wind-pipe
Red paint spraying
On the grass
It is a song all alone
A solo fragment (121)

By comparing Lawino's song to the last cry of a ram to be slaughtered, Ocol symbolically sees the plight of the oppressed women as a farce, a joke that should be ignored: Song of the woman/Is the mad bragging of a defeated General,/Ten thousand men/Dead, dying,/The others scattered (122). The venom of resentment, hatred, and vengeance continues to smolder in the spirit of Ocol so much so that Lawino, according to Ocol, is a value-less chattel of which to be disposed. He despises, disparages, casts aside, and excludes his once loving wife because of a "modern woman." Because of the so-called modern woman who represents a foreign ideology, Ocol, the son of the custodian and guarantor of African cultural values becomes very hostile, vengeful, reactionary, and violent towards his African wife who represents what Africa stands for.

Ocol's beliefs, actions, feelings, knowledge, achievement, (he is a civilized and educated African), and adjustment have created a radical new vision of his world. There is a dislocation between the inner culture which Lawino encapsulates, and the outer and artificial culture which Ocol and Tina encompass is clearly demonstrated. Ocol, the poet/persona attests to this: Song of the woman/Is sour sweet, /It is pork gone rancid, /It is honeyed/Bloodied sour milk/In the sinking/Maasai gourd (124). This oxymoron is a poetic device par excellence. In a self-betraying statement, Ocol unconsciously indicates the reality and authenticity of Lawino's song. He says that her song is both sweet and bitter because, first she is telling her husband, Ocol the truth about the reality and authenticity of his cultural values; secondly, it is bitter because she is telling him the bitter truth that he is losing his cultural bearings. Again, her song is honey-sweet and at the same time sour milk because there is the unpredictable continuity of the past, present, and future, the knowledge that while the past must determine the future, one is unable to see exactly how in casual terms: We will obliterate/Tribal boundaries/And throttle native tongues/To dumb death (124). The theme of life as changing and the sub theme or motif of the continuity reinforced by the symbol of "native tongues" and the alliteration, "...dumb death" bring out the individual identity and character of Ocol as someone who does not realize that his fantasy is filled with holes. He is unaware that he is losing his cultural bearings. He is ignorant of the fact there is no solution in the modern world to worries about personal identity, tradition, and cultural crisis.

The excitement of early love has turned into arguments, abuses, insults and calumny. Happiness has degenerated into sadness; love into hatred. The poem offers a disillusioned view of marriage and love: Song of the woman/Is the mad bragging/Of a defeated General, (126).

In the second poem in *Song of Ocol*, the poet/persona turns his war cannon towards Africa. In his characteristic manner, he denigrates and debases African cultural values. In other words, he dilutes the very culture that accounts for his existence. The poem starts with a rhetorical question:

What is Africa
To me?
Blackness,
Deep, deep fathomless
Darkness;
Africa,
Idle giant
Basking in the sun,
Sleeping, snoring,
Twitching in dreams
Diseased with a chronic illness,
Choking with black ignorance,
Chained to the rock
Of poverty (125).

Africa is a dense symbol with metaphorical possibilities; it is a synecdoche; it is personified because it is not a geographical expression but a metaphysical landscape. In this stanza, the persona demonstrates the binary opposition which is common in postcolonial discourse: Africa/the west; white/black; Orientalism/Occidentalism; man/woman; the colonizer/ the colonized. In this light, hybridity takes centre stage by highlighting notions of identity, culture and nation as coherent and unified entities that exhibit a linear historical development. This concept of hybridity is the dilemma in which the persona in *Song of Ocol* finds himself, and this is a state of "in between-ness."

Caught in the web of the ideological vision of the west, the persona joins the ranks of Joyce Cary, Joseph Conrad and other western writers who had perceived Africa as a fantasy which is not realistic. If Africa exists at all, it is: Deep, deep fathomless/ Darkness/ Africa/ Idle giant/ Basking in the sun/Sleeping, snoring/Twitching in dreams. As "a civilized" and someone who has been brain-washed by western ideology and philosophy, Ocol does not see anything good in Africa. Postcolonial cultural nationalism needs to be more sophisticated and critical than the simple sentiments expressed by Ocol.

Africa is described in the poem as a child who is yet to attain maturity. As a child, she is a lover of toys: Child/Lover of toys/Look at his toy weapons/His utensils, his hut.../Toy garden, toy chickens/Toy cattle/Toy children (125). Everything about Africa is diminutive; everything about Africa is unrealistic. In this poem there is the desire to be settled, to be home, to be done with exile, alienation, and the pains of life, but paradoxically, Ocol is a cultural bastard because either way, he will not be accepted. There is an increasing focus on the culturally brainwashed Africans as dangerous threats to the survival of African cultural heritage. He is an uprooted African without anything to which he can return; he is without any society since he has rejected Africa as superstitious, underdeveloped, and uncivilized. He needs to keep defining himself: Stuck in the stagnant mud/Of superstitious,/Frightened by the spirits/Of the bush, the streams/The rock/Scared of several corpses…(125).

There are striking explorations of the grotesque and macabre indicating evidence of cultural genocide caused by one of Africa's children. This is clearly demonstrated in the angry, highly virulent, and aggressive tone regarding African culture and belief system in which the persona castigates and denigrates Africa: To hell/With your Pumpkins/And your Old Homesteads/To hell/With the husks/ Of old traditions/ And meaningless customs, (126). This is a poem about repression and suppression of one's cultural values due to the deceptive darts of an alien culture: Like beggars/you take up white men's adornments,/Like slaves or war captives/ You take up white men's ways/Didn't the Acoli have adornments?/Didn't black people have their ways? (47-8)

Ocol's emotional outburst with regard to the African way of life is his proclaimed differences of his attitude which are usually more minor shifts of opinion and adjustments than radically new visions of the world. Ocol is concerned with the need for change, renewal and adaptability, but he forgets that the pumpkin in the old homesteads is the cultural bastion that must not be uprooted; it is the very foundation on which his cultural values are rooted. It is also the fertile soil on which his cultural values thrive to show p'Bitek's poetic vision through exit politics.

Bradley W. Wing, in *Degendering and Regendering: Recomposing Masculinities through Ant-Sexist Masculinity Projects,* highlights the tenets of Exit politics as the counter-culture and feminism, gender projects that take the form of explicit resistance to pressures to actively engage with appropriate hegemonic masculinity projects; projects which distance men from their fathers and other men and come to identify with mothers and other women and come to renounce masculinity by attempting to become non-sexist individuals. (100) Trying to throw more light on the concepts of degendering and regendering, Wing states:

> Degendering and regendering are essentially meant to instill in men those qualities which will offer new model relationships with both women and men possible based on openness, emotional vulnerability, empathy and trust. This is a herculean task as Connell points out, "...demasculinization (or more strongly put- the annihilation of masculinity)- even when it accompanies some attempts at regendering-can be quite unsettling for men, and the discomfort they feel in response to the 'gender vertigo' that accompanies degendering may lead them to set limits on the changes they are willing to make. (101)

Okot p'Bitek hides behind Lawino to push through his degendering agenda. Lawino thinks that if Ocol, her beloved husband sees her as a human being and not a woman, peace, love, and tranquility will flourish. The woman like the man has an important role in society and should be treated with some respect. In *Song of Lawino*, the persona states: When your mother lifts her breast/And asks you/Did you suck?/If your father lifts his penis/Towards you!/Know that you are in deep trouble (165-6). The breast and the penis are pivotal and archetypal symbols that reiterate the concept of regendering and degendering. The man's cradle is tied to the woman's breast; as a consequence, the man should accord the woman some respect. It is only by doing this that gender differences can be kept at bay. The woman's breast signifies love, compassion and food, while the penis symbolizes force and trouble. These two organs are representatives of the world view of the two genders.

Renewal, desire, interest, women, wholeness remain p'Bitek's concerns although the specific framework or philosophy of life, especially seen from the standpoint of Ocol will alter to allow fragmentation and the impossibility of bringing both the male and female genders into harmony. The postcolonial binary concept of man/woman finds expression in p'Bitek's poetics. The persona once again reiterates:

No one wrestles with his father
No one looks down
On his mother,
You cannot abuse your mother!
Because it was that woman
Who hewed you out of the rock
And moulded your head and body (166).

A critical look at the above stanza shows that if there is mutual respect between the two genders, men who are carried away by the culturally ascendant expectation will renounce it. In this regard, they will resist hegemonic standards and prescribed roles which are socially and culturally defined. The man is who he is because of a woman: You sucked those wrinkled breasts/And that's what made you/The big man you are (166). In the spirit of feminist literary criticism which is inundated with cross-fertilization of ideas as Susan Manly has illustrated, women struggle to escape the confines of gender subjectivity by expressing the "fictionality of both feminity and masculinity." (qtd in Habib, 669.) The argument sustained here is that the constructed nature of gender is a strategic one; and if writing and thinking could demonstrably be seen to transcend the body, then there would be no argument for excluding women from the mainstream of the public sphere.

Consequently, it is important to restate the argument that has undergirded and sustained this study. This study has argued that Okot p'Bitek in *Song of Lawino* and *Song of Ocol* uses Lawino and Ocol as allegorical figurations to comment on gender inequality caused by the social and cultural constructions of the postcolonial woman. Lawino is a gargantuan and symbolic woman who represents the oppressed and culturally and socially excluded women from the public sphere.p'Bitek uses Lawino to subvert both the social and cultural construct ascribed to the women by trying to undo gendering to be able to restructure gender relations along more egalitarian and inclusive lines; and that explains why she is treated with realistic intensity. Again, p'Bitek in his two poetry collections writes with the consciousness and conviction that envision a non-hierarchical society. This study helps to reveal that de-gendering and re-gendering are meant to create stability and harmonious existence between the two genders in the society. These two concepts become vital tools used to work out less hierarchical and dominating ways of being men in the world. The second revelation of this paper is that, if writing and thinking could demonstrably be seen to transcend the body, there would be no argument for excluding women from the public sphere. Furthermore, the study revealed that borrowed traditions constitute a grave danger and a huge threat to the African way of life. Ocol and Clementine's lifestyles as seen in some of the poems in these collections are ridiculous, ludicrous, shameful, degrading, and artificial. They demonstrate and signify the negativity of western culture. This study also debunks the uncritical aping and acceptance of an alien culture which plays a destructive role in the lives of the African. Besides, this study proposes degendering and regendering within the postcolonial society if the women are to be accorded the respect that they deserve. Finally, from the foregoing submission, it is evident that p'Bitek's use of language helps to establish the relationship between Lawino and Ocol in the poems. The admixture of fantasy and realism in both collections demonstrates Lawino's grasp and mastery of African cultural values and aesthetics in spite of her illiteracy, and this makes her more likable and more positive than the despondent Ocol who is an allegorical figuration of cultural imperialism.

Works Cited

P'Bitek, Okot. *Song of Lawino*. East Africa Pub. House Ltd, 1960.

_____*Song of Ocol*. East Africa Pub. House, 1970.

Achebe, Chinua. *Morning Yet on Creation Day*. Heinemann, 1975.

Barry, Peter. *Beginning Theory*. Manchester U. P., 1995.

Bhaskar, Roy. "How to Change Reality: Story vs. Structure –A. Debate. In Jose Lopez and Garry Potter (eds) *After Postmodernism*. London: Athlone Press, 2001.

Chinweizu. *Anatomy of Female Power: Masculinist Discussion of Matriarchy* Pero Press, 1990.

Chinweizu, J. Onwuchekwa and M. Ihechukwu. *Toward the Decolonization of African Literature*. Fourth Dimension Press, 1980.

Conrad, Joseph. *Heart of Darkness*. Blackwood Magazine, Edinburgh 1899.

Connell, Raewyn. *Gender and Power: Society, the Person, and Sexual Politics*. Stanford U. P., 1987.

Ezenwanebe, Osita C. "Issues in Women's Liberation Struggles in Contemporary Nigeria: A Study of Ezeigbo's *Hands that Crush Stone*" (2010). *Journal of International Women's Studies*, 16(3), 262-276. (2015).

Ferguson, Kathy. E. *The Feminist Case against Bureaucracy*. Temple U. P., 1984.

Fonchingong, Charles C. "Unbending Gender Narratives in African Literature". *Journal of International Women's Studies*, 8(1), 135-147. (2006).

Fonlon, Bernard. "The Idea of Literature." *Abbia*. CEPER, 1982.

Funk and Wagnalls. *Standard Dictionary of the English Language*. Funk and Wagnalls, 1983.

Habib, M. A. R. *Modern Literary Criticism and Theory*. Blackwell, 2005.

Heron, G.A. 'Introduction' to *Song of Ocol*. East Africa Pub. House Ltd, 1960

Kayoka, C.M. "The Women in Kiswahili Literature: A Feminist

Approach". Unpublished paper, University of Dar es Salaam. (2000).

Liyong, Taban I.O. "Lawino is Unedu." In "The Last Word." East Africa Pub. House, 1969.

Lyatuu, J. Usawiri wa Wanawake katika Fasihi ya Kiswahili: Ulinganifu wa Waandishi wa Kike na wa Kiume Uchunguzi katika Riwaya teule. Unpublished M.A Kiswahili dissertation, University of Dar es Salaam. (2011).

Matteru, M. L. B. "The Image of the Woman in Tanzanian Oral Literature: The Survey, *Kiswahili,* University of Dar es Salaam: Institute of Kiswahili Research, 49 (2):1-31 (1982).

Mbughuni, P. The Image of Women in Kiswahili Prose Fiction, *Kiswahili,* University of Dar es Salaam: Institute of Kiswahili Research, 49(1)15-24. (1982).

Messner, Michael. "Boyhood Organized Sports and the Construction of Masculinity" In *Journal of Contemporary Ethnography Chicago, IL; University of Chicago Press,* 1990.

Mkomwa, A. "Usawiri wa Mwanamke katika Misemo Iliyoandikwa katika Vipepeo," Unpublished MA Kiswahili dissertation, University of Dar es Salaam. (2014).

Momanyi, C. Nafasi ya Mwanamke katika Ushairi wa Shaban Robert" in Y.M. Kihore (ed.) *Kiswahili,* University of Dar es Salaam: Institute of Kiswahili Research, 64(53-63). (2001).

Moran, Mary "Our Mothers Have Spoken: Synthesizing Old and New Forms of Women's Political Authority in Liberia". *Journal of International Women's Studies,* 13(4), 51-66. (2012).

Nwale, Pascal Newbourn. "Where is the Foundation of African Gender?" The Case of Malawi" In *Nordic Journal of African Studies,* U. of Malawi, 2002.

Ojaide, Tanure. "Point of View". In *Callalo.* The John Hopkins U. P., 1986.

Omari, Shani and Senkoro, Fikeni E. M. K. "Imaging the Woman through Tanzanian Women's Maxims". *Journal of International*

Women's Studies, 19(3), 119-134. (2018).

Available at: http://vc.bridgew.edu/jiws/vol19/iss3/10

Stratton, Florence. *Contemporary African Literature and the Politics of Gender.* New York and London: Routledge Taylor and Francis, 1994.

Tutuola, Amos. *The Palm Wine Drinkard.* Faber and Faber, 1952.

En.m.wiktionary.org.wiki; Access date: 18 December 2020.

Wing, Bradley W. "Degendering and Regendering: Recomposing Masculinities through Anti-Sexist Masculinity Projects." PhD Dissertation, Missouri, Columbia, 2008.

Chapter 3

Fela Anikulapo-Kuti: Anticolonial and Postcolonial African Revolutionary, Visionary, and Musician.

Thomas Jing

Introduction

Afrobeat superstar Fela, as he was popularly known, died on August 2, 1997 (Stanovsky, 1998). Fela was a very talented if somewhat controversial musician and activist. Admired and feted, even by the likes of musical giants in their own right such as South Africa's Hugh Masekela, Cameroon's Manu Dibango, Mali's Salif Keita, and Congo's Lokua Kanza (Moon, 2008) as well as dreaded and avoided like a plague by politicians and statesmen, he left no one indifferent. He was arrested 200 times by different regimes; and the government of General Muhammadu Buhari sentenced him to ten years in prison (Adenekan, 2006). Fela might have been an "eccentric," as the late Biafra leader Ojukwu once characterized him (Nwangwu, 2008), but he was also a virulent anti-colonial and postcolonial critic and one of Africa's finest musicians whose message transcended his Yoruba ethnicity to address issues concerning Nigeria, Africa, and black people. His struggle against oppression and exploitation had global impact; and today, long after his death, Afrobeat, the music idiom he pioneered and championed throughout his life, reverberates throughout the world. But who was Fela Anikulapo-Kuti? To what extent was he an anti-colonial and a postcolonial musician? To understand the man and his music, it is important to know his family, the city in which he was born and raised, the Nigerian ethnic group to which he belonged and whose rich culture and traditions inspired a lot of his music; and, of course, Nigeria and Africa, his country and

69

continent respectively. The struggles of all these worlds helped to inspire and shape his character and music. Using an anti-colonial and a postcolonial lens, this article attempts to capture the man, his music and struggles.

Fela, the Nigerian and African

Fela embodied Yoruba, Nigeria, Africa, and the black world. I believe that to understand him, it is fitting to start with a contextual examination of the country in which he was born and so valiantly fought for; to wit, Nigeria.

Located on the Gulf of Guinea in the West Coast of Africa, the Federal Republic of Nigeria is a former British colony and Africa's most populous nation (200.334.397 according to World Population Review). Long before it became a Western colony, it had played a central role in the Transatlantic Slave Trade that was responsible for the dispersal of numerous Africans to other parts of the world. The interethnic and religious conflicts which once served as a catalyst to this sad state of affairs still persist to this day even though Nigeria came of age as an independent country in 1960. Nigeria is very rich in human and natural resources and is home to some of the most ancient and dynamic African cultural traditions. However, it has been unable to use these assets to fight against poverty and underdevelopment. In 1966, Lee Kuan Yew (2000), the Father of the Singaporean Miracle, had wondered what would become of this country, for it held out such great potentials and constituted one of the brightest spots of Africa (p. 356). The answer to his musing was provided by the *CIA Factbook* which noted that "after independence in 1960, politics were marked by coups and mostly military rule" and that "the government continues to face the daunting task of institutionalizing democracy and reforming a petroleum-based economy whose revenues have been squandered through corruption and mismanagement."

These failures provided Fela with grist for some of his most virulent lyrical denunciations of those in power and the Nigerian society. Veal (2000) states that "at his outdoor beach and stadium concerts in Lagos, he led audiences in choruses of 'Ole' (Thief) as he sung (sic) the names of each post- independence head of state..." (p. 230).

The story of the beginning of modern Nigeria commences with the outlawing of the Transatlantic Slave Trade. Britain outlawed the trade in 1807 but "the ...trading did not end until 1860" when it "was gradually replaced by other means of trade in form of such commodity ... as palm oil" (Adeuyan, 2011, p. 5). To give teeth to its shift in policy, the British government undertook several measures, including military, to put an end to the outlawed trade. Thus, it was on slave-trading ground that in 1851, Kosoko, King of Lagos, was forced off his throne and replaced by his more tractable uncle Akitoye (Crowder, 1966, p. 150). This new policy led to the gradual opening up of the interior to direct trading relations between African producer and European buyer. Despite initial reservations on the part of the British Government, "by 1850 British trading interests were concentrating in two regions of what is now Nigeria: Lagos, the gateway to the rich forests of Yorubaland; and the Delta ports..." (pp, 151-152). Adeuyan (2011) has noted that "after initial contact with Great Britain in 1849, Lagos became a colony of the British Crown in 1861" (p. 6). With the notorious colonial "Scramble for Africa" by the various European powers, Sir George Goldie, said to be the "the founder of modern Nigeria" (Smith, 2015; Crowder, 1966), "would take on the role of pushing further inland, first through his United African Company... and later with the Royal Niger Company which would be chartered by the British government..." (Smith, 2015, p. 42) in 1881. By 1900, what is today the whole of Northern Nigeria had become a newly formed British protectorate, with Lord Lugard, Goldie's lieutenant and driving force in its creation, as its High Commissioner. It was Flora Shaw, a journalist and the lady with whom Lugard had struck up a relationship, that suggested that Britain's territories along the River Niger be given the name Nigeria (Ibid, p.45); a combination of "Niger" and "area."

Early in 1900, Goldie's Royal Niger Company had been bought out by the British government and its activities transferred to the Colonial Office. However, Ki-Zerbo (1975) has pointed out that it was Lugard who brought together the three parts of Nigeria, that is, the Colony of Lagos, the Protectorate of Southern and Northern Nigeria, into one in 1914 (p. 443).

Crowder (1966) maintains that "the World War projected Nigerians out of a colonial backwater into a modern world in which, because of the exigencies of war, Nigeria became suddenly important…" (p. 270). One other important thing that the war achieved among Nigerians, especially those who had participated in it, was to fire up their spirit of nationalism by changing their perception of white people (Ki-Zerbo, 1976, p. 470). This and other factors caused people to start to oppose the imperial project for real.

The rise of Nigerian nationalism did not mean that old challenges had suddenly vanished. Cracks and ethnic fault lines that always existed but had hitherto remained buried underneath the surface when the British were in charge started to emerge in the run-up to the country's independence. Following WWII, when in 1951 Britain divided the country into three distinct administrative regions – Northern, Eastern and Western regions - each with its own House of Assembly, the division helped to pave the way for regional nationalism.

The three major political parties that emerged for the 1959 general elections were the Northern People's Congress (N.P.C.) with Sir Ahmadu Bello – the Sardauna of Sokoto - and Sir Abubakar Tafawa Balewa as the party's flag bearer for the election; the National Council of Nigeria and Cameroon (N.C.N.C.) with Dr. Nnamdi Azikiwe as its leader, flag bearer; and the Action Group led by its leader, Chief

Obafemi Awolowo who emerged as its leaders (Adeuyan, 2011, p. 320). Even though Nielsen (1966) argues that "tribal problems and the fusing of small groups into larger political units have of course been characteristic of the process of nation-building throughout history" (p.24), none of these political parties could genuinely boast of a Pan-Nigerian appeal. Thus, Ki-Zerbo (1976) points out that it was after withdrawing from the Nigerian Youth Movement (NYM) created by Nnamdi Azikiwe in 1945 that Awolowo founded the Yoruba cultural movement the *Egbe Omou Oduduwa* whose purpose was to establish Yoruba autonomy within the Federal Republic of Nigeria (p. 494). Fanon (1963) argues in connection with national liberation that the truth of its success lies in the whole social structure being changed from the bottom up (p. 35) and that "in decolonization, there is…the need of a complete calling into question of the colonial situation" (p. 37). Were the leaders of the various political parties ripe enough to deal with decolonization in the new Nigeria? In the preface to Fanon's *Wretched of the Earth* (1963), French philosopher Jean-Paul Sartre has argued that if national revolution is cut short and the native bourgeoisie takes over power, the new state, in spite of its formal sovereignty, remains in the hands of the imperialists (p. 11). In Nigeria, this danger was real since Donaldson & Pui-Lan (2002) argue that "the post independence native elites, revolutionaries, and leaders of the new nations emerged fully cloaked in the colonial garment and devoted to the structures and policies of the former colonizers" (p. 101). Whatever the case, this was the Nigeria in which Fela was born. He, therefore, embodied the colonial, the anti-colonial and postcolonial phases of Nigeria's historical and political evolution.

Colonialism, anti-colonialism and postcolonialism

Fela was born in 1938, when British colonial venture in Nigeria was in full bloom; and he died in 1997, twenty-seven years after the country obtained political independence in 1960. As a product of the colonial, anti-colonial and postcolonial periods, who better to sing about and challenge the ills of these eras than a musician with his background! To determine the extent to which he was an anti-colonial and a postcolonial fighter, it is important to start off by defining the terms *colonialism*, *anti-colonialism* and *postcolonialism*.

Hall (2013) states in representation that sometimes meanings depend on the difference between opposites: man versus woman, primitive versus civilized, etc. With this argument in mind, the definitions of the terms "anti-colonialism" and "postcolonialism" will be pitched against those of "colonialism." What is colonialism and is it the same as imperialism? Young (2001) argues that "…a characteristic of postcolonial writing is that the terms 'colonial' and 'imperial' are often lumped together, as if they were synonymous terms" and that "this totalizing tendency is also evident in the way that colonialism and imperialism are themselves treated as if they were homogenous practices." Cannella and Viruru (2013) note that "both colonialism and imperialism involve the takeover, subjugation and control of one group by another" and that "…colonies established for the purpose of settlement can be characterized as colonial projects, and those established for the purpose of exploitation as imperial projects" (p. 14). Whatever both terms represent, Edward Saïd (1994) maintains that imperialism "means the practice, the theory, and the attitude of a dominating metropolitan centre ruling a distant territory, 'colonialism,' which is almost always a consequence of imperialism" (p. 9). He summed up both practices thus: colonialism, even if understood as distinct from imperialism, still involves acts of geographical violence on human beings and operated not only as a form of military rule but also simultaneously as *discourse* of domination. To Young (2001), imperialism has numerous meanings but is most often "characterized by an exercise of power, either through direct conquest or (latterly) through political and economic influence that effectively amounts to a similar form of domination." He adds that "typically, it is the deliberate product of a political machine that rules from the centre, and extends its control to the furthest reaches of the peripheries…" and that "unlike colonialism, imperialism is driven by ideology and a theory of sorts…" (p. 27). Noting that the result of imperialism is colonialism, Cannella and Viruru (2013) have concluded that

…colonization transformed and impoverished the structure of economies, generated privileged knowledges and discourses, and established imperialist institutions. Peoples, cultures, and countries changed. When decolonization occurred, there was no possibility of achieving some form of precolonial state of being. (p.13)

Even though from some of these definitions imperialism is the driving force of colonialism, it (imperialism) transcends physical decolonization. The purpose of this article is to focus on aspects of both practices which have affected Nigeria adversely and which constituted the basis of Fela's musical denunciations.

For Barker (2003), the view of French philosopher Michel Foucault is that power is productive, that is, engendering the forces that challenge it. It was thus out of colonial exploitation and oppressions that the anti-colonial struggles arose. Young (2001) expounds on this idea by noting that

The period from the 1880s onwards was also marked by increasing intellectual as well as political resistance to colonialism in the colonies themselves, and it was colonized people themselves that henceforth spearheaded anti-colonial sentiments, to much greater effect than European anti-colonial activists had ever achieved. In part this was a product of the impact of colonial rule itself; the disruption that capitalism brought to trading and industrial relations in the colonies created a class of bourgeoisie that utilized the knowledge learned at the new educational institutions introduced under colonial rule, the spread of literacy, and the increase in newspapers, in order to combat feudal and imperial rulers alike. (p 100)

According to him, "independence was the object of that (*anti-colonial*) struggle, and the assumption was that it would fully realize the ideal of self-determination" (p. 45).

Attributing imperialism to the "modernity" project of the Enlightenment, Smith (1999) has maintained that knowledge and culture were just as important as raw material and military strength. For the colonized who were subjected to cultural indoctrination through the policy of assimilation, as it was the case of those in former French colonies, culture and its psychological effects still loom large in their critique and discourses. Cannella & Viruru (2013) points out that "the French spoke a language of equality yet imposed their own views of humanity on others without hesitation" (p. 15). It was this inclination which underpinned the emergence of the Negritude philosophy, described by Leopold Sédar Senghor, one of its key proponents, as "the cultural patrimony of, the values, and above all the spirit of Negro African civilization" (Kesteloot, 1974, p. 102). The rise of Negritude is not surprising, for Aimé Césaire (1972), one of the philosophy's originators, stated that "…we lived in an atmosphere of rejection and developed an inferiority complex," adding that "…the black man was searching for his identity" (p. 76). Thus, Young (2001) states that Francophone anti-colonial activists articulated the cultural and psychological effects of colonialism as they were experienced by those subjected to them. Questions they raised were: how does it feel to have your culture devalued and appropriated, your language debased into a vernacular, detached from all forms of power which are accessible and enacted only in foreign languages (p. 274)? It is, therefore, not surprising that it was Fanon (1963) who articulated militant anti-colonial activism with the tradition of black psychological redemption and black empowerment central to the tradition of Marcus Garvey and Negritude. Though

Fela was from an Anglophone country, his political outlook, as reflected in the lyrics of his music, seemed to owe more to Francophone thinkers such as Fanon (1963), Aimé Césaire (1972), and Diop (1996). Negritude philosophy, a pillar of Francophone thought, was greatly influenced by the Harlem Renaissance of the twenties, especially by Alain Locke's *The New Negro* (first published in 1925). In turn, Negritude influenced the black power movement of the sixties, a fount from which Fela drank deeply during his trip to the US and meeting with Sandra Izsidore.

It is difficult to talk of Fela in terms of anti-colonial or postcolonial before his trip to the US in 1969. "In 1969 I was completely almost unintelligent because I had no original African contribution to make," Fela stated, adding that "An African meeting an English should have something to offer" and that "Africans should be taught to be able to contribute their own mind, their own culture, their own philosophy" (Veal, 2000, p. 75). To determine the degree of transformation he experienced while in the US and how this contributed to his postcolonial outlook, it is essential to define the term "postcolonialism." Seen from the angle of theories, postcolonialism

> ...emanated from the rise of Western empires in the eighteenth through the twentieth centuries, their scramble to divide the world among themselves, the strategies of subjugation and resistance engendered by colonialism, and the chain reactions that have been in motion ever since. (p. 100)

Ashcroft, Griffiths & Tiffin (1999) note that there are controversies surrounding the term "post-colonial." They point out that there are those who believe that it refers only to the period after the colonies became independent and those who argue that it is best used to designate the totality of practices, in all their rich diversity, which characterize the societies of the post-colonial world from the moment of colonization to the present day, since colonialism does not cease with the mere fact of political independence and continues in a neo-colonial mode to be active in many societies (p. xv).

Looking at the term by taking his cue from anti-colonialism, Young (2001) states that

> since anti-colonial revolutionaries were themselves increasingly in touch with each other in different ways during the course of the twentieth century, a political and theoretical convergence took place that laid the basis for the field of 'the postcolonial.' (p. 274)

Ashcroft, Griffiths & Tiffin (1999) agree with Young, maintaining that 'post-colonial theory' has existed for a long time before that particular name was used to describe it, for once colonized peoples had cause to reflect on and express the tension which ensued from this problematic and contested, but eventually vibrant and powerful mixture of imperial language and local experience, 'post-colonial theory came into being' (p. 1). To these scholars "all post-colonial societies are still subject in one way or another to overt or subtle forms of neo-colonial domination, and independence has not solved this problem" (p. 2). Donaldson and Pui-Lan (2002) make a valid point when they state that "the political independence of former colonies did not mark the end of colonialism" (p. 101). Saïd (1994) agrees, arguing that "the nations of contemporary Asia, Latin America, and Africa are politically independent but in many ways are as dominated and dependent as they were when ruled directly by European powers" (p. 19). Which African musician expressed this syndrome of cultural, material and psychological dependency on former colonial powers better than Fela?

Fela, the Anti-colonial and Postcolonial Musician

The world's reaction to Fela's death was evidence of the larger-

78

than-life stature of the fallen hero. "He was a fighter who incurred the wrath of a string of Nigerian regimes," states Tom Moon (2008), adding that "his songs...were filled with passionate chants about military corruption." Vakunta's (2012) observation is even more poignant when he points out that Fela's "...musical novelty is anchored on a medley of thematic considerations – sex, gender, social stratification, oppositional politics, abuse of power, disempowerment, social identity, cultural authenticity, Afrocentrism, imperialism and more." To Stapleton and May (1986), "Kuti...almost alone among the modern musicians of post-independence black Africa in the 1970s, felt restrained by neither the niceties of supportiveness nor the fear of reprisal" (p. 64). Perhaps, it was in recognition of his struggles that "in a list featuring icons such as Nelson Mandela, Pablo Picasso and the Beatles, Time Magazine, in 2006, named Fela Anikulapo-Kuti (1938-1997) as one of the heroes of the last sixty years" (Dosunmu, 2010, p. 1).

As outlined, Fela's overall attitude was pitched against a history that includes histories of slavery, of untold, unnumbered deaths from oppression and neglect, of the enforced migration and diaspora of millions of people, of the appropriation of territories and land, of the institutionalization of racism, of the destruction of cultures and the superimposition of other cultures (Young, 2001). Young (ibid) argues that postcolonial cultural critique involves the reconsideration of this history, particularly from the perspective of those who suffered its effects, together with the defining of its contemporary social and cultural impact (p. 4). As Vakunta (2012) puts it, "Fela assumes the posture of the spokesman of the wretched of the earth... He sang about a vast array of social issues – dictatorship, corruption, abuse of power..."

Fela's death might have given Africa's corrupt class a cause for celebration, but in his music, in the seeds of rebellion against tyranny that he sowed, and in the relevance of the message he imparted, he continues to stalk them. He was resurrected roughly a decade later when his life was the focus of *Fela*, a 2008 Off-Broadway performance which premiered on Broadway at the Eugene O'Neill Theatre in November 2009 until January 2011. In addition to his two sons, Femi and Seun, bands such as Antibalas, Kokolo, NewenAfrobeat, Chopteeth, Chicago Afrobeat Project and many others scattered all over the world have remained loyal to his musical tradition (Dosunmu, 2010).

Fela was an explosive cocktail of interlocking influences and ideas, some of them very potent. To understand his contributions to anti and postcolonial struggles in Africa, it is important to explore his roots. Who was Fela and where did he come from? Which were the influences that shaped his life and how did they affect his music and the message he conveyed through it? What were his contributions to anti and postcolonial struggles on the African continent and even beyond?

Fela was Nigerian and belonged to the Yoruba, an ethnic group described by Thompson (1984) as "... black Africa's largest population, and ...creators of one of the premier cultures of the world." Veal (2000), identifies Fela as "...a product of Yoruba history," noting that "his personal story is inextricably intertwined with the history of postcolonial Nigeria" (p. 19). But who are the Yoruba? Scattered across south-western Nigeria are the Yoruba (Ki-Zerbo, 1978) who trace their common origin to a mythical king called Oduduwa. From Ile-Ife, believed to be their original homeland and still revered to this day as their common cultural and sacred spiritual centre, they spanned out, reigning over other city-states such as Owu, Sabe, Popo, Ketu, Oyo, Ijebu, Egba, Nago, Ijesha, Ondo, Shabe, etc. (Crowder, 1966, Ki-Zerbo, 1978, Adeuyan, 2011). Veal (2000) points out that the current cultural meaning of the term *Yoruba* is relatively recent and that prior to the nineteenth century the various subgroups inhabiting the area might have more accurately been described as autonomous kingdoms united more by similar socio-political organization, common language, and common cultural practices than by any broad, shared sense of ethnicity (p. 22). It was out of this medley that Oyo emerged as a powerful kingdom in the sixteenth century and its king, known as the Alafin, became the supreme ruler of what is much of now called Yorubaland (Crowder, 1966, p. 56). By the nineteenth century Yorubaland had lapsed into a civil war and the economic and military lustre of Oyo started to dwindle, leading to the emergence of new centres of power among which was Abeokuta, founded in 1830 (Veal, 2000, p. 23) and Fela's birthplace. Adeuyan (2011) argues that the Oyo wars and slave raids were complementary exercises among the Yoruba of the nineteenth century (p. 5) and that this was important in the growth of Abeokuta. Weakened by internal divisions and wars, Oyo became vulnerable to Dan Fodio's Fulani invasion seeking territorial and religious expansion as well as the capture of slaves. The scholar further points out that, cities located on slave routes to the coast such as Ijebu and Abeokuta bore the brunt of these invasions. This situation prompted the Egba, the original inhabitants of Abeokuta, to seek refuge under the rock of Olumo; hence the term *Abeokuta* standing for "the city under the rock." The Egba were soon joined by other refugees fleeing from the epicenters of these conflicts and their numbers soon swelled. Forced by this circumstance and with no place to run to, the people of Abeokuta emerged from their hiding places and coalesced around a courageous and enlightened leader called Shodeke. Nevertheless, with the slave raids still raging all around, they reached out to the British, the dominant European power in the region, for protection and for arms to defend themselves. The "cordial relation with the British would enable Abeokuta to obtain not only Western arms for protection, but also Western knowledge, which was increasingly becoming essential in this period of developing cross-cultural contact" (Veal, 2000, p. 23). Shodeke went on in 1841 to extend an invitation to the British to establish mission schools in Abeokuta, which was the first in the Yoruba hinterland. With its Western foundation thus laid, Abeokuta was poised for even greater external influence, especially when Ajayi Crowder, a freed slave of Yoruba extraction and a graduate of Fourah Bay College in Sierra Leone, arrived. He brought with him other Yoruba who had been rescued and educated by the British and this influx contributed immensely to Abeokuta's image as a modern centre for both Christianity and Western education. Among the biggest beneficiaries of this influence was the Ransome-Kuti, Fela's family.

Not very much is known about Rev. Canon Josiah J. Ransome-Kuti, Fela's grandfather and the man through whom the Kuti family burst into prominence. Veal (2000) refers to him as a "…an Anglican pastor, a pioneer of the Christian church in Yorubaland," adding that "it was through his encounter with British missionaries that Christianity entered the Ransome-Kuti family..." (p. 27). It was at Fourah Bay College, where he studied, that he was exposed to Western music. Olaniyan (2004) states that he was a musician whose accomplishments laid the foundation of the musical tradition in the family. Even though Fela's father did not make music a profession, he inherited his father's love for the art and considered Western musical training an important part of education (Veal, 2000). Wole Soyinka, 1986 Nobel Prize laureate in literature and a member of the family (Adenekan, 2006), concurs with Veal's assessment, stating that the reverend was manic in his treatment of music and his ears picked up unerringly the source of a wrong sound.

From the foregoing analysis, in the Ransome-Kuti family Africa and the West met and sometimes collided. No family member expressed this clash as overtly as Fela and his mother, from whom his initiation into anti-colonial politics seemed to have originated (Stapleton and May, 1989; Stanovsky, 1998). According to Veal (2000),

> Fela's mode of expression reflected a family tradition most obvious in the lives and works of his parents. First is the tendency towards activism and derisive criticism typified by his mother…, an anticolonial women's rights activist with a strong antiauthoritarian streak. (p. 18)

Fela's break with the family tradition of studying medicine and settling instead for music provided him with the tool he needed to embark on his anti-colonial and postcolonial journey. "As far as Africa is concerned music cannot be for enjoyment; it must be for revolution," Fela declared in the *youtube* video *Interview with legend Fela Anikulapo-Kuti about music, politics and freedom*, adding that when Africans suffer and smile, it is a slave mentality. He thus sees music as "the weapon of the future" (Dosunmu, 2010). He captured the conflicting attitude of Africans smiling while they suffer in the song *Shuffering and Smiling* (1978).

Young (2001) argues that "if colonial history, particularly in the nineteenth century, was the history of the imperial appropriation of the world, the history of the twentieth century have witnessed the people of the world taking power and control back for themselves" and that "postcolonial theory is itself a product of that dialectical process" (p. 4). In the same vein, Veal (2000) points out that "the notion of 'tradition' in Africa has become highly charged as a result of the massive disruptions wrought by slavery and colonialism. Ashcroft, Griffiths & Tiffin (1995) buys into the argument when they state that "...what we refer to as post-colonial cultures is the historical phenomenon of colonialism, with its range of material practices and effects, such as... slavery, displacement, emigration, and racial and cultural discrimination" and that "these material conditions and their relationship to questions of ideology and representation are at the heart of the most vigorous debates in recent post-colonial theory" (p. 7). In Africa, in the postcolonial atmosphere, Veal (2000) points out that musicians have been important negotiators between contested notions of 'traditional' and 'modern,' 'black' and 'white,' and 'Africa' and 'the West,'" adding that "these contradictions manifested themselves in various ways within Fela's stated ideology" (p. 18). Fela captured the postcolonial essence in the song *Why Black Man Dey Suffer* (1971), tracing the origin of black suffering to European enslavement of Africa.

83

Even though Fela was an admirer of notable pan-Africanist, Ghana's Kwame Nkrumah, he did not start preaching revolution in his music right from the start. To Veal (2000), Fela's musical transformation went through many stages. Stapleton and May (1989) agree, noting that at Trinity College in London where he enrolled in 1958 to study music, it was classical and other Western musical forms that he spent most of the time learning and practising. Heselgrave (2017) points out that "...Kuti's first success was as a singer in a popular Highlife band..., specialized in uplifting party tunes that reflected the hopes and dreams of the fledgling independent nation." Dosunmu (2010) adds that he formed "a jazz quintet at first, and later, highlife jazz fusion band called Koola Lobitos" (p. 2). By 1968, Fela began calling the music Koola Lobitos played "Afrobeat," described by Stanovsky (1998) as a "...distinctive fusion of West African highlife, jazz, funk and traditional African tribal music..." and by Dosunmu (2010) as a genre which "blends anti-establishment lyrics with Yoruba traditional music and Western forms, particularly jazz" (p. iv).

Stapleton and May (1989) maintain that from a music perspective Fela's trip to the US in 1969 was not quite a success. However, "one positive aspect of the American visit for Fela...was his friendship with a black American woman named Sandra Izsidore," an activist who "...introduced Fela to the ideas of such people as Malcolm X, Angela Davis, the Last Poets, Stokeley Carmichael and Eldridge Cleaver" (p. 67). Sandra has expounded on her meeting with Fela in an interview done during *Fela!*, by declaring that "I met Fela in 1969 here in Los Angeles. I knew that he could teach me all I didn't know about my heritage, only for me to find out years later that I was the one who was teaching him." But even more compelling, is Fela's own admission in an interview he granted shortly after the US sojourn.

It's crazy; in the States people think the black power movement drew inspiration from Africa. All these Americans come over here looking for awareness. They don't realize they're the ones who've got it over there... (Stanovsky, 1998)

The spell cast by Sandra and radical black nationalists in the United States over Fela led to a series of even deeper radical transformation of the musician, starting with name change. A common colonial disruptive practice going back to the days of slavery is to erase the identity of subjected persons or places by imposing the names of the colonizing or enslaving masters (Bennett, Jr., 2000). Thus, before the explorer David Livingstone gave the name Victoria Falls to that renowned geographical landmark in Zambia and Zimbabwe, it was called Mosi Oa Tunya ("The Smoke which Thunders" in Shona) by the natives. In a counter narrative to diffusionism, the idea that knowledge was a one-way traffic from the West to the Other, anti-colonialists have raised the issue of "substitution," a practice in which local models were substituted and replaced with those of the Europeans (Pratt, 2004).This practice impacted names, especially in African communities whose members had been baptized into Christianity. So, in spite of her anti-colonial streak, Fela's mother was called Frances Abigail Olufunmilayo Thomas Ransome-Kuti. Ashcroft, Griffiths & Tiffin (1995) have explained this irony by pointing out that "despite the 'imitation' and 'mimicry' with which colonized peoples cope with the imperial presence, the relationship becomes one of constant, if implicit, contestation and opposition" (p. 9). Veal (2000) and Dosunmu (2010) maintain that it was through a British missionary that the name "Ransome" entered the Kuti family. Fela was born Olufela Oludotun Olusegun Ransome-Kuti which he changed, as Stanovsky (1998) explains: in 1975, "Fela and his mother Africanized their family name, substituting Anikulapo, a Yoruba name meaning 'one who carries death in a pouch,' for Ransome." Fela thus became Fela Anikulapo-Kuti. In line with his Africanization drive, he changed the name of his band from Koola Lobitos to Afrika 70 (Stapleton & May, 1989). It is easy to conclude from this idea of changing names that he was inspired by the examples of Malcolm X (to Malkik-El Shabazz) and

85

Stokeley Carmichael (to Kwame Touré). As evidence that he took the name issue very seriously, he raised the matter in the lyrics of *Upside Down* (1976). In the song, he contrasted people of other countries who identified themselves with their national names with Africans who did not bear African names and attributed the tendency to the fact that in Africa everything was "Upside Down."

Another colonial practice that has come increasingly under fire in the postcolonial dispensation is the issue of language. Fela's use of broken English has sometimes been attributed to his attempt to transcend a narrow tribal base in order to reach a broader audience. Stapleton and May (1989) have acknowledged that "by 1972 Fela was one of the biggest names in Nigeria, and indeed West Africa: because he sang in broken English rather than Yoruba, his records were understandable in all Anglophone countries" (p. 67). While some scholars (Ibid, 1989) have tended to interpret this gesture with wise economics, there is an even deeper reason. Through his music, he championed the cause of the poor and what better way to do so than through a language they understood.

By choosing a local language over that of the colonial master, he aligns his thinking with a postcolonial writer such as Ngugi wa Thiong'o (1986) who argues that language is always more than a simple medium of communication and that "the domination of a people's language by the language of the colonizing nations was crucial to the domination of the mental universe of the colonized" (p. 6). Fela fought hard for an African renaissance but as some scholars have argued, no people have ever achieved a true renaissance using somebody else's language (Diop, 1996 & Asante, 2007, p. 116).

According to Young (2001), one way to view the postcolonial is that it "is a dialectical concept that marks the broad historical fact of decolonization and the determined achievement of sovereignty – but also the realities of nations and people emerging into a new imperialism context of economic and sometimes political domination." Perhaps it is such a view which had prompted Fanon

(1963) to state earlier that in decolonization "...there is the need of a complete calling in question of the colonial situation" (p. 37). Part of the tragedy of modern Africa, especially of Nigeria, is that independence has brought nothing but untold suffering to its people. The ruling class has subjected the continent to various forms of exploitation and, in the process, has sometimes acted worse than the colonial masters have. Corruption, tribalism, exploitation of the masses, cultural alienation, religious hypocrisy, embezzlement of state funds, graft, theft by government officials and politicians, police brutality are but a few of the problems associated with postcolonial Africa (Ayittez, 1998, 2005; Soyinka, 1996). It is against this backdrop that Fela directed a good part of his wrath. Vakunta (2012) has stated that "Fela advocated alternative discourses in his lyrics, he vocalized the need for a political new deal, a sane economic order and respect for the social contract." In *Zombie* (1977), he lashed out at the unimaginative leadership of the military which has ruled and ruined Nigeria and likened soldiers to zombies who only act on command and display a total absence of any initiative. "*Zombie no go turn until you tellem for turn...*" (my transcription), he chanted. The culmination of this absence of leadership is confusion which he captured in an earlier song *Confusion* (1975). In *Sorrow, Tears and Blood* (1977), he continued his war against military and police brutality: *Army dem come; Confusion everywhere.*

He also directed his anger against the masses that sheepishly flocked behind Christianity and Islam, two foreign religions which "...had been guilty not merely of physical atrocities on African soil, including enslavement of the indigenes, but a systematic assault on African spirituality in the contest for religious hegemony" (Soyinka, 2012, p. xi). Turning his back on the Anglican Church in which he was brought up, he crafted a religion which he called "Africanism" as an alternative to the foreign religions. "He has nothing but disdain for Christianity's promise of paradisiacal solace as compensation for hard times on earth" (Vakunta, 2012). He takes on those who follow these religions blindly in *Shuffering and Smiling* (1978), pointing out the irony and hypocrisy in which religious leaders such as bishops and the pope as well as the Imams live well while exhorting their congregants to forget about such pleasure on earth to reap greater rewards in heaven: *Suffer, suffer, suffer for world...; Enjoy for heaven Christians go deyyab* (my transcription)

His decolonization drive also targeted Africans he believed were guilty of alienation by adopting foreign habits and cultures. He took up this aspect in the song *Gentleman* (1973) in which he condemned those Africans determined to be seen as "gentleman" and thus acted unusually or adopted a dress code unsuitable for the steaming tropical environment: *Africa hot, I like em so; I know what to wear but my friend don't know.*

His crusade against such self-abnegating mentality continues in the song *Buy Africa* (1996) in which he called on Africans to produce and consume their own goods and not spend their time gawking at and consuming products manufactured in other countries. This tendency towards extroversion, he attributed to *Colonial Mentality* (1981) in which brainwashed Africans shunned things African and identified with things foreign. He traced the root of this problem in the song *Teacher Don't Teach Me Nononsense* (1986) where he pointed out that in other countries, at school children are taught their own culture and it is only in Africa that things are different because in school children are taught another man's culture.

Among the dissonant messages which characterized Fela's anti and postcolonial message, were his views on women, for he did not believe that they were equal to men. Olaniyan (2004) has highlighted some of his thoughts in this regard.

Class liberation, an agenda he devoted all his creative efforts to advancing is not against nature, but 'women's lib' is. It is 'against the natural order of the world.' And of course is un-African: 'It comes from European religions. Their religions didn't teach them properly. They teach that men and women are equal in the house, for better and for worse. No man, that's bullshit...' (p. 121)

Fela exposed some of his views on women in the song *Lady* (1972): *She want salute man she go; sit down for chair, She want take piece of meat before anybody...* Fela's view about African women exposed the depth of his ignorance on the subject. His mother and Sandra Izsidore, just two women from whom he learned a lot, should at least have convinced him that if anything at all African women have proved to be even better than their men. As the prophet of "Africanism," he should have known that black history provides numerous examples to corroborate this point of view. Even before his mother embarked on her anticolonial crusade, black women such as Queen Zinga Mbandi, Yaa Ashantewaa, Empress Taitus, Sojourner Truth, Harriet Tubman, Angela Davis and many others had long graced history books for their exploits. Oddly enough, he attributed the quest for man-woman equality to Christian religion which, as a matter of fact, many scholars have held responsible for promoting Western patriarchal views. According to Diop (1990), Western patriarchy devalued and debased women and a common example is the biblical story in which "Eve is responsible for the fall of humanity from the grace of God..." (Dove, 2003, p. 168). These are some of the views that, through colonialism, Western patriarchy and Christianity introduced and promoted in Africa which was largely a matriarchal society (Diop, 1990)

To conclude, if we share Young's (2001) view that post-colonialism designates the perspective of tricontinental (three continents of Africa, Asia and South America) theories which analyze the material and epistemological conditions of postcoloniality and seek to combat the continuing, often covert, operation of an imperialist system of economic, political and cultural domination (p. 58), Fela, through his music, epitomized that "combat" in Africa. Whatever flaws might have emerged during his emancipatory journey, it is Olaniyan (2004) who has summed up the artist best. To the question "Why is Fela important?" The scholar responds that the body of work the name represents captures the essence of the "postcolonial incredible" in ways no other African popular musician did.

References

Adenekan, S. (2006, Feb. 15). Dr Beko Ransome-Kuti. *The Guardian Online*

Adeuyan, J. O. (2011). *The Journey of the First Black Bishop: Bishop Samuel Ajayi Crowther 1806 – 1891*. The United States of America: AuthorHouse

Asante, M. K. (2007). *Cheikh Anta Diop: An Intellectual Portrait*. Los Angeles: University of Sankore Press.

Ascroft, B., Griffiths, G. & Tiffin, H. (1999). *The Post-colonial Studies Reader*. London and New York: Routledge.

Ayittez, G.B.N. (1998). *Africa Unchained*. United States of America: Palgrave Macmillan.

Ayittez, G.B.N. (2005). *Africa in Chaos*. United States of America: Palgrave Macmillan.

Bennett Jr., L. (2000). *Before the Mayflower: A History of Black America*. Chicago: Johnson Publishing Company, Inc. (Original work published in 1962)

Césaire, A. (1972). *Discourse on Colonialism*.Trans. Joan Pinkham. New York: Monthly Review Press.

Chilisa, B.C. (2012). Indigenous Research Methodologies. Thousand Oaks, California: Sage Publication, Ltd.

Crowder, M. (1966).*The Story of Nigeria*. London: Faber and Faber limited. Original work published in 1962

Crowder, M. (1967). *Assimilation in Senegal*. Great Britain: Richard Clay (The Chaucer Press) Ltd.

Donaldson, L. E. & Pui-Lan, K. (Ed. 2002). *Postcolonialism, Feminism & Religious Discourse*. New York: Routledge

Diop, C.A. (1990). *The Cultural Unity of Black Africa.*Trans. Presence Africaine. Chicago: Third World Press.

Diop, C. A. (1996). *Towards the African Renaissance.*Trans. Eguna P. Modum. Britain and USA: Karnak House.

Dosunmu, O. A. (2010). *Afrobeat, Fela and Beyond: Scenes, Style and Ideology* (Unpublished doctoral dissertation). Faculty of Arts and Sciences: University of Pittsburgh

Dove, N. (2003). Defining African Womanist Theory. In Ama Mazama's (Ed.) *The Afrocentric Paradigm.* (pp. 165-184). Trenton, NJ: African World Press, Inc.

Fanon, F. (1963).The Wretched of the Earth. Trans. R. Philcox. New York. Grove Press

Hall, S. (2013). *Representation: Cultural Representation and Signifying Practices.* London: SAGE Publication Ltd. (Original work published 1997).

Heselgrave, D. (2017). Sorrow, Tears and Blood: Afrobeat the Music of Post-Colonial Nigeria. Retrieved from
http://thefestival.bc.ca/sorrow-tears-and-blood-afrobeat-and-the-music-of-post-colonial-Nigeria

Izsidore, S. (2009, Sept. 21). Sandra Itzsadore on *Fela!.* Retrieved from youtube *http://www.FelaonBroadway.com*

Izsidore, S. (2010, May 25).The Fela We Didn't Know…Ex-American Girlfriend Reveal all the Intimate Details! Retrieved from *youtube*

Kesteloot, L. (1991). *Black Writers in French.*Trans. Ellen Conroy Kennedy. Washington, D. C., Howard University Press.

Ki-Zerbo, J. (1978). *Histoire de l'Afrique Noire.* Paris: Hatier.

Kwame, N. (1964). *Consciencism.* London : Heinemann

Moher, J. W. (2015). Muhammadu Buhari vs. Fela Kuti : Nigeria's New President-elect Once Jailed a Music Icon. *Washington Post,* 2015, April 1

Moon, T. (Aug. 4, 2008). Fela Put His Passionate Resource Politics in the Groove. Retrieved from *AfricaResource*

Ngugi wa Thiong'o. (1986). *Decolonizing the Mind.* London: James

91

Currey.

Nielsen, W. A. (1966). *Africa*. New York: Atheneum

Nwangwu, C. (1997). The Life and Times of Controversial Afrobeat Superstar. Retrieved from *USAAfricaonline.com*

Nwangwu, C. (Aug. 4, 2008). Afrobeat Superstar. Retrieved from *AfricaResource*

Olaniyan, T. (2004).*Arrest the Music! Fela and his Rebel Art and Politics*. Bloomington and Indianapolis: Indiana University Press

Pratt, M. L. (2004, September). The Anticolonial Past. *Modern Language Quarterly*, Vol. 65(3), pp. 443-56.

Saïd, E.W. (1979).*Orientalism*. New York, United States of America: Vintage Books Editions.

Saïd, E.W. (1994).*Culture and Imperialism*. New York, United States of America: Vintage Books Editions.

Smith, L.T. (1999). *Decolonizing Methodologies*. Dunedin: University of Otago Press.

Smith, M. (2015).*Boko Haram: Inside Nigeria's Unholy War*. London: L.B. Tauris & co.Ltd

Soyinka, W. (1996).*The Open Sore of a Continent.A Personal Narrative of the Nigerian Crisis*. Oxford, New York: Oxford University Press

Soyinka, W. (2012). *Of Africa*. New Haven and London: Yale University Press.

Stanovsky, D. (1998). Fela and his Wives: The Import of a Postcolonial masculinity. Appalachian State University. Retrieved from *English.class.ncsu.edu/jouvert/v2/TAN.HTM*

Stapleton, C. & May, C. (1989) *All African Stars: The Popular Music of a Continent*. Great Britain: Paladin

Thompson, R. F. (1984). *Flash of the Spirit*. United States of America: Vintage Books Edition.

Vakunta, P. W. (2012). Fela's Rebel Afrobeat: A Pedagogical perspective. *Journal of African Literature Association*, Vol. 6, No. 2

Veal, M. E. (2000).*Fela: The Life and Times of an African Music Icon*. Philadelphia: Temple University Press.

Wane, N.N. (2007, July). Mapping the Field of Indigenous Knowledges in Anti-Colonial Discourse: a Transformative Journey in Education. *Race Ethnicity and Education.* Vol. II (2)

Yew, L. K. (2000). *From Third World to First: The Singapore Story 1965-2000.* New York: HarperCollins Publishers.

Young, R.J.C. (2001) *Postcolonialism: A Historical Introduction.* Oxford, UK: Blackwell Publishers.

Chapter 4

Fodéba Keïta and *Les Ballets Africains*: Dancing To Freedom

Thomas Jing

Introduction

Today, terms such as *djembe* and *djembefola* are gradually making their way into mainstream English vocabulary. What do these words signify? Where do they come from and how have they laid the foundation for the explosion of different African dance ensembles scattered across Africa and other parts of the world? These achievements owe their origin largely to the Guinean revolutionary and visionary playwright and choreographer Fodéba Keïta who founded *Les Ballets Africains*, the hugely popular dance group in Paris in 1952. Fodéba Keïta, one of the continent's towering giants, remains largely unknown while many people in Africa know Kwame Nkrumah, Nelson Mandela, Fela Kuti, and Miriam Makeba. In addition, even the few who know Fodéba Keïta tend to do so in the light of his repugnant political reputation; he played an important part in creating the postcolonial repressive political machinery in Guinea which ended up consuming him. This investigation elects to examine the man from the angle of culture, wherein he achieved almost as much as, if not more than, Nelson Mandela did in politics or Nigeria's Aliko Dangote has done and is doing in business. At a time when few people thought Africa had a culture, let alone one that could attract world attention and be celebrated, he stunned the global community by proving otherwise. *Les Ballets Africains*, the dance troupe he started, took the world by storm. It changed many people's perceptions of Africa. Who was he? Where did he come from?

Finally, what had he in mind when he started the dance troupe? In an online biography of *Les Ballets Africains*, Steve Huey notes that "Les Ballets Africains is now a cultural institution, highly respected for the quality of their performance and artistry." How did Fodéba go about it? Which factors drove him in this endeavour? How huge was his cultural, economic and social contribution to Africa and the world? And above all, how has his dance ensemble evolved over time? In an interview published in March 2007 by *Maximum Ink*, Madison's Music Magazine online, Hamidou Bangoura, Director of Les Ballets Africains, stated that "it's important to share our culture with the rest of the world." This article seeks to provide some answers to the questions above-raised as it dabbles into the world of dance, of African dance, and its relevance to community organization and educational promotion. In this research, the term "Africa" is seen from an Afrocentric perspective in that "Afrocentricity appropriates all African history in the United States and elsewhere..." (Asante, M.K., 1993, p. 17). Sometimes, black and African will be used interchangeably to refer to people whose forebears originate from the continent of Africa and who self-identify with Africa.

My Journey into the World of a Dance Icon

Stokes (2013) has noted that "you can also prove that you are a credible speaker by discussing your personal experience." Drawing from this approach, my journey into the life of Fodéba Keïta, the Guinean visionary and revolutionary choreographer who founded the dance troupe *Les Ballets Africains* in Paris in 1952, begins in Ndop, in broadway, at a time when it was still largely a rural farming community. It begins with my own cultural epiphany which turned out to be my informal initiation into African folkdance. Ndop, located about 250 miles northwest of Yaoundé, the capital of French Cameroon, was the seat of the local government since the days of the British colonial administration. My father, a blacksmith, had moved there in the forties from Bamendankwe, his birthplace.

Neither my father nor my mother had been to school; but they knew the value of good education. My uncle, my mother's older brother, was Cameroon's first civil engineer; and her father was very fluent in German, having attended a German school in Bimbia, a district along the coast of Cameroon; and having served as tax collector and interpreter when Germany administered my country as a colony (Ki-Zerbo, 1978; Rudin, 2013). The idea of having such towering figures for a father and a brother might have caused my mother not to consider any career option for me that was not illustrious. This is another way of saying that I had to be Western educated. In ways that I could never have imagined, this stance had far-reaching implications on my personal development.

Since I was born and raised in Ndop. This setting was central in shaping my worldview. I grew up knowing very little of my parents' own village. Ndop is a vast fertile plain set in the midst of hills and was once at the crossroads of Tikar and Chamba migration. These two major ethnic groups in the area were largely responsible for the current ethnic configuration of the Western Grassfields of Cameroon. As a cultural crossroads, an administrative headquarters, and economic hub, this district often hosted numerous important events. One of such events was the annual Agro-pastoral Show, an occasion used to showcase the most modern food production and processing techniques as well as the best farming implements. Important as agriculture and animal husbandry were and still remain to this day in this part of the Cameroons, organizers knew back then that it needed more than one activity to attract the kind of population that often made such events a success. So, in addition to agricultural activities, the occasion was also used to promote other aspects of development such as culture.

Fortunately, the kind of obsession with which colonization attempted to destroy local cultures in most parts of Africa had really not taken hold in this part of Cameroon. Lord Lugard, a pillar in

British imperial venture and one of the initiators of Indirect Rule, attempted, through this policy, to ground British control over the territory by using local leaders. Since local leaders were in charge, the policy helped in reducing friction and in preserving and even promoting local cultures. Part of this policy carried over in the post-colonial dispensation when local leaders saw cultural preservation and promotion as a means to enhance their people's progress and development (Che, 2013, pp. 27-30). It came as no surprise therefore that during Agro-pastoral Shows, there were cultural manifestations and competitions among the participating ethnic groups in the region. In no other aspect of culture was the competition fiercer than in traditional dances.

Even though I watched and sometimes participated in traditional dances, they really did not mean much to me. I had overheard my parents proudly talking about the extraordinary performance of Tamukung Dance from their village. Out of a sense of ethnic pride and loyalty, it was normal for them to talk that way, so I attached no particular significance to the gesture. It was a perception that was about to change and alter the way I viewed culture and folkdance.

The Agro-pastoral Show was fast approaching. A few days before the event, Jing Ngwanueh, my uncle and the manager of Tamukung, came to Ndop to register the dance for the competition. Since he was someone I greatly admired and held in high esteem, the registration immediately aroused my curiosity, which only seemed to grow unrelentingly, when on the eve of the Agro-pastoral Show, members of Tamukung troupe arrived in our compound in a "mammy wagon": an old truck converted into a kind of bus. A huge hall used by natives of Bamendankwe residing in Ndop for their weekly meetings had been set aside for the dance troupe. As soon as they alighted, they began to haul huge sacks to the hall. The sacks were so many that I began to wonder what could be in them. That was to remain a mystery until the next day as I went to bed, but I could not sleep, waiting for that next day to come quickly. It did.

The earlier part of it was spent focusing on events directly related to agriculture. My parents and uncle had given me some money to change into several coins to appear rich; and with a dress to match my new status I sauntered onto the Agro-pastoral Show ground. It was jammed with people, many of whom had come with some precious items to exhibit. Squeezing myself like a maggot through the human jumble, I finally got to a wide path that had been opened up in front of the stands. I picked my way on this path to avoid the squeeze, drifting with the human flow and feasting my eyes on all the marvels the diverse worlds of agriculture and culture had to offer.

Rambling in the hot tropical sun and eating all kinds of snacks and goodies soon took their toll. Since it was in the late afternoon that the folkdance competition would begin, I decided to rush back home for a quick nap. I was fast asleep when someone eagerly woke me up. It was my mother. "What are you still doing here?" she asked in amusement. "Tamukung is already in the Agro-pastoral Show ground and would soon begin dancing," she announced.

Very frantically, I jumped out of bed and headed straight for the showground which was just nearby. I arrived just when the musicians were busy setting their xylophones, a twenty-two-piece instrument of thick, hard, red, noisy tropical wooden bars played by four strapping villagers. It was to be accompanied by a drum conceived in genuine Tikar tradition, with a tall anthropological tale to recount. Standing at about 1.20 m above the ground, with a long rope for the player to strap round his waist to keep it in place while he pounded it away, this one seemed very special. Tapering downward from the membrane to the midsection, it began to broaden at the base, giving it a kind of dumbbell shape. Every inch of the way, on that hard mahogany wood out of which it was carved, it had different kinds of village motifs etched on the surface all round it: a king in ethnic garb sitting on his throne, a thatch house, a chameleon, a pair of gongs, and a woman pounding food in a mortar. These images summed up community life and captured the very essence of these cultural competitions.

I was still busy taking in the musicians and their instruments when my ears caught a rattling note. I looked up in the direction from where the sound had emanated. My word, what was I seeing! Half hidden by a segment of the grandstand where the dignitaries were sitting, on a path that had been cleared to let in the various dance groups, was what I had waited for so long to see. Almost blending in with the surrounding population, but still standing out well enough for a person to see was Tamukung.

Lined up in a single file according to their heights, they were about fourteen of them, all dressed up in some of the finest of very traditional dancing regalia. Brand new, the outfits the dancers had on were designed out of the alternating blue-white stripe Ndobo fabric, with the edges of the arms and bottom rimmed with cured goatskin and red cloth. This was a ritual dance that had been transformed into a recreational one. So, they all had their faces covered and they sported some of the most beautiful dancing head masks I have ever seen. They were gaudy Tikar masks, crafted by some of the best masters in the trade, with many of them encrusted with copper embellishments, beads, and cowries, the trademarks of the greatest of these artists. Their dancing whisks, of horsetails set on carved hardwood and sometimes, ivory handles, were decorated with beads in the grand style of the Bamouns-Bansos and Bamilekes (three major Tikar groups). As for the seeds used to make the rattles strapped around their ankles, they were something else. Fat and flat and woven into a thick cluster, their vibrations could scare the devil out of hell during dancing. I was very impressed.

Shortly after I had breezed in, the voice of the announcer proudly rang out with those magic words: "Tamukung of Bamendankwe!" I adjusted and held my breath. The xylophones immediately struck up; and then the drum rolled in and rumbled in one of the most beautiful melodies I had ever heard. It was thunderous and the ground was shaking. With the *kam*, the lead dancer, leading the way in a prancing gait, and the other dancers in tow, Tamukung strutted into the ground

100

like Zulu warriors.

"*Atungsiri built his house and spent the night outside...*" the old lines of a popular village lore to shame a chicken thief, which I would hear so often after, were hammered out of the xylophones in the language of my forefathers. I could literally feel my head swelling with pride. My own people could put it all together so beautifully. And as the dancers strutted their stuff, the spectators voiced their approval in countless cheers.

In the cultural competition, Tamukung won first prize, a feat this dance would repeat in numerous other occasions and competitions. After the event, bursting with pride, l let it be known to anyone who cared to listen that Tamukung came from my parents' village, a place I had never actually known. By associating with the dance, this gave me a sense of pride, of belonging, and of identity.

With my experience in The Cameroons and the one in South Africa, where I lived for four years and where dance had played an important part in the anti-apartheid struggle, I was quick to make a connection between art and emancipation. So, traditional dance was the first thing that came quite naturally to my mind when I read about the alarmingly high school dropout rates prevalent among African-Canadians as well as some of the reasons given to explain this sorry state of affairs. With this background knowledge of dance and the predicament of black students, I did not even think when I was called up to write about any venerated Black revolutionary or visionary.

Fodéba Keïta, the Visionary

Writing in *Maximum Ink*, Madison's Music Magazine online, Sarah H. Grant gives this glowing description of *Les Ballets Africains*:

The women sway like churning butter. The rattle and djembe pick up the rhythm and they thrust their arms back and forth as if repelling the air. They are the essence of, gyrating and stomping with beads of sweat pouring down their strong visages. A man with long braids play the kenkeni to the beat of the throbbing heart. For Les Ballets Africains, music is celebration.

Davies (2008) emphasizes the role of the troupe by noting that: "the company carries the enormous responsibility of representing African culture to the world, meeting a demand reminiscent of the insatiable appetite for African art that existed in the 20th century."

The journey of the troupe started in Siguiri in Guinea-Conakry in French colonial West Africa where Fodéba Keïta was born on January 19, 1921, the son of a male nurse. After completing Junior Elementary School in Conakry, the country's capital, in 1937, he attended École Normale Supérieure William Ponty in Senegal, an institution where French African schoolteachers and colonial cadres were trained. Founded in 1855 in Saint Louis as École des Otages (Verbatim: School for Hostages) on the initiative of General Faidherbe, it was renamed in 1903 after William Merlaud-Ponty, a former Governor General of French West Africa, by Governor Jean-Baptiste Chaudie of the French Colonial Government. Today, the school flaunts among its most notable alumni a good number of prominent African personalities and heads of states: Félix Houphouet-Boigny and renowned writer Bernard Dadié of Côte D'Ivoire, Modibo Keïta of Mali, Hubert Maga of Benin Republic, Hamani Diori and Boubou Maga of Niger, Maurice Yameogo of Burkina Faso, Diallo Telli, the first Secretary General of the Organization of African Unity (OAU), and Abdoulaye Wade of Senegal, just to name a few. In 1913, the school experienced the first of its several relocations when it was moved to the Island of Goree. From its very beginning, the school was started to propagate the French language. By the time it became known as École William Ponty, it had broadened its activities to include the training of Africans who would serve as intermediaries between the colonial administration and the local population. Sabatier (1978), however, sums up one of the main goals of the institution by noting that it was to create "…a carefully limited number of indigenous auxiliaries whose loyalty as well as competence would be beyond question." To Charry (2000), it "...was an important means of indoctrinating West Africans with French culture" (p. 47). With an increasingly bulging student population from French West and Equatorial Africa, a plan to move the school to a more spacious location was set in motion in 1923; but it was only in 1938 that this attained fruition when the institution was set in the remote and rustic environment of Sebikotane. The move also witnessed a shift in French colonial policy, from the idealistic one of completely assimilating Africans into the French culture to that of association through which Africans received French education but were profoundly rooted in their own indigenous identity (De Jong, Quinn & Bach, 2014). Kringelbach (2012) notes that in 1935, the new director of the school, Charles Beart, had introduced "school theatre" to the curriculum of the institution and "the students were asked to write plays with explicit aim of illustrating their 'native' traditions." The idea behind this decision "was to encourage them to preserve a connection with local cultures and with rural life in particular" (p. 145). These plays were staged in school during the "Fete D'Art Indigene" (Native Art Festival). This youth theatre had a profound impact on the lives of the students and "one student, Guinean poet Fodéba Keïta, was to transform this youth theatre into live *national heritage*" (p. 146).

Fodéba Keïta entered the École William Ponty in 1940 and graduated from it with a teaching degree in 1944. Yet again, one wonders what life could have been during those years. Charry (2000) paints a portrait of what life was like in the school while he was there:

> Students at École William Ponty in the 1940s, such as Fodéba Keïta (founder of Les Ballets Africains), were exposed to European music and culture and became important forces in modernising African music in Senegal and Guinea. (p. 47)

A great student of music, poetry and theatre, he taught

successively in Tambacounda and in Saint-Louis in Senegal after his graduation before leaving for France to pursue further studies. He arrived in Paris towards the end of 1948, not long after the creation of *Présence Africaine* (1947), a momentous event in his life as a writer. He enrolled at the Faculty of Law at the University of Paris. The negritude movement was in full bloom and he "…became a part of the flamboyant cohort of Francophone students around Léopold Sédar Senghor, Alioune Diop and the emerging negritude movement" (Kringelbach, 2012, p. 146). Negritude, an anti-colonial movement initiated by Paulette Nardal, the first black woman to enroll at the prestigious Sorbonne University, was described by former Senegalese President, Léopold Sédar Senghor, one of its greatest theorists, as "…the cultural patrimony, the values, and above all the spirit of negro African civilization" (Kesteloot, 1991, p. 102). The politician-scholar added that "…his return to his African past, his sudden resentment of his own Frenchness and his search for virtue in the African personality was the result of his realization that he assimilated, and was not being assimilated" (Crowder, 1967, p. 52). Aimé Césaire (1972), described as "the High Priest of Negritude," explains that Negritude was real resistance to cultural assimilation (pp. 70-78).

Tossed in the eye of this anti-colonial maelstrom, his political outlook started to take shape and even influence his art. He had allegedly received scholarship from the French government to study theatre art but switched to law in Europe; and rumours have it that his scholarship was rescinded. For lack of funding, he dropped out of his studies in law with just a certificate. He then invited his friend and compatriot Kante Facelli, a guitarist, arranger, and music interpreter, over to Paris and, teaming up with the Cameroonian singer Albert Mouangue, the trio formed the group Fodéba-Facelli-Mouangue in 1949. A playwright, choreographer, poet, composer, and storyteller, Fodéba Keïta was aware of his numerous strengths and wanted more and so became an avid researcher and writer of plays towards which he directed the bulk of his energy. His revolutionary vision received a major boost from like minded individuals around him at the time. Kringelbach (2012) points out that

Assan Seck, poet David Diop, actor Maurice Sonar Senghor (Léopold Sédar Senghor's nephew), actress Annette Mbaye d'Erneville, dancer-actors Feral Benga and Habib Benglia also gravitated around the movement (*negritude*) and discussed ways of embodying Negritude ideas on stage. (p. 146)

It was, therefore, out of the desire to capture his vision on stage that he founded *Le Théâtre Africain* de Keïta. He, however, quickly realized that with theatre, he would not be understood outside Francophone countries and so made the momentous decision of using dance as a vehicle for the transmission of his message. In an RFI broadcast dedicated to renowned African artists dubbed *Les Grandes Voix D'Afrique* (Great Voices of Africa), in an episode that focused on "Keïta Fodéba: du Merveilleux au Tragique" (Keïta Fodéba: From the Marvelous to the Tragic)," it is stated concerning his choice of dance as medium for his message that

> It is first and foremost to show the Mandingos the basic importance of songs, of music, and of dance. By so doing, by bringing together singers, dancers, and acrobats, the troupe wanted to present to the entire world, the expression of traditional cultural, moral, and intellectual values of the African society. Since dance is more than a succession of gestures. (My translation)

Under the impulse of this reasoning, the theatre group morphed into *Les Ballets Africains* de Fodéba Keïta. When Guinea became independent in 1958, his increasing political involvement caused him to hand the group over to the state as a gift and it was renamed *Les Ballets Africains de la République de Guinée* and it toured the world as the nation's 'cultural ambassador' (Ibid).

It is worthwhile to note that for a person in the midst of an anti-colonial struggle, the choice of the word "ballet," the very epitome of Western dance, to describe an African dance troupe was jarring. However, in an article Fodéba published in the UNESCO cultural magazine *Courier* of January 1959, he defended his apparently ironic stance.

Ballet, in its Western conception, is an original choreographic creation. Our popular African dances hardly yet correspond to this. But if ballet is 'a form of artistic and cultural expression developed by man in his endless quest for new means of expression, in his yearning to create forms which are ceaselessly renewed according to his genius and abilities,' African dance as a means of expression and of exteriorization can be identified with ballet. (p. 20)

This critique of naming seemed particularly pertinent and might have influenced him. It was probably in a bid to show his Africanity, that he was still very much grounded in African traditions, that he is believed to have made the claim that he was from a family of griots (oral praise-singers and historians) and took the name Keïta, a noble branch of the Mande. While many Guineans question the veracity of his claim, their conduct might just have been influenced by the desire to get back at him for what he had represented in the repressive machinery that operated in Guinea following the country's independence in 1958.

His selection of dance in the midst of other art forms still required further elaboration for a number of reasons, not least because of the era and context in which he was operating. It was an era in which dance, especially African dance, was pretty much vilified (Ajayi, 1998), the reason for this being very much influenced by a strong version of the Cartesian mind/body dichotomy, with the reason/emotion divide as a corollarydangote. According to Kringelbach (2007) "…dance was viewed as a 'primitive' form of expression pertaining to the domain of emotion" and as a result the "so-called 'primitive' peoples were assumed to dance more than people from more sophisticated societies because their lives were led by emotion rather than by reason" (p. 3). Even more intriguing was the fact that Fodéba Keïta was first and foremost a poet surrounded by poets: Aimé Césaire, Léopold Sédar Senghor, Leon Gontras Damas, David Diop, etc. of the Negritude Movement. What's more, with the creation in 1947 of the publishing house Présence Africaine by the Senegalese Alioune Diop, the environment to write and get published could not have been better. Poetry aside, he could have also drawn inspiration from other parts of the world where other forms of written expression were being pressed into service by Africans as a weapon of choice in the fight for freedom. Alain Locke, described as the "Father of the Harlem Renaissance," the black cultural revolution that took place in America in the 1920s, had taken the world by storm with his publication of *The New Negro* in 1925. This work had been translated into French by Paulette Nardal and had played no small part in influencing the formulation of the Negritude philosophy. In 1938, Jomo Kenyatta had published *Facing Mount Kenya*, described by renowned Polish anthropologist Bronislaw Malinowski in his introduction to the book as "instructive contributions to African ethnography by a scholar of pure African parentage" (p. xiii). In 1948, South Africa's Alan Paton published his classic *Cry, the Beloved Country*, an anti-colonial work critical of apartheid in his country. Was Fodéba Keïta completely oblivious to these developments? Whatever the case, even with all the influences listed, he settled for dance and provided additional reasons, some of them very potent, to justify his selection when he stated that "to make Africa and all the variety known, we have chosen dance, not only as an excellent means of universal expression but also because, with us, it is connected with all the other arts" (1959, p. 20). In other words, he went for the total package. Dance in Africa remains largely a people's art par excellence and has widespread application in that it encompasses other art forms such as music (Ajayi, 1998; Argenti, 2002, 2007; Bebey, 1975; Flaig, 2010; Ntaimah, 2012), sculpture

107

(Argenti, 2002; R. F. Thompson, 1974), story-telling (Ebron, 2002), theater (Layiwola, 2003), aesthetics (K. W. Asante, 2000; R. F. Thompson, 1974), and spirituality (Gunn, Jr., 2006; Ajayi, 1998; R. F. ti, 1974). The relevance of dance to Africans has also been identified by Kariamu Welsh Asante (1998) when she states that "dance in Africa is not a separate art, but a part of the whole complex of living" (p. 4). Fodéba Keïta (1959) concurs, referring to African dance as an emanation of the people while to Ajayi (1998), it is a microcosm of culture.

Having made his choice, it was a long journey towards the creation of *Les Ballets Africains*; and in which endeavour, he gained inspiration from both Africa and Europe. The preparation had inadvertently started during Fodéba's school days at École William Ponty where during the holidays students were sometimes required to collect the dances, poetry and songs of their villages and to present them upon their return to school as part of their training in poetry and theatre art. Keïta retraced that step after the troupe was moved to Guinea from Paris in 1958, but this time with a sense of purpose. He added to it, the sophistication of his European training in dance and theatre. Above all, he had the backing of and funding from the Sékou Touré government, a vehemently anti-colonial outfit that had overtly rejected De Gaulle's offer to make Guinea part of the French Community. With all of this, Fodéba Keïta scoured the backcountry of Guinea, sampling, auditioning, and recruiting the finest drummers, dancers, storytellers, poets, and choreographer, grist for his neo-traditional dance venture. Kariamu Welsh (2004) describes neo-traditional dances as "…those dances that are created in the spirit or likeness of traditional dances but … are not bound to all the aesthetics and cultural rules of that society" (p. 19). Green (2011), on her part, views them as "…dances that make use of elements of traditional dances, but not necessarily in the same context as they are found in the traditional culture" (p. 24). Concerning folkdances, Buckland (1999) points out that "removal from their former contexts alters their meanings; but the movements of the staged dances maintain a cultural validity which can act as a window through which more understanding can be gained of the people who perform them" (p. 100). Fodéba Keïta's efforts required some tinkering, borrowing, and modernizing (Andrieu, 2014), that culminated in *Les Ballets Africains*.

Fodéba (1959) laid bare the purpose of his ensemble, stating that the ongoing tendency of an African folklore company such as (his) must be "to display to the whole world the cultural values of both these two Africas; the traditional and pre-colonial Africa of our forefathers and the Africa of today which is gradually being impregnated with Western civilization." According to Juang and Morrissette (2008), among some of the first members of the troupe were Kante Facelli, Raphael Wigbert, Conte Seydou, and Touré Ismaël. Both scholars point out that in the early 1950s, notable artists were recruited, such as Italo Zambo of Guinea and Papa Ladji of Mali, one of the troupe's most famous drummers. Between 1951 and 1955, the dance travelled to Holland, Luxembourg, Denmark, Norway, Germany, Italy, Spain, Austria, France, Belgium, and Switzerland. The two scholars maintain that the early songs Fodéba composed celebrated the history and culture of Africa and went on to becoming true classics: for example, *Minuit*, *Aurore Africaine*, *Chanson de Djoliba* and *Sine Mory*. Cohen (2012) describes the troupe as "the world's first professional and internationally touring African performance company" (p. 12). However, in spite of its initial burst of success and popularity, French ethnomusicologist Gilbert Rouget, in an article published in the black Journal *Présence Africaine* in 1957, under the title "La danse africaine et la scène" (African dance and stage), decried the absence of "genuineness" in the dance. In the face of this critique, Fodéba Keïta struck back, thus becoming a spokesperson for African culture. "Genuine, in fact, compared to what? To a more or less false idea which one has conceived about the sensational primitiveness of Africa?" he questioned before

109

proceeding to show that his performance was authentic. "No! Authentic folklore is that which truly represents the more characteristic aspects of the existence it wishes to bring to life on stage" (Andrieu, 2014; Fodéba, 1959).

By the time the dance ensemble first burst onto the New York scene in 1959, "the company had risen to fame during the 1950's, touring Western and Eastern Europe, French West Africa, South America and the Middle East with shows featuring West African music, stories, and dance stage in modern arrangements and choreography" (Ibid). The arrival of *Les Ballets Africains* in America could not have been timelier. It was not the first time that Africa was providing part of the solution to the cultural yearnings of African Americans. Green (2011) argues that "besides Asadata Dafora, the person credited as the first to bring African dance to the shores of the United States; there were several others who had an influence on the art form" (p. 25). Cohen (2012) also cites Efiom Odok, a Nigerian-born artist working in Harlem and one of Josephine Baker's contemporaries with a group called Calabar Dancers as well as the well-known Nigerian-born group leader and recording artist, Yoruba drummer Babatunde Olutunji (p. 14). Thus, "genuine American interest in African performance had grown since the early 1930s" but this "was still in its nascent stages when *Les Ballets Africains* arrived in 1959" (p. 14). One of the critiques that have been levelled against the Civil Rights Movement of the 1960s in the US is that it had no cultural program apart from appealing to African Americans to integrate into the dominant society. Malcolm X, who reached the height of his cultural and social power in the 1960s, challenged this view. Of African Americans, he reasoned that "...the adaption of our ideas, attitudes, language, and history to the social and cultural imperatives of the African people was the first requirement of our comprehensive transformation" and African culture went on to gain respectability with Malcolm X's pronouncement that "...we were an African people despite all of the claims to the contrary by the African

American establishment" (Asante, M.K. 1993, pp. 26-27). It was out of this tradition of revolutionary change that the Kawaida philosophy of black cultural reconstruction of Maulana Karenga was born. It is against this backdrop that the importance and relevance of the arrival of Fodéba Keïta's troupe should be assessed. The arrival marked a shift in African dance from the dances of Nigeria and Ghana to the energy-charged, physically challenging dances and music from Guinea (Cohen, 2012, p. 15). *Les Ballets Africains* was the first group from French-speaking Africa

Fodéba Keïta, Dance, and Emancipation

Introduction

Hanna (1988) points out that dance is potentially very potent (p. 13). Kringelbach & Skinner (2012) confirm this by arguing that "dance does not simply 'reflect' what happens in society or serve a particular 'function' but that it is often central to social life as music and other universal forms of expression" (p. 2). Both scholars go further to state that it "is not fixed outside the bodies of performers and is therefore malleable enough to be manipulated according to context, ideology, and purpose" (p. 14). My investigation of the life of Fodéba Keïta and the dance troupe he created focuses mainly on the historical and emancipatory aspects. As such, dance should be largely understood as an art that rejects "inequality, the oppression of disenfranchised groups, the silencing of marginalized voices, and authoritarian social structures" (Fraleigh & Hanstein, 1999, p. 105). In a recent edition of "Danse D'Afrique" (African Dance), which met in Bamako in Mali from October 10 to November 04, 2019, French choreographer Angelin Preljocal remarked that in just a few years African choreography had really become contemporary. Talking to the Paris-based African magazine *Jeune Afrique*, she noted that "this year we are treated to a truly contemporary dance: it deals with social issues, from politics to economics, to urgent daily issues," adding that

111

"even if it emanates from tradition, it is not like before in which tradition was recycled in order to disguise modernity" (Andrieu, 2010, my translation). So, cursorily, how has the revolutionary vision of *Les Ballets Africains* impacted politics, culture, economics, society and education?

Cultural

Alan Merriam (1959) posits that in Africa, dance is culture and culture is dance. Culture is defined in cultural studies in terms of "shared meanings or shared conceptual maps" (Hall, 2013, p. 4). Seen from this angle, dance became a perfect tool for effectively creating and engaging entire communities in the anti-colonial struggle. *Les Ballets Africains* was created in the thick of the anti-colonial struggle and went on "to represent the culture of Africa by being an ambassador of love and truth through presenting the folklore of Guinea to the world, preserving the traditions that were being forgotten by urban city youth and reuniting people across ethnic barriers" (Juang and Morrissette, 2008). This role was hardly surprising, given that at the time of Guinea's independence in 1958, the leader of the country, Ahmed Sékou Touré, had emphasized the preservation of the African culture through a broad rehabilitation of traditional languages, dance, art, and drumming in the school curriculum. A well-nurtured prejudice had maintained that Africa took no part in shaping civilization and was accused of being without history and without culture. "Africans were considered to be a people without history, without any civilization worthy of the name … (Crowder, 1967, p. 2).

Such prejudice and many others were products of the modernity project, an emanation of the Age of Enlightenment. This was a period in which scientific and technological developments had endowed Europeans with tremendous power and a feeling of superiority. "European intellect, culture and understanding of the world were considered more advanced – superior to the others"

(Cannella and Viruru, 2004). With the power and feeling of superiority, they set out, conquered other lands, and subjected their people to their own ways of viewing the world; first through interruption, which entailed "the negation of the historical process of the dominated people, by means of violently usurping the free operation of the process of development of the productive forces" (Cabral, 1974, pp. 41-42) and then through European cultural assimilation, which for the "native populations …. turns out to be only a more or less violent attempt to deny the culture of the people in question" (p. 40). Crowder (1967) elaborates on cultural assimilation by noting that

> …the French when confronted with people they considered barbarians, believed in their mission to convert them into Frenchmen. This implied a fundamental acceptance of their potential human quality, but a total dismissal of African culture as of any value. (p. 2)

In America, the story was no different for black people. African American historian Lerone Bennett, Jr. (2000) has demonstrated how black people were stripped of their culture when they arrived in the Americas as slaves. Dance in particular came under European cultural assault and violation in African life. European missionaries, explorers, traders, and administrators attacked African folkdances (Ajayi, 1998; K. W. Asante, 2000), describing them as lewd, primitive, barbaric, and imitation of fornication. K. W. Asante (2000) argues that they did so precisely because dance "facilitates all phenomena in African societies" and also because their impressions of these dances "were largely related to their own /imperialist/ ambitions." Ajayi (1998) concurs, noting that, "given the cultural importance of dance in many of these cultures (*African*), it was politically expedient for the colonizers to prevent their survival" (p. 4).

In colonial America, during the era of enslavement, African folkdance was often discouraged in black communities, sometimes

113

by the very leadership of these communities. For example, in 1787 the Free African Society, the first African American organization in the United States, "opposed singing and dancing" in order to "improve the morals of its members" (Neufeldt & McGee, 1990, p. 11). Even when dance was taught in schools, hooks (2003) argues that it was usually European dances, such as ballet since it was "imperialist white-supremacist capitalist patriarchal values /which/ were taught in Southern black schools..." (p. 1). The result of this was that "Black parents didn't want to send their daughters to... Negro Dance Group" for fear that they "would be taught ancestral African dancing" (Harnan, 1974, p. 51).

When *Les Ballets Africains* arrived in America, the Civil Rights Movement and the Black Power Movement were taking place at the same time as that of the independence of some African countries from Western colonial rule. Juan & Morrissette (2008) maintain that with the arrival, black youths and practitioners of arts made connection with the African dance that it was presenting as a part of reclaiming their heritage and rights to an African identity. *Les Ballets Africains* was instantly received with tremendous enthusiasm and strong connections across cultural and linguistic barriers. This for a reason Cohen (2012) provides: "Given Africa's earlier, long-standing status as a source of shame and dismay ... this new interest in African dance constituted a radical shift" (p. 13). The impact of these dances in the US was, therefore, far reaching. Papa Ladji, master-drummer of Malian extraction, became the first of the Guinean-master teachers to travel to the USA in 1958 and his role as a cultural ambassador and transmitter started in 1959 when he met with artists like Chief Bey and Charles Moore. He also worked with other artists, such as Babatunde Olutunji, Pearl Primus, Yusef Lateef, master-Cuban drummer Mongo Santamaria, Nina Simone, Art Blakey, and many more. What was even more spectacular was that these developments led to the creation of the first generation of traditional African folk artists and djembe players to teach the ensuing generation, as well as of the first traditional African cultural arts schools, one of which was the International African American Ballets (IAAB), established around 1974. Many of the alumni of this institution spread throughout the country and became master teachers and founders of dance groups. For example, Amaniyeo Payne, a former member of IAAB, became the artistic director for Muntu Dance Theatre of Chicago which started in 1972. Similarly, Chuck Davis founded Dance Africa and the African American Dance Ensemble in 1968. This product of IAAB is based in Durham in North Carolina. In addition to the artists outlined, Juang and Morrissette (2008) state that

> Melvin Deal's African Heritage Dancers and Drummers is another example of a generation that has taught youth since the early 1960s. African American legends, such as Baba Robert Crowder, Arthur Hall, the Ishangi Family African Dancers, and other related djembe traditional ensembles, have raised the appreciation for African culture in the United States.

In Africa, the contribution of *Les Ballets Africains* to cultural emancipation was no less spectacular. Cabral (1973) argues that imperialist domination, by denying the historical development of the dominated people, necessarily also denied their cultural development (pp. 42-43). However, with independence, African countries had a lot of political and cultural catching up to do. In October 1975, UNESCO, meeting in Accra in Ghana for an African intergovernmental conference, stated that, "the major cultural problem which Africa faces is the one of its cultural identity", for "to affirm the cultural identity of a people is to give meaning to their lives and to lay a foundation to their political independence" (*Présence Africaine*, 1976, p. 9). Coming twenty-two years after the foundation of *Les Ballets Africains*, this belated conference was certainly inspired by the achievements of the ensemble. Davies (2008) maintains that the company's productions fuse traditional African dance, music, oral culture, and acrobatics across various genres, from comedy to drama, adding that the dancers perform to the strong percussive rhythms of such traditional Guinean drums as the djembe, the doudoun, and the kenkeni, as flutes and, of course, voices. She insists that "even in the company's most acrobatic sequences, it remains true to the principles of African dance by honoring the socio-historical roots of the art."

Political and Historical

Fodéba was aware that dance could be used for mass mobilization and political liberation. He took advantage of the status that he had been afforded by *Les Ballets Africains* to become politically involved and to fight for the independence of Guinea. He knew, as did notable African American choreographer and dancer Pearl Primus (1998), that dance was the soul of the African people. Some important events in the tortuous history of black resistance to domination and tyranny lend credence to this declaration. For example, Bennett, Jr. (2000) points out that it was during a voodoo dance ceremony that the successful slave revolt which culminated in Haiti's independence in 1804 was plotted (p. 108). In more recent times, *Amandla* and *Mayibuye* (SAHO, 2015) served as road ambassadors to the ANC during the anti-apartheid struggle in South Africa.

As a storehouse of African history, Green (2011) is right on point when she states that, "African dance is part of an oral tradition that is handed down between generations by a mouth to ear process" (p. 17). Given this importance, it is easy to see why some ensembles, with *Les Ballets Africains* and *Ballet National du Senegal* leading the way, have contributed far more than the noises of African politicians and administrators in asserting and promoting the continent's cultural identity and independence abroad. Initiation, dance and music, from their inception, formed three realities which blend together into one, which is life and its activities, in traditional black-African conception (Mveng, Njob, Samuel, 1969, p. 9). It is not surprising, therefore, that during the colonial era "many dances were banned because of fear of indigenous rebellion, fear of the unknown which created problems in colonizing other cultures" (Davila, 2009, p. 63). According to Ajayi (1998), the destruction of these dances served as a cultural reinforcement of the military defeat and helped to facilitate the act of ruling over the subjugated people (p. 4).

Thus, with its emergence *Les Ballets Africains* was effective in creating a strong national identity that integrated elements of the different ethnic dance forms in a way that established uniformity and provided a criterion or standard of African theatre performance that has served as a model for all Africa. As a tool for integration, it even went farther than that. Even though the main repertoire of the troupe drew from Guinean legends and folklores, it also reflected the rhythms and dances from other West African countries, such as Mali, Mauritania, Senegal, the Gambia, Guinea-Bissau, Sierra Leone, Liberia, Côte d'Ivoire, and Burkina Faso, with some of these cultural aspects dating back to the 13th century during the days of the old Empire of Mali (Juang & Morrissette, 2008). So, in this way the Ballets became effective tools to create not only a strong national identity but a continental one as well.

Social

For Davies (2008), the productions themselves of *Les Ballets Africains* tackle social issues from an African viewpoint. Some of these productions were already exploring issues of the environment even before they became topical: for example, *The Bell of Hamana*. Another aspect in their repertoire was education, as a means for individual and societal development: for example *Silo: The Path of Life* (2007). Another important and very contemporary issue that featured in their performance was that of genital mutilation. Gastineau (1999) illustrates in this performance.

After a dazzling display of drumming and parades of masks great and small, a remarkable event occurred: The initiates rejected the

117

ritual female circumcision. One gesture rang out like a shout: a girl stood and emphatically refused. An entire dance devoted to this followed that the statement was made by a national, government-funded ensemble deepened the point.

Evolution, an item on their repertoire bearing the signature of Bangoura, focused on the Guinean woman, held as equal to man in all. Gastineau (Ibid) gives this description to drive home the point: "the initiates (*young girls*) closed Act I with an impressive display of female power in an extended drumming exchange" in which "…they faced off a stageful of drumming men and more than held their own."

The application of dance goes far beyond these specific aspects. It has been used as a means for community building and involvement (A. Kipling. Brown, 2008, chapter 7; O. C. Banks, 2010; Vissicaro, 2004, 2009). Since it unites different art forms, it is multi-layered and is therefore capable of attracting people with diverse interests, thus engaging a broad spectrum of the population. In this, it does not only transcend ethnic and national barriers but occupational as well. This was an aspect that resonated well with the message Papa Ladji conveyed during his training sessions in the United States. His clarion cry of "African People for Americans and Americans for Africans" reached many across ethnic barriers (Juang & Morrissette, 2008). Through such community mobilization, dance becomes an effective counter-hegemonic art. According to the American *Bureau of Justice Statistics*, 1 in 3 black men can expect to go to prison in their lifetime. Similarly, while black people make up 13% of the population of the US, they constitute 40% of those who are imprisoned (K. Bell, 2016). Here, the relevance of dance to mobilize black children and inculcate certain values required for their survival should not be underestimated.

Economic

Africans have been constantly reminded by Western propaganda that they did not have a culture; even in the postcolonial dispensation their governments have paid scant attention to it. Green (2011) points out that "being a dancer, musician or a theater person was frowned upon in Africa" and that "parents did not want their children to go into the arts or theater" (p. 19). In some cases, she went on to recount, people of the arts such as griots were denied burial in the cemetery for fear they would contaminate the burial ground and so were buried in the hollow of a baobab tree. A patent and contemporary example of this kind of rejection was that of Maurice Sonar Senghor, the nephew of late Senegalese President Léopold Sédar Senghor as well as the founder of the National Ballet of Senegal. After he spurned his father's wish to go into the study of law and opted instead for dance and theater, his father stopped paying for his education and disinherited him. Similarly, Afrobeats superstar Fela Kuti, who pursued music instead of medicine in keeping with family tradition, was rebuked by his parents. More recently, renowned Nigerian author and feminist, Chimamanda Ngozi Adichie, has expressed how she had to flee Nigeria to the United States because her parents wanted her to study medicine when she had already made up her mind to become a storyteller. I wanted to believe that such an attitude was only prevalent among Western-trained African middle-class families until Mamady Keïta, lead drummer for Ballet D'Joliba, testified that he "was disowned by his family for joining the ballet" (Flaig, 2010, p. 18).

Today, for a continent that produces and exports virtually nothing, it is mainly culture that has become her saving grace. Even though many African universities are still to set up real department for African arts and culture (dance, music, and movies), music remains one of the most important exports of the continent, with countries such as South Africa, Nigeria, Senegal, Cameroon, Guinea, the Democratic Republic of Congo, and Côte D'Ivoire hauling in substantial amount from the industry. With substantial government funding and promotion, the arts could easily become a huge source of financial gain. *Les Ballets Africains* fits in this picture.

119

Les Ballets Africains is arguably the most popular dance group in the world and the impact it has had on the economy of not just Guinea but the entire Senegambia region is huge. African master drummers and dancers are selling like hotcakes in rich Western countries where they have opened dance and drumming schools in countries such as the United States, Germany, Belgium, and France, to name just a few of them. For example, in Belgium Mamady Keïta started his own drum school called *Tam Tam Mandingue*. Flaig (2010) points out that "between 1992 and 2008, Keïta has established (at least) twenty-three, official *Tam Tam Mandingue* schools worldwide…" (p. 23). Apart from tuition fees, CDs, drums crafted in Africa and other dance and music paraphernalia are sold. This is extremely good news for African craftsmen and drum makers who might not have had a market for their products. In addition, countries such as Guinea, Gambia, Mali, Senegal, etc., have become dance Meccas for African drumming and dance students from countries as far as Japan, Australia, the US, South Korea, Argentina, Germany, etc. During their stay in these African countries, these students help in promoting the local economy by spending money on accommodation, on food, dance, and music items, as well as a wide range of services. It is only when African culture becomes economically relevant and viable that people will strive to preserve and promote it. This is far from being an exhaustive analysis of the economic benefits of *The Ballets Africains*.

Education

Proponents of cultural imperialism, which is the universalization of one group's experience and its culture and its establishment as the norm (McLaren, 2003), have often downplayed the importance of the cultures of other communities in their lives. It was Carter Woodson (2006), who first drew attention to the dangers of educating black people away from their own cultural traditions. He argued that the 'educated Negroes' have the attitude of contempt toward their own people because in their own as well as their mixed school Negroes are taught to admire the Hebrew, the Greek, the Latin and the Teutons and to despise the African. A group of black students based in the City of Regina in Canada who were interviewed in 2016 identified five main areas in which they believed African folkdances could be relevant in their lives: viz. family/community organization, cultural inclusion, group identity, gender issues, and the prevention of low self-esteem and high dropout rates (Jing, 2017). Hanna (1999) points out other importance of dance to education by noting that it can facilitate learning of other academic disciplines and life skills and that not only can students learn the discipline of dance, but they can also learn about dance through dance; and that through dance education students can discover and address personal and public concerns about health, gender, ethnicity, self, and their national identity (p. 2).

Anyone would be taken aback by the disproportionately high school dropout rates prevalent among some minority communities, such as the black and First Nations communities. Concerning the black community, this is the picture Hampton (2010) paints in connection with education:

As elsewhere in the country, many Black youth in Québec are not engaged in public schools, leaving them unable to make useful connections between the education they receive at school and their lived experiences – with the exception of the clear connection between the disenfranchisement and alienation they experience at school and that which they and their families experience in wider society. Even Black families who have been in Québec for multiple generations face an unemployment rate and a proportion of low-income households more than double those of the general population. 3. Nearly half of Québec's Black youth drop out of high school. A 2004 study demonstrated that a group of Black students in Québec who started high school between 1994 and 1996 had a 51.8 per cent graduation rate, compared to 69 per cent for the population as a whole. 4. (p. 105)

The situation of inexplicably high school dropout rates is not peculiar to Quebec. Dei et al. (2007) point out that "in the 1990s, North American society is facing the challenge of providing education for an increasingly diverse population" and that "the issues of race, ethnicity, class, gender, and sexuality present significant challenges and lessons for Euro-Canadian/American schools" (p.3). Consequently, "despite the efforts of the 1990s, at the dawn of the twenty-first century, the situation for Black learners in Canada had not significantly improved" (Hampton, 2010, p. 105). Focusing mainly on the Ontario Public School System, Dei et al. (2007) have conducted a study on the phenomenon of black students who constitute a disproportionate number of those who leave school prematurely.

The Canadian experience is identical to those of African Americans and blacks in South Africa. According to the *Journal of Blacks in Higher Education* (JBHE), college graduation stands at 42%, 20 points below the one for whites, that is 62%. Such discrepancies set the mind to working and identifying culture, or the lack thereof, as the main reason for the situation. This was received with a very common pushback from some members of the society. Many people, spoken to in connection with the situation, were quick to point out that if culture is responsible for creating the situation, how come Asian students, who navigate the same cultural currents as blacks and Native students in Canada and the United States, do well in school? This question is more mischievous than it appears. It is a racial indictment; and, in the worst of times, it often comes with a liberal dose of scientific half-truths and baseless allegations designed, in the main, to deflect accusations of white cultural hegemony and imperialism and to entrench the top-dog mentality. As a result, it requires a rebuttal sufficiently robust to put it to sleep. Strangely enough, in the question lies the answer.

Drawing on data from Statistics Canada 2002, a study jointly conducted by Teresa Abada, Feng Hou and Bali Ram in 2008 to determine differences in levels of academic achievements among the children of immigrants showed that the highest rates of university graduates between the ages of 24 and 34 born of immigrant parents were the Chinese with 69.5 %, followed by the Indians with 65.2%. As outlined, this finding seems paradoxical as these two groups operate in a "foreign" cultural environment; but follow the argument. In the search for an explanation to such discrepancy, the present research found out that the two groups which showed significant dropout rates and low academic performance, blacks and First Nations students, have had a cultural experience in North America different from that of the two Asian communities. Historically, native-born North American blacks and First Nations have operated in a virtual indigenous cultural vacuum dominated by two deleterious forces operating in tandem; to wit, the destruction of their cultural institutions and then their forcible assimilation into the dominant Eurocentric culture. Focusing on Africans of the Diaspora (native-born North American blacks), Karade (1994) insists that they were "…stripped of their fundamental social structures and mores" (p. 5). This experience is different from that of the Chinese or Indians who have always retained their own culture in this continent even as they navigate the treacherous streams of cultural hegemony and exclusion. This argument takes on greater weight when a distinction is made between the school performance of African-born and diaspora black students. Those from Africa generally experience high graduation rates and perform well in school. With data from the United States Census Bureau, Wachira Kigotho (2015) has conducted a study titled *A Profile of Sub-Saharan African Students in America*. His findings show that, compared with America's overall foreign-born population, the foreign-born from Africa had higher levels of educational achievement between 2008 and 2012. Similarly, in *The Foreign-Born Population from Africa: 2008-2012*, a survey conducted jointly by Christine Gambino, Edward N. Trevelyan and John Thomas Fitzwater (2014) at the US Census Bureau, 41% of the African-born population had a bachelor degree compared with 28% of the overall foreign-born population in the US. According to another analysis of the Census Bureau by the *Journal of Blacks in Higher Education (JBHE)*, African immigrants to the United States were found more likely to be college educated than other immigrant groups. The journal continues by noting that 48.9% of all African immigrants hold a college diploma, a figure which is slightly higher than the percentage of Asian immigrants to the US, nearly double the rate of native-born white Americans and nearly four times the rate of native-born African Americans. In Canada, students of African immigrants came third, after the Chinese and Indians, with a university graduation rate of 55.9% (Abada, Hou & Ram, 2008).

What these findings show is that there is a significant link between cultural preservation and high academic performance. Ngugi wa Thiong'o (2009) argues that "…cultural subjugation is more dangerous (*than political and economic*), because it is more subtle and its effects longer lasting" and that it can lead to a pessimism that fails to see in a person's history any positive lesson in dealing with the present (p. 109). The Chinese in North America have often attributed their academic excellence and economic success largely to Confucian ethics (N. Smith, 2015). So, coming back to the explanation of the discrepancy between African-born and native-born North American blacks, one should point out that a Yoruba student from Nigeria, for instance, apart from bringing his or her own ethical and cultural values enshrined in the *Book of Ifa* (Karade, 1994, pp. 14-20; Soyinka, 2012, pp. 104-169), has never been methodically exposed to the blitz of Eurocentric indoctrination and brainwashing as well as anti-black hostility which over the centuries have dogged Africans and contributed significantly in eroding self-esteem and ethnic worth. The point of cultural complementarity is taken up by renowned Jewish historian Max Dimont (1962) who notes that "Jewish renaissance" came about in a two-way flow dynamic in which the Biblical Jews maintained their Torah-based faith while embracing

Hellenic philosophical rationality they had previously rejected. In other words, the Jews did not discard Judaism; they only supplemented what they had with something they borrowed from the Greeks (pp. 192-200). North American blacks and First Nations people were forced to abandon who they were, leaving a cultural void which was gradually filled with an unending barrage of denigrating and demoralizing morass and negative discourses designed mainly to rob them of their own history and heritage as well as to entrench white colonial stranglehold and values. Anti-black and - Native attitude prevalent in most North American school environment today stems largely from long years of very hostile and corrosive colonial narratives which have often been directed against the two groups.

The students interviewed in Regina identified low self-esteem as the main cause of high school dropout rates. Copeland, Jr. (1995) argues that "a positive self-image (*self-esteem*) cannot survive without culture;" that "culture is a part of who and what we are;" and that "in the city, minority youth are often discouraged from learning about their history" (p. 9). The process of steering a group away from its history has been referred to as "de-historicizing" (Abdi, 2012). Copeland, Jr. (1995) argues that, "the ethnic culture to which a youth belongs establishes the image that...he or she must have pride in and rally around" (p. 9). He equates lack of self-esteem to "personal inferiority," (p. 84) which he associates with the notion of "plantation ghost," a term coined and used by clinical psychologist Na'im Akber to describe "people so dehumanized and psychologically torn from belief in their own mental abilities that they become brainwashed into thinking they are still a slave, when actually they are free". As a result, "these individuals roam through life seeking the mentally safe bondage of the plantation, where someone else thinks for you and tells you when to come and when to go" (p. 85). If in Africa dance is culture and culture is dance, the relevance of dance to education becomes unquestionable.

Conclusion

The political role of Fodéba Keïta has come under severe attack, especially from his compatriots. Even though he fought hard for the independence of Guinea and actually composed the country's national anthem, these great political achievements were completely overshadowed by his terrible record in promoting tyranny. He was instrumental in setting up the notorious Boiro Camp where numerous political prisoners in Guinea were tortured and eliminated. It is, however, in culture that he shines with exceptional lustre with his creation of *Les Ballets Africains*, a dance ensemble whose impact and reach is global. Today, in many parts of the world, the djembe and other African drums resonate and many African master drummers and dancers have gone on to have illustrious careers thanks to the pioneering, visionary and revolutionary efforts of Fodéba Keïta in the creation and promotion of African dance. Whatever political crimes he might have committed, his cultural contributions are enough for him to be forgiven. After all, leaders, such as Mobutu, Idi Amin, Macias Nguema, Bokassa and many others, had nothing to show for the devastation of their countries.

Bibliography

Abada, T., Hou, F. & Ram, B. (2008). Différences entre les groupes dans les niveaux de scolarité des enfants d'immigrants. *Études analytiques – Documents de recherche, Statistique Canada*, No 11F0019M au Catalogue, No 308.

Abdi, A. A. (2012). *Decolonizing Philosophies of Education*. USA: Sense Publishers.

Ajayi, O.S. (1998). *Yoruba Dance*. New Jersey: African World Press, Inc.

Andrieu, S. (2014). Les Valeurs de la Création Chorégraphique Ouest Africaine (The Values of West African Choreographic Creation).

La Revue des Musiques Populaires (French Journal of Popular Music Studies), Vol. 10 (2), 2014

Argenti, N. (2002, Aug.). People of the Chisel: Apprenticeship, Youth, and Elites in Oku (Cameroon). *American Ethnologist.* 29 (3), pp. 497-533.

Argenti, N. (2007). *The Intestines of the State: Youth, Violence, and Belated Histories in the Cameroon Grassfields.* Chicago: The University of Chicago Press.

Asante, K. W. (1998). *African Dance: An Artistic, Historical and Philosophical Inquiry.* Trenton, NJ: African World Press, Inc.

Asante, K. W. (2000). *Zimbabwe Dance.*Trenton, NJ: African World Press, Inc.

Asante, M.K. (1993). *Malcolm X as Cultural Hero and other Afrocentric Essays.* New Jersey: African World Press, Inc.

Bangoura, H. (2013). *An Interview with Hamidou Bangoura, Artistic Director of Les Ballets Africains.* Retrieved from company website www.lesballetsafricains.net.

Banks, O. C. (2010). Critical Postcolonial Dance Pedagogy: The Relevance of West African Dance in Education and Media Studies in The United States. *Anthropology & Education Quarterly*, 41(1), pp. 18-34.

Bebey, F. (1975).*African Music: A People's Art.* Trans. Josephine Bennett. Westport, Conn.: Lawrence Hill and Company.

Bell, K. (2016). *United Shades of America.* CNN Reality Show in San Quentin Prison. California, USA.

Bennett Jr., L. (2000). *Before the Mayflower: A History of Black America.* Chicago: Johnson Publishing Company, Inc. (Original work published in 1962)

Buckland, T. J. (1999). *Dance in the Field. Theory, Methods and Issues in Dance Ethnography.* Great Britain: Macmillan Press Ltd.

Cabral, A. (1974). *Selected Speeches.* New York: Monthly Review Press.

Cannella, G.S., Viruru, R. (2004). *Childhood and Postcolonization.* New York: Routledgefalmer.

Cesaire, A. (1972). *Discourse on Colonialism*. Trans. Joan Pinkham. New York: Monthly Review Press.

Charry, E. (2000).*Traditional and Modern Music of the Maninka and Mandinka of Western Africa*. Chicago and London: The University of Chicago Press

Che, C. C. (2013). A Concise and Analytical History of Mankon Kingdom: About 1197-2012. Bamenda: Agwecams Printer.

Cohen, J. (2012). Stages in Transition: Les Ballets Africains and Independence, 1959-1960.*Journal of Black Study*, 43(1), 11-48.

Copeland, Jr. N. E. (1995). *The Heroic Revolution: A New Agenda for Urban Youthwork*. Nashville Tennessee: James C. Winston Publishing Company Inc.

Crowder, M. (1967). *Assimilation in Senegal*. Great Britain: Richard Clay (The Chaucer Press) Ltd.

Davida, D. (2001). *Kealiinohomoku's Legacy: The Postmodern Dance Event*. Retrieved from *Author's Blog*. Montreal.

Davies, C.B. (2008). African Ballet. *Encyclopedia of African Diaspora Vol. I: Origins, Experiences, and Culture*. Santa Barbara, California: ABC-CLIO Inc.

Davila, D. E. (2009). *Critical Folkdance Pedagogy : Women's Folkdancing as Feminist Practice* (Unpublished doctoral dissertation). University of Illinois at Urbana-Champaign, Illinois.

Dei, G.J.S., Mazzuca, J., McIsaac, E., Zine, J. (Eds.). (2007). *Reconstructing 'Dropout'*. Toronto, Canada: The University of Toronto Press.

De Jong, F., Quinn, B. Bach, J-N. (2014). Ruines d'Utopie: L'Ecole William Ponty et L'Université du Futur Africain. *Politique Africaine* 2014/3.No. 135. Pp. 74-94

Dimont, I. M. (1962). *Jews, God and History*. New York: Signet Book New American Library.

Diop, C. A. (1996). *Towards the African Renaissance*. Trans. Eguna P. Modum. Britain and USA: Karnak House.

Ebron P. A. (2002). *Performing Africa*. New Jersey: Prince University

Press.

Flaig, V. H. (2010). *The Politics of Representation and Transmission in The Globalization of Guinea's Djembe* (Unpublished PhD Dissertation). University Of Michigan: Musicology.

Fodéba, K. (1959). The True Meaning of African Dances. *The UNESCO Courrier. January 1959*, No. 1 (pp. 18-24). Paris: UNESCO.

Fodéba, K. (1960). The men of dance. In Samuel J. Friedman (Ed.), *Ballets Africains*. New York : David H. McIlwraith.

Fodéba, K. (1994). *Aube africaine et autres poèmes africains*. Paris : Présence Africaine.

Fraleigh, S. H. (1987). *Dance and the Lived Experience: A Descriptive Aesthetics*. Pittsburgh, Pennsylvania: University of Pittsburgh Press.

Fraleigh, S. H. & Hanstein, P. (1999). *Researching Dance: Evolving Modes of Inquiry. Pittsburgh*, Pa.: University of Pittsburgh Press.

Gambino, C., Trevelyan, & Fitzwater, J. T. (2014). The Foreign-Born Population from Africa. *American Community Briefs*, Issued October 2014. US Census Bureau Report.

Gastineau, J. (1999, Oct.) *Les Ballets Africains*. Paramount Theatre: Denver Colorado

Grant, S.H. (2007, March). An Interview with Hamidou Bangoura. *Maximum Ink online*:
Madison

Green, D. (1998). Traditional Dance in Africa. In K. W. Asante (Ed.), *African Dance : An Artistic, Historical and Philosophical Inquiry* (pp. 15-28). Trenton, NJ: African World Press, Inc.

Green, D. (2011, Sept.). The Saga of African Dance and Black Studies Departments. *The Journal of Pan African Studies*, Vol. 4, No. 6.

Gunn, Jr., W. F. (2006). *Rhythmic African Spirituality In Sports, Dance, Music And Art*. USA: The Kemetic Institute For Leadership And Human Development.

Hall, S. (2013). *Representation: Cultural Representation and Signifying Practices.* London: SAGE Publication Ltd. (Original work published 1997).

Hanna, J. L. (1988). *Dance, Sex and Gender.* Chicago: The University of Chicago Press.

Hanna, J. L. (1999). *Partnering Dance and Education.* Maryland: Human Kinetics.

Hampton, R. (2010). Black Learners in Canada. *Race and Class.* Institute of Race Relations., 52(1), pp. 103-110.

Harnan, T. (1974). *African Rhythm American Dance. A Biography of Katherine Dunham.* New York: Alfred a. Knopf.

Jing, T. (2017). *An Afrocentric Cultural Study of Buum Oku Dance Yaoundé and Perceptions of its Relevance to African (-Canadian) Students Between the Ages of 18 and 25 in the City of Regina* (Unpublished doctoral thesis). Regina: The University of Regina

Journal of Blacks in Higher Education. (2015). *African Immigrants have the highest academic achievement in the US.* Retrieved from www.atlnightspots.com/african-immigrants-have-the-highest-academic-achievement.

Juang, R.M. & Morrissette, N. (2008). *Africa and the Americas: Culture, Politics, and History, A Multidisciplinary Encyclopaedia Vol. I:* Connecticut: Greenwood Publishing Group

Karade, B. I (1994). *The Handbook of Yoruba Religious Concepts.* San Francisco, CA/Newburyport, MA: Weiserbooks.

Kesteloot, L. (1991). *Black Writers in French.* Trans. Ellen Conroy Kennedy. Washington, D. C., Howard University Press.

Kigotho, W. (2015, Sept., 18). A Profile of Sub-Saharan African Students in America. *University World News*, Issue No 382.

Kipling Brown, A. (2008). Common Experience Creates Magnitudes of Meaning. In Shapiro's (Ed.), *Dance in a World of Change* (Chapter 7). USA: Sheridan Books.

Ki-Zerbo, J. (1978). *Histoire de l'Afrique Noire.* Paris: Hatier.

Kringelbach, N. H. (2007). "Cool Play": Emotionality in Dance as a

Resource in Senegalese Urban Women's Association. In H. Wuff (Ed.) *The Emotions: A Cultural Reader*. Oxford: Berg.

Kringelbach, N. H. (2012). Moving Shadows of Casamance : Performance and Regionalism in Senegal. In Neveu Kringelbach and Jonathan Skinner (Eds.) *Dancing Cultures: Globalisation, Tourism and Identity in the Anthropology of Dance* (Chapter 7). Oxford: Bergham.

Kringelbach and Skinner. (2012). The Movement of Dancing Culture. In Neveu Kringelbach and Jonathan Skinner (Eds). *Dancing Cultures: Globalisation, Tourism and Identity in the Anthropology of Dance*. Oxford: Bergham.

Layiwola, D. (2003, Sept. 13). Conceptualizing African Dance Theatre. *Paper presented during CODESRIA 30th Anniversary Conferences*. Ibadan: Institute of African Studies.

McLaren, P. (2003). *Life in Schools: An Introduction to Critical Pedagogy in the Foundation of Education*. United States of America: Pearson Education, Inc.

Merriam, A. P. (1959). Characteristics of African Music. *Journal of International Folk Music Council* 11(1959), pp. 13-19.

Mveng, E. & Njob, C. Samuel, K. (1969). *Danses Traditionnelles Camerounaises*. Yaoundé: Centre Fédéral et Linguistique.

Neufeldt, H. G. & McGee, L. (1990). *Education of the African American Adult: An Historical Review*. New York: Greenwood Press.

Ngugi wa Thiong'o. (2009). *Something Torn and New. An African Renaissance*. New York: *Basic Civitas Books*.

Ntaimah, P.T. (2012). *The Oku Trail: Tracing Roots, Footprints and the Edification of a Cultural Space*. London: AuthorHouse.

Présence Africaine. (1976). *Hommage à Léopold Sédar Senghor: Homme de Culture*. Paris : Présence Africaine.

Welsh, K. (2004). *African Dance*. United States of America: Chelsea House Publishers

Rudin, H. R. (2013). *Germans in the Cameroons: A Case Study in Modern Imperialism*. India: Isha.

Sabatier, P. R. (1978). "Elite" Education in French West Africa: The Era of Limits 1903-1945.

The International Journal of African Historical Studies. Vol. 11. No 2 (1978). Pp. 247- 266

SAHO. (2015). Amandla Cultural Ensemble. *South African History Online: Towards a People's History.* Cape Town, South Africa.

Soyinka, W. (2012). *Of Africa.* New Haven and London: Yale University Press.

Stokes, J. (2013). *How to Do Media and Cultural Studies.* Thousand Oaks, California: SAGE Publications, Inc.

Thompson, R. F. (1974).*African Art in Motion.* California: University of California Press.

Vissicaro, P. (2004). *Studying Dance Cultures around the World: An Introduction to Multicultural Dance Education.* Dubuque, Iowa: Kendal/Hunt Publishing Company.

Vissicaro, P. (2009). Dance, Community, and the Reconfiguration of Space: Resettlement Strategies among African Refugees in Phoenix, Arizona, *Review of Human Factor Studies,* 15(1) pp. 48-66.

Woodson, C.G. (2006). *The Mis-Education of the Negro.* Deweyville, Virginia: Khalifah's Booksellers and Associates. (Original work published in 1933)

Chapter 5

Instincts in Lieu of Senses:
Francis B. Nyamnjoh's *Married But Available*

Benjamin Hart Fishkin

If love, sex, romance and farcical misadventure were all components of an Olympic sport, then the characters of Mimboland in Francis B. Nyamnjoh's *Married But Available* (*MBA*) would all be decathletes and they would win every single medal at the 2020 Tokyo Summer Games. They are liberated, expressive and have developed a penchant for risk taking in their private lives because they are restrained, constrained, limited and censored in their public, political, and economic lives. The result is short-term satisfaction and a consequent long-term eroding of the control, order and stability that surely any parent would want for their children. The central theme or discourse is that this course of action is actually not liberating despite appearances to the contrary. Physical passion is relevant only as a substitute, stifling permanent liberation and lasting freedom. While immensely entertaining, this novel is a study of sociology and it relates to the psychoanalytic work of Jacques Lacan in his 1938 essay entitled "The Family Complexes in the Formation of the Individual". In Lacan's eyes, there is a distinction between the family and a biological pairing. The principle or concept that he developed is that "The human family must be understood within the quite particular order of reality constituted by social relations (Lacan 11). In other words, in terms of how people in France and elsewhere are structured, the human family is an institution rather than a connection of blood, chromosomes or any other nucleotide sequence. The individual who is devoid of sexual restraint, and who spurns all combinations of accepted morals and forms of behavior,

133

does so because this is the only area of his/her existence in which he/she has any measure of control. Lacan calls this problematic, albeit understandable, behavior "…a paradoxical economy of instincts" and it has volcanic repercussions (Lacan 5). An autocracy, despite the worst intentions of the worst individual with unlimited power, is a form of government brutality that cannot help but give rise to some form of liberation or its quest.

For the Anglophone Cameroonian to be truly successful, and keep insanity from the door, he/she must find (at least) one area of daily life where compromise is not an option. Nyamnjoh's characters empower through self-expression. This is the only reason why they do not unravel and blow away. They refuse to comply with the dilemma of psychological imprisonment in order to preserve their cultural identity. Nyamnjoh reveals this frustrating tension in one of his other novels, *Mind Searching* (*MS*) where men go to Sunday Church Service "…to honour their appointments with young women…" (*MS* 4). This is symptomatic of a much larger problem—a circumstance where national and global politics have reduced society to rubble and brought about a damaging shift in family dynamics. With deregulation, *La République du Cameroun* has sort of a "Wild West" quality to it and that has forced people to be led by their wits, and other extremities, because there is no structure and there is no legal system. People wander through the city punch drunk and in their incoherence exacerbate their already considerable rudderlessness. If life in Sawang is described as "…the bumpy reality of a city hardly at peace with itself…" making love becomes a potent, yet fleeting narcotic, and some would say an act of lunacy, that offers a temporary sanctuary of peace and escape that doesn't exist while the eyes are open (*MBA* 9).

At the heart of the matter is inclusion and what happens when people do not get it. This notion of where the African belongs and what is happening to his/her past is a big part of *Married But Available*. The novel is a psychological minefield of characters who are quarantined and disregarded, hemmed in at every move, until they explode with a series of bad decisions that always have unimaginable repercussions. An extensive and exceedingly comprehensive memory bank does not help them. Prince Anointed, the archivist at Puttkamerstown Achieves, speaks of an academic conference called "The Missing State in Mimboland" (*MBA* 25). Who pray tell has caused or stepped in to fill this vacuum? All the while, the metaphor of important things neglected, forgotten, lost and destroyed by ministerial indifference hangs in the damp and mildewed air, obviously meant to extend to the whole nation (*MBA* 24 -25). In a glimpse of what is to come, the "...lack of an interrupted power supply unit to control surges..." makes the one working computer in the woefully understaffed archival office ineffective and unreliable (*MBA* 26). Nyamnjoh, in a scholarly article entitled "Incompleteness: Frontier Africa and the Currency of Conviviality", reduces this relationship to that of the baby and its babysitter where history and institutional verification are removed from the latter (*JAAS*, vol. 52. n°. 3 253). Normally the author's deduction is a simple one; the baby, infant or child is young, beautiful and inexperienced and needs the guidance of the babysitter so it can develop the talents and traits it will need to form healthy relationships. But, the real world is no fairytale and this baby thinks it already knows the happy ending it is entitled to inherit. When Nyamnjoh breaks it down as a scholar who is part detective and part social anthropologist it is so messy, so complex, so incommensurate and so elaborate in its scheming and intrigue that the roles between a selfish child and compassionate adult are quickly reversed. The baby, here a variable for the west or western civilization, is so blind and unaware of its shortcomings that it demands attention and thrusts and imposes itself on the global stage as if it were master in someone else's home. This has the resonance of a genuine baby who demands all of the ice cream in the ice cream parlor or all of the candy in the candy store even though the result will be disastrous (*JAAS*, vol. 52. n°. 3 254). The infant is so incomplete that, the facts notwithstanding, it demands credit, respect and recognition for completeness and superiority while remaining oblivious to how long the babysitter (Africa) has been in the business of accumulating wisdom and spirituality (*JAAS*, vol. 52. n°. 3 254). This is why *MBA*'s first in-country scene involves Prince Anointed and the rats, cockroaches, and white ants that have infested his record keeping (*MBA* 26). The baby presumes to know more than the babysitter in a tale of hubris and misplaced pride that someone else will have to pay for.

The cause of all of this disarray worthy of dystopia is misplaced anger, envy or even wariness. This is what is at the root of Lilly Loveless's graduate research. The ingenuous thirst for experience from the West voyeuristically and covertly observes an unsuspecting exotic populace in the east and threatens to steamroll and subsume it (or is it the other way around?). Her PhD on "Sex, Power and Consumerism in Africa" shows how these two extremes tend to flip, change, and shift. However, the unsettling voice that rings in everyone's inner ear is, will the elements contained within the title of Lilly Loveless's dissertation free and liberate the people in Mimboland i.e. *La République du Cameroun* and British Southern Cameroons or will they make the people of Mimboland more like white people? Nowhere are these battle lines more clearly drawn than when she and Bobinga Iroko go to a nightclub in Sakersbeach and the name of this congregation of sweaty dancers is literally Black & White. Lilly Loveless is reticent, careful about avoiding danger and risk and clearly uncomfortable with all of the sexual dancing and the base pounding beat of the music, but Bobinga Iroko is not. Bobinga Iroko, is a name that constitutes two species of the strongest type of wood. They represent strength and stability; having deep roots. This is the culture of the babysitter, the mentor, the teacher. Yet, it is the aptly named Lilly Loveless. She views herself as the authority on knowledge, coming from a Western school and living in a bright capital city with all of its plastic conveniences. She is instantly over her head as the narration hints through a dialogue between Lilly and her partner. "'If you were dancing for survival, you'd die before the day breaks,' her partner mocked—Lilly Loveless was cautious not to rush into things" (*MBA* 82). When the music pours out over the dance floor, she cannot believe her ears. All songs seem part of Lilly's theme, but are largely absent from her life. The ideas border (roughly) on who has the most lovers and why so many women are fighting for one man. That said, one song over the nightclub's loudspeakers says more about the mixing of white and black than any other. A struggling man finds out that his brother is scheduled to be appointed to the higher reaches of the government and he is overjoyed in his fantasy as to how his life is going to change. This instance is capture in the following lines:

> The young man envisions his brother's appointment changing his life in a big way— 'my life is going to change', 'at last I am going to relax' like a baobab of achievement and power, as 'suffering has ended'. The days of trekking, sandwiches, and struggle in overloaded taxis are over. He anticipates riding in his own car, an air-conditioned Mercedes, going into the inner cities to fetch vulnerable girls-especially those who turned him down when he was nobody—who can't resist anyone with a car (*MBA* 85).

Love has an economic component and here you see it in the form of a foreign car. *Adbrands* describes the Mercedes badge as arguably carrying more status than any of its competitors (mercedes_de.htm Web). The government official's brother shows that this emphasis on flashy items that can be bought and displayed has migrated southward across the Mediterranean and over much of the African continent. Those in Muzunguland (a thinly veiled euphemism for France or the Western world) rarely approach clandestine affairs without a casualness, a randomness and a lack of discernment and there is a relationship between this and the way money changes hands.

The Mimbolander is, or once was, different. Much of *MBA* could not have been written a century ago. It is no wonder that Lilly Loveless's scholarship is financed in part by a society named for Michel Foucault, a champion of theories on control, coercion and impulse. Foucault famously did not have much patience for the bourgeois (who surely could be eager to make monthly payments on a Mercedes for eighty-four months) and might well have been more interested in the government officials' brother *before* his brother's promotion—when he lived in the ghetto. What he liked or had an affinity for were those at credit risk, those on the periphery, those who needed collateral and those who did not operate in the center of society. This required a trip to the third world and this is why Lilly Loveless is interested in tribal communities and travels to seek them out. She is looking for a certain kind of knowledge that she cannot find in her likely suburban home. She has no familiarity with the facts, truths and principles in Paris and has "…practically forgotten her boyfriend of two years…" (*Married But Available* 5). She has no power and although she does not know it—like our baby—Lilly Loveless is trapped by social institutions. Foucault, if aware of her, would put Lilly Loveless behind a one-way glass. She thinks she is researching a subject, but in reality she *is* the subject of a very penetrating gaze. The visitor needs her conflicts resolved. She has spent much of her twenties getting knots in her rope and this (their removal) is the true under the surface purpose of her fieldwork. It is a connection or interconnection with Africa that can be the remedy that will untie them. While she does not mean any harm, this presumed and uncredentialed diplomat of civilization views herself as a person with comparatively few restraints. If Francis B. Nyamnjoh, in his 2015 article "Incompleteness: Frontier Africa and the Currency of Conviviality", conveys the European or Western sentiment that Africa hopes to emerge "…albeit tentatively, from hopelessness to hope, darkness to promise[,]" then Lilly surely is an acolyte of this philosophy ("Incompleteness: Frontier Africa and the Currency of

Conviviality" 254). Not only is Africa crucial to its own development, survival and liberation it is crucial spiritually to Lilly Loveless's ability to enjoy her life. Knowledge is transferred but the boundaries, the cultures and the conversations are scrambled.

Nyamnjoh's special ability as a narrator reveals more than Africa's hidden, secretive pressures; he digs up out of the soil the very problems the continent needs to be liberated from and concludes that they are international and global in nature. A power, a government or a state tells the people what they cannot do, but in order to develop a resistance the critic has to determine who is stating this, where they are located and if there is some implicit danger that is not being stated and from which people we must be liberated. Does Lilly, who is operating with the best of intentions, hope to uncover the identity of the Cameroonian? Alternatively, is the task that lies before her to write about, to manage and to control love, sex and passion in part of the world where this component of an individual's life is the only privately expressed characteristic that is not a regulated commodity?

It is no accident that to develop as a scholar Lilly Loveless must get on an airplane. This says something about the international power relationship from which the African must develop immunity. Spending six months in Mimboland to do fieldwork is a luxury not easily reproduced or reciprocated by the Mimbolander. The British Southern Cameroonian must resist by realizing that he/she is being molded and shaped by a system which relegates him/her to the status of a minority shareholder. What is worse is that this is a secret. William Blake once said "I must Create a System, or be enslaved by another Man's; I will not Reason and Compare: my business is to Create" (Wilson 4). Blake was talking about more than poetry, painting, printing and engraving. The African in general and the British Southern Cameroonian in particular must fight against complacency in the one and only area that has no surveillance.

In Part 2, Chapter 5 of George Orwell's *Nineteen Eighty-Four* a couple meets in secret in an undisclosed room above a junk-shop.

The room, Orwell says, dirty or clean was paradise. The only place where anyone has any form of privacy, the only place where one is not observed is the bedroom (Orwell 150). It is an oasis. Nyamnjoh refers to this as "…a resting place…You mean sugar daddies and sweat mamas…where they bring their catch…" (*MBA* 14). And so begins Lilly Loveless's scholarship. Mountain Valley is a restorative place where men and women use aliases to pursue sexual exploits while painstakingly protecting their identities. The need to keep these things stealthily and surreptitiously hidden is pure Nyamnjoh and this point is central to psychoanalytic criticism. Desire is sustained, and it can even be enjoyed, just as long as no one else can see it. If the Cameroonian cannot enjoy his/her job, his/her language, his/her literature, his/her theatre and his/her journalism the form that is left to them is relegated to what takes place behind closed doors. As a consequence, issues that swirl around sex, love, marriage, divorce and love affairs are extremely complicated; far more complicated than they would be if the Cameroons were not ruled by a leader whose power is absolute.

In a telling remark from *Nineteen Eighty-Four* Winston tells Julia, "You're only a rebel from the waist downwards…" (Orwell 156). This is a remark that must be looked at more carefully. It says something about love and it says something about the mechanics and inner workings of a dystopian society. There is no intellectual component in this kind of a love; instead the partners have a temporary connection that is disinterested in the larger problems around them. They are desperately and fearfully grasping at a final alternative. There is no thinking, there is merely an undiscerning instinctual reaction and both Nyamnjoh and Orwell are stating that this is not the way to have a successful relationship. It is a way to ensure that this political and intellectual torture will continue and ratchet up in direct proportion to the individual's willingness to surrender to it.

Just after touching down at Sawang International Airport, before she even leaves the airplane, Lilly Loveless is given a box of 250 condoms by a woman about to commence work involving HIV/AIDS prevention (*MBA* 6). With a big smile the woman with a newly minted European reproductive health degree states, "life's too sweet and too short to waste" (*MBA* 7). This is liberation, or a substitute for what it used to be. This is an invitation, a siren song, to give in to a course of action that may not ultimately set her free from control. It certainly won't be thought about, deliberated or examined with any depth. Nyamnjoh uses words like "...snatch what was left of life from the jaws of HIV/AIDs..." but this is by no means an upbeat or energetic appraisal (*MBA* 7). I would add or translate the phrase to mean "...snatch what you can right now..." It seems to be saying, in an imported message, that physical love or the act of sex is one of the only remaining upbeat ingredients in the collective cupboard of the African. There is so much to drag a person down that you simply have to take every fleeting moment of happiness and release wherever you can get it. There are so many drawbacks, unenforced rules, and neglected regulations that make daily life harder and create a modern dystopian tragedy. For example, Lilly begins her trip in Mimboland by being introduced to crater size potholes, stink, refuse mountains, flies, maggots, rats, and floating sewage (Nyamnjoh 9). The country is described by Francis Nyamnjoh as "...the peaceful armpit of Africa..." (Nyamnjoh 9). Lilly lands in a world where nothing seems to be going right, where the only thing that thrives is unpredictability. In her doctoral research about sex, power, and consumerism she quickly realizes that all three (often at the very same time) are a means of escape. *Married But Available* is not a novel about sex, love, marriage, divorce, marriage, and cheating, but rather a novel about the core social and psychological deficits that drive people to them.

Surely this is an academic area of research that surprises and piques the curiosity of the reader, but what is initially really unexpected or unusual is where it comes from. The fact that our prospective PhD travels from overseas, and that her mother fears the

141

trip and does not want her to go, says something about the two nations and the speed and velocity with which ideas travel back and forth between them. There is a multilayered liberation struggle; I consider this both a war of ideas about the past involving history, politics, and memorials and a collision of social mores in the present involving dating, sex, marriage, contraception and consumerism. The more than five decades since British Southern Cameroons ' 1961 declaration of independence are characterized by an unraveling and a steady dismantling of traditional standards, systems, and calibrations. The biggest problem has been creating a genuine, bilingual nation in a nation where only a portion appears to want it. This is what happens when one state has two colonial legacies. The majority of official administrative business in the Cameroons is conducted in French. Consequently, we have had a slow but purposeful removal of the social identity of the English speaking populations in North-West and South-West of the Cameroons. What is left is fear and turmoil. A worried mom—Lilly's overprotective Mom—refers to a new journey to Mimboland as "Lilly's impending African misadventure" (*MBA* 4). The translation is "I am afraid of all the fun she is going to have in a world she could not be going to had we (France) not been there before." We are told that on an earlier vacation to Africa, Lilly Loveless came back with "a few screws rearranged" (*MBA* 4). *Married But Available* is a detailed study of the unceasing head on collision that has caused this irrevocable displacement.

With the above mentioned collision and its consequences, it does not take long to see that fewer and fewer romantic partners are actually sharing lives together in satisfying companionships that endure. Nyamnjoh's novel has to do with a lack of coherent association that was once presumed, understood and expected. As an educator, I cannot help but feel that this has to do with a focus on immediate and instant gratification without any planning whatsoever for the future. But this is not a traditional African trait. These are not characteristics of the culture. This is not the normative gentility, grace, education and training that has been cultivated and curated for centuries. Where do short term, sometimes very short term, incentives come from and what has happened to grown up and time tested lessons of spiritual connection, compassion, empathy and unity in the former British Southern Cameroons? The answer is tied up in the young people and their desire for a brand new kind of life—one that is professional, prosperous, and visible to those who do not have it.

Humans are hardwired to want things, but the distaste for delay is not something peculiar to the traditional. African. If one goes back far enough time and trust in this part of the world were in abundant supply. What arises in *Married But Available* is evidence that the abandonment of spiritual reverence for one's ancestors has given way to things that you can see. For example, to keep and hold a girlfriend Nyamnjoh's creation of a character named Innocent buys her an apartment. In it he buys her top of the line tech including "...a TV set, a compact disc set, a fan, a Moulinex blender, a fridge, a wool carpet...body lotions, perfumes, shoes, jewelry, clothes and airtime for the cute little cell phone he bought her as a birthday present" (Nyamnjoh 51). This is a Western attribute which, at some point, became an Eastern affliction. But how did this happen? How did issues involving debt, consumerism, and immediacy cross the South Atlantic Ocean? What unforeseen problems can be caused by such a shift? In Adam McKay's *The Big Short*, a 2015 film for Paramount Pictures about the American housing bubble, we see a story ain't never been told, a youthful mortgage broker trumpets loudly "Trust me, I'm not driving a 7 Series without strippers. No one on the pole has good credit and they are all cash rich." In 2007 and 2008 this is what passed for expertise. To the uninitiated (myself included) a 7 Series is a BMW 7 Series. They cost more than $80,000 and the impression given in *The Big Short* is that no one ever owns one outright. This overlapping or intersection of the strippers (sex), the

143

brokers (power) and the luxury sedan (consumerism) goes a long way towards pointing out what arouses action, activity and motivation for American's and, by a long extension, Nyamnjoh's characters. Such baubles, trinkets and shiny objects serve as sparkling distractions which take their eyes off the prize. The narrator reminds the reader that,

> Her (Eunice) friends were proud and dressed expensively. Seeing this, her taste for nice dresses increased and so she vowed to date a man who could give her much money, and a man with whom she will face fewer problems. One day as she was coming back from school a BMW 'S' stopped and offered to help her to her destination. The man inside gave Eunice an appointment in a hotel. She acted accordingly and they established a relationship. Brother, as the man prefers to be called, is the right man for her. He is married, but he lavishes Eunice with cash, as she and her youthful exuberance bring out the full meaning of his flashy BMW as a symbol of his achievements. She now affords expensive dresses. He equips her house, and her church and God have taken second place (*MBA* 138).

This is but one of many stories that Britney tells to Lilly Loveless. Britney serves as both the receptionist of the Mountain View Hotel and the former's research assistant. Relationships, like those involving Eunice and Brother, are motivated by one universal stimulus and it is not love. These are stories about reality and they have been with us for centuries. "First and foremost, affairs in our environment are encouraged by money" (*MBA* 49). With each passing moment Nyamnjoh tells us about vicious interplay that would shock even the most jaded listener. One Saturday, while celebrating Britney's birthday over a sumptuous and elaborate breakfast, Lilly asks Britney what interviews are to be discussed that day. "More on how materialism can drive us," is the reply (*MBA* 137). The key word here is "drive". It serves as a literary *double-entendre*. Sure, it can mean to prompt, to induce, to spark and to arouse but it also refers to an automobile and the prestige it brings to the male driver. In a romantic setting the male may well feel that "I have to drive" (which in this case is slang for making all of the important decisions and having full control). The phrase or term BMW does not necessarily refer to Bavarian Motor Works that is more than a century old and is based in Munich. The capitalized letters, according to Francis B. Nyamnjoh, also can mean "Beer, Men and Women" (*MBA* 138). To take the etymology even further Lilly Loveless makes the argument "It also means Break My Window and take me home, and if things work out, Be My Wife" (*MBA* 138). The emphasis is always on "me", the speaker, and never the spirit or health of the community. The values involve status, like the thin and exceedingly temporary condition of "owning" a home in *The Big Short*, and never substance. Taste is always imported from somewhere else as Eunice, a student at a local government high school, is influenced by how her friends attire themselves in expensive dresses made and manufactured in Europe. This is an untenable situation where the victim is unaware that she is being psychologically, politically and financially swindled of her unique self-conception.

While no one disputes Eunice's attractiveness she does not seem to be willing to act in her own best interest. Also, she does not even seem to be aware that she has alternatives. Not only does she begin an affair with a decidedly middle-aged stranger the only thing he brings to the table with him is his German car or the equivalent luxuries from the West. She has compromised herself twice; once for money and second for things that can be bought from the very nation(s) that have colonized her people and made them subservient. One gets the impression that Eunice has absolutely no idea of this, no awareness of the existence of The Berlin Conference of 1884-1885 which sliced and divided Africa amongst many European nations and she does not have any awareness that the conference and Brother's car have a common denominator. That is a lesson that was not taught to the lower sixth students at her high school.

The point here is not to blame Eunice, but rather to delve into the more complicated question of how she got this way. Has she, in her lifetime, had any other values? If the answer to that question is "Yes" then where have they gone? If women, very young ones, tend to dress expensively and value a certain sort of prestige surely some important items must be discarded in the process. An expert computer technician who works for Mastercard, Visa and Apple can scrub a computer's hard drive to the point where it has no information. The computer once had information and now that it is scrubbed it is empty. The problem with Eunice is that she has always been empty. She begins as a *tabula rasa*. What has happened to the African history that precedes her and why does she now have the notion that there is prestige in things that can be bought with money? The answer is connected to the fact that the archives in Mimboland are in shambles. No one knows the past, no one cares about what has happened and no one is fully aware that this impatient disinterestedness in history and a careful analysis of cultures is what they must be liberated from before they can attain the desired development of this nation in a cesspool of underdevelopment.

The quandary or predicaments listed here are not confined to Africa. They can be seen all over the world. What we have in *Married But Available* is a lack of self-reliance, a dearth of problem solving and a pervasive passivity that casually hopes things will improve when there is no evidence to back this up. Is this any different than Eugene O'Neill's *The Iceman Cometh*? Both are set in bars, one in lower New York in 1912 and the other in Mimboland nearly a century later. All Nyamnjoh does is add humor, better lighting, an altered accent and more powerful Mimbo-Wanda beer. Is this any different from Geoffrey Chaucer's *The Canterbury Tales* where the sexual exploits and class tensions of medieval England are traded for the very same mischievous and licentious entertainments sought by a people with more colorful clothing, braided hair and more debt? These are flat characters with universal traits. The author presents them as a way to show everyone what is *not* there; realistic figures who struggle with temptation, people who plan responsibly, individuals who budget and members of state who read. One never gets the impression that Nyamnjoh's characters are even aware of an entanglement with the West, even as they are speaking on cute cellphones, paying for minutes with sim cards, buying CDs, MP3s, DVDs, and flash sticks and displaying to the world that they have more money than sense (*MBA* 98). Bobinga Iroko argues that cellphones are "…instruments of exploitation…" (*MBA* 164). This has all sorts of implications because there are so many ways in which a person can be used. "The cellphone has also proved very useful in rigging elections because the rigging of elections is the favourite[sic] pastime of our politicians…And do not forget using the cellphone to eliminate critics, subversives and political opponents…" (*MBA* 164).

Also, a cellphone may be a convenience for a mother with a newborn baby. It may be something essential in the case of an emergency or an automobile accident, but such an import, and others like it, makes the user willing to yield to the supervision of another. This docility is bad for business, bad for everyone wherever they are located. For starters, it is expensive and the monthly fees, which head west, are a motive in and of themselves. Additionally, cellphones accelerate the love affairs, making it easier for people to avoid the detection of their spouses or partners regardless of the moral viewpoint one might have. Then, there is the issue of status. The owner of a cellphone shop in Puttkamerstown tells Lilly Loveless that "…most of the women who own phones get them from men, who also feed the phones regularly with airtime…" which may not be the healthiest of situations and then "…because it is expensive to run, you sometimes find people with cell phones who go for months without making a single call. Still they are proud of their phones and usually they want to display it for people to notice they have a cell phone" (*MBA* 159). This is the most troubling transformation of all.

147

People buy cellphones just so others can see them, envy them and be jealous of the carrier. Is this any different from children noticing the brand names of clothing worn by their classmates from Missoula to Madison to Cleveland? The very nature of competitiveness, consumerism and complicated affairs are the reasons why these relatively recent technological advances have revolutionized the landscape of Mimboland for the worse (*MBA* 158).

The insidiousness of this insurrection is far more pervasive than a single item that can be bought at a corner shop. Yes, the sale of cell phones is an issue, but it is by no means the only one. Many items and concepts have shepherded colonialism to Africa and elsewhere. As a cultural anthropologist at the University of Virginia, Charlottesville, Ira Bashkow has studied and researched in Papua New Guinea about the problems that are thrown up when one population emulates the other. According to Bashkow,

> Today people's ideas of whitemen's culture are also formed through experiences in the town and in PNG cities; through encounters with the modern black elite who are regarded as "heirs" to the former colonial masters (Latukefu 1985, 49); through books, newspapers, videos and advertisements (Foster 2002; Gewertz and Errington 1996); through schooling and Christianity; and through people's own experiences of 'turning whitemen'… (52).

It may be a different part of the globe, but the circumstances and the carefully concealed snares are the same. The black man looks outward and seeks to copy other people without being aware of what he is losing or even if he is losing anything. The people tend to play follow the leader, putting up only a modicum of resistance before falling quietly into line. The purpose of a novel like *Married But Available*, even though it does contain a great deal of laughter, is to unsettle, to shock and to shake people free of their false feeling of quiet pleasure or security. Life is not a wonderful thing. It is far from ideal. The text is there to present realism to those who do not want to see it.

Many of these problems are difficult to comprehend, but perhaps the hardest and deepest of them all is that "…skin is changeable…" (Bashkow 58). On the surface, this is impossible. Skin cells do not change. Pigmentation and the genetics that produce it do not vary. But upon a closer look that is not what Bashkow is talking about. He is talking about human culture, social structure and even behavioral finance. People can be irrational, emotional and unhinged when they are under stress and that is precisely what happens under colonialism. Pressure, whether the individual is aware of it or not, influences decision making and this can cause people to instinctually misbehave, lash out, relinquish self-control and do so in an instant. This ability to act "unpredictably" or in a way that nobody would expect shows how a person can externally espouse characteristics of a race that is not their own. In *The Meaning of Race and Modernity in the Orokaiva Cultural World* it is made clear that "…people with black skin could be whitemen…" (Bashkow 58). Alternatively, whites in the southwestern Pacific Ocean could change their construction as a result of being around people who behave differently than they do as well as look different from them. This crosspollination takes place so subtly and so imperceptibly that only those who are truly given to critical self-examination can realize what is happening and how terrible the consequences may be.

Thus, most of the characters in *Married But Available* don't seem to see that they are losing part of themselves in the bargain. Over and over again Lilly Loveless says the equivalent of "I smell danger," or that trouble is imminent (*MBA* 116). Often these impending obstacles are brand new ones and their overhanging problems are nothing like those experienced in the past. For example, life at the university has changed. Francis B. Nyamnjoh hints at this in his earlier novel *Souls Forgotten*, but it is in *Married But Available* that he delves into the lives, and one would say spectacular misadventures, of the students. The University of Mimbo is not a place to be, a place to study or a place to drink Manawa beer. It is a place "…to be fleeced…" (*MBA* 178).

Whatever one thinks about the ideal of being in love he/she is soon disabused of his/her illusions. Money almost always changes hands between the young women and their often older boyfriends. This must not be misconstrued for money has always been a temptation, but here, there and everywhere business is conducted with such brazenness that there is no sense of shame. It's a wonder that, upon commencing a relationship, a new couple does not shake hands in the company of an attorney and a stenographer. Things are so official that they have lost not only innocence, but the pretense of being innocent. There is really no discernable spark of character. Rarely are there displays of genuine feelings. The entire playing field of courtship has changed as a result of colonialism. The data that corroborates Lilly Loveless's dissertation, more often than not, shows adults behaving like adolescents and then hoping that someone else will come along and clean up the mess they had made.

Where the West gets involved with this is by marrying the concepts of science and indentured servitude and then farming them out to a part of the world that has never seen such dysfunction before. A girl in Mimboland, not even completely out of her teens, is perpetually "in play" and willing to trade without hesitation every one of her assets for a style of life to which she has never been accustomed. Women are fickle, says the Duke of Mantua in Giuseppe Verdi's opera *Rigoletto*. This may well be the nineteenth century playbook from which people are to embrace the irrational, inconstant, unfeeling and confusing entanglements that Nyamnjoh displays for his lovers of anything other than emotion. "La donna e mobile" could surely play in the nightclubs of Sakersbeach if the voice of its soaring tenor had a Jamaican accent and a beat behind it. When Lilly is taken to one of the many nightclubs featured in Nyamnjoh's *Married But Available* the setting and the characters all have a sense of mischief. The language, despite the tropical flair, is dangerous. Beneath a veneer of fun and excitement are all sorts of problems. She sees corrupt customs officers, businessmen, politicians, intellectuals, police, and military figures. Everyone wants something and this is the playing field where romance begins or is often realized. This is "…a tropical paradise for parasites…" (Nyamnjoh 33). In such a setting women can be trouble, often shrewd, outsmarting men and keeping their options open despite statements to the contrary.

As a feather in the wind,
She changes her word,
And her thoughts.

She's always sweet,
Her face is pretty,
Whether she's laughing or crying
Or telling a lie.

If a man trusts her
He'll always be miserable,
If he confides in her,
Watch out for his heart! (Verdi)

As a consequence, sex, love, desire, and tomfoolery are part of this story too. In *Rigoletto*, like *Married But Available*, there is no fidelity and there is always a storm of bad behavior ready to wreck everything. It is no wonder that in this Southern Cameroonian novel, Lilly Loveless learns about conversations dripping with resentment. People are now pursuing a new type of wealth and will do anything to obtain it. Meetings between men and women are laden with buyer's remorse. When it comes to love, one man laments that his girlfriend appears only at brief intervals, without warning and when it suits her. Even then she quickly gathers food, takes it with her to eat by herself

151

and charges the bill to him. He is unable to plan at all and while ensconced in this restless, tumultuous or disordered state of affairs he realizes that when they do meet in person "…her buttocks do not touch the chair long enough for me to blink" (*MBA* 178). She is an apparition and the two function as deceptive warring factions. The very lack of face-to-face time, and how they communicate, says a great deal about their relationship. Information moves from one party to the other via Beepers, busy signals, sim cards, ringtones and cellphone "airtime" (*MB* 178). Things are not developing. They are devolving. In an exchange about the business world worthy of the *Wall Street Journal*, *Barron's* or *The Financial Times* we learn about the role of technology, science, installment payments and their codependence with sex, access and the maintenance of a relationship. In terms of the young University of Mimbo student who often vanishes, her man is constantly buying her airtime at MIM$500 and she does not even say thank you (*MBA* 178). He calls her the chairman of MIMBEEP, or the Mimbo Association of Beepers, because that is how they exchange information (*MB* 178). Francis B. Nyamnjoh never loses sight of who is buying these items, who is paying for them, how fanciful they are, and where they come from. The process of buying is what people need to be liberated from. Flaunting one's consumption, and using what one consumes as a means to laud it over others who would like to be part of the privileged few, is the trap that has forever changed the emotions that motivate men and women. The African is a victim not of an invading army, but that of a mentality. The loss of the capacity to anticipate consequences, and in *Marred But Available* this manifests itself in sex that is based on persuasion, bribery and cunning but never affection, kindness and an act of mutual compassion and feeling, is a symptom of global social change. The Mimbolander has developed the idea that the way to happiness is through objects; without knowing that he/she has become part of a market created by someone else.

The problem that has developed in the not too distant past is that people have exchanged symbols for solid decisions. Instead of having wealth, people tend to chase it and, in the process, broadcast their lack of progress cum development. The Cameroons, despite its boundless economic potential, appears to have participated in a form of materialism and consumerism in which someone else is having more fun. An attraction for things that are temporal, for things that last for a relatively short period of time, has subordinated a wide swath of the population while handing control and influence to people who live far away and speak another language. Not only is this relationship not symbiotic, it is unknown to those who stand to suffer the most. Post colonialism, and the imperialism that propels it, did not stop slightly more than half a century ago with the handing over of power to the colonized look alike. Instead, it has changed shape and transformed to the point where physical weaponry like bayonets, machine guns and shrapnel are not the most effective weaponry. In a step that was highly unanticipated, thoughts and intellectual misdirection have proved to be the best way to enslave with chains that are not made of metal. It is from this blindness, this willful and almost eager disregard for the facts, that people must be liberated. Buying clothing, perfume, sex, telephones, cars and hair care products does not provide lasting freedom, only an extensive perpetual hangover which exchanges a rich and vibrant culture for red ink, impotence and rudderlessness.

Works Cited

"Executive on a Mission: Saving the Planet." *Adbrands.net*, www.adbrands.net/de/mercedes_de.htm. Accessed 12 July 2017.

Bashkow, Ira. *The Meaning of Race and Modernity in the Orokaiva Cultural World*. U of Chicago P. 2006.

Lacan, Jacques, "Family Complexes in the Formation of the Individual" http://www.lacaninireland.com/web/wp-content/uploads/2010/06/FAMILY-COMPLEXES-IN-THE-FORMATION-OF-THE-INDIVIDUAL2.pdf

The original French edition of the article was published under the title LA FAMILLE in Encyclopédie française (A. de Monzie, Editor), Vol.8, Paris 1938

Nyamnjoh, Francis B. "Incompleteness: Frontier Africa and the Currency of Conviviality" *Journal of Asian and Africa Studies*, vol. 52, no. 3, 2017, pp. 253-270

_____ *Married But Available*. Langaa RPCIG, 2009.

_____ *Mind Searching*. Langaa RPCIG, 2007.

Orwell, George. *Nineteen Eighty-Four*. Signet Classics, 1950.

The Big Short. Directed by Adam McKay, performances by Christian Bale, Steve Carell and Ryan Gosling, Paramount, 2015.

Verdi, Guiseppe. *Rigiletto* "La donna e mobile" Opera Lyrics

Wilson, Eric G. *My Business is to Create: Blake's Infinite Writing*. University of Iowa Press, 2011.

Section II

North America

and

The Caribbeans

Chapter 6

Language, Freedom, and the Revolutionary Visionary: The Writings of Zora Neale Hurston

Bill F. Ndi, Benjamin H. Fishkin, &
Adaku T. Ankumah

Visionaries and revolutionaries are most often the most misunderstood people of their times. Worse still, not even those one would expect to side with their stance ever do. Revolutionaries and visionaries generally live before their time. In the case of Zora Neale Hurston, it is not surprising that, thirteen years after her death and burial as a worthless orphan, or even a stray dog, Alice Walker would travel to the state of Florida to unearth the grave wherein she laid buried under dirt and dead leaves in a snake and rodent infested bush. Even to find Zora Neale Hurston's grave, Alice Walker had to impersonate a niece and cook up a story as to why it was important for her to find out where her beloved aunt was buried. And having found the grave, Alice Walker helped erect a tombstone on which she honored Zora Neale Hurston as "A Genius of the South." Thus, Alice Walker's endeavor made it easy to find Zora Neale Hurston's grave at the Garden of the Heavenly Rest where according to Stuart McIver, "the lone vertical tombstone stands out conspicuously, which is only fitting because Zora Neale Hurston was no ordinary mortal" (Web). Not only was she not just an ordinary mortal, but also she was one who deserves her place amongst heraldic revolutionary and visionary black voices. The authenticity of the language with which she captures Black folk life brings her works to the center. This was at a time when the best of her days thought such language should be left on the margin. Even more so characteristic of Zora Neale Hurston should be added Stuart McIver's portraiture of her as "a complex, often contradictory woman, equally at home with New

York's poets, playwrights and jazz musicians, rural Florida's turpentine workers and migrant laborers, and witch doctors in New Orleans and the West Indies" (Web).

Furthermore, Zora Neale Hurston's use of language, akin to the ordinary folk, breaking linguistic conventions and writing practices, yet the multifaceted nature of meaning warrants her canonization to the sainthood of postmodernism. It is Zora Neale Hurston's assertion of independence and freedom to identify with her oppressed lot, doing something to shift the stead while at the same time not condoning those who simply spend time complaining. Her understanding and defense of authenticity in holding and portraying an unadulterated version of her folks' speech patterns reveals how much she understood that acts of betrayal begin with translation. Exploring the use of language in her works and her stranglehold on the theme of freedom that in life made her to be at home with people from a variety of casts and climes will go a long way to unpack how much of a revolutionary and visionary Zora Neale Hurston is. It is not to say credence would be given here to her biographical information, most of which is public knowledge and readily available. Can one fully discuss Black revolutionary and visionary voices while discarding or neglecting the works of Zora Neale Hurston? Do her writings not bring to bear upon her refusal to despise Black instrument of meaning as well as the privation her people have suffered in time, space, bodies, etc.? Have these socio-historical forces not stolen from Black people most of that which has been God-given to them?

Zora Neale Hurston was part of "a cadre of Harlem's young and talented Black artists [who] refused to take direction from Du Bois. They called themselves the "Niggerati" in 1926" (Kendi 324). Therefore, it should not come as a surprise for a founding member of this movement to stand vehemently opposed to white assimilationism and to media-suationism. Writing about Zora Neale Hurston and the Niggerati movement, Ibram X. Kendi further highlights her studies with Franz Boas and her subsequent rejection of his assimilationism from whence she became "the penultimate antiracist mouthpiece of rural southern Black culture" (324). He also hammers home the driving force behind these revolutionary and visionary artists:

> These youngsters were formulating a literary and social space to total artistic freedom and tolerance for differences in culture, color, class, gender, race, and sexuality. The Niggerati was quite possibly the first known fully antiracist intellectual and artistic group in American history. Its members rejected class racism, cultural racism, historical racism, gender racism, and even queer racism, as some members were homosexual or bisexual. (324)

From the above it is evident that Zora Neale Hurston's preoccupation in her writing is with her humanity as well as the humanity of others. She seems not to dwell on the differences or similarities that push humans apart or bring them together. Hurston's career shows that Black artistry does not need a nous of whiteness to be art in its own right nor does it need some kind of avowal and approbation from white folks. This thinking is directly in line with that of her longtime friend Langston Hughes who charged the "younger Negro Artist" to "change through the force of his art" (qtd. *in* Kendi 324). Yet again, Kendi, in summing her life works and passions, and in opposition to the Du Boisian double consciousness underscores that "Anthropologist Zora Neale Hurston was one of few Black intellectuals writing for popular audiences who was not suffering from this race prejudice, this cultural assimilationism sweeping the academy in the 1930s and 1940s" (345).

Zora Neale Hurston's stance unveils an uncanny insight into the passive and active interlinked forms that permeate colonial, post-colonial, and neo-colonial alienation in a bastardized way that returns the hitherto enslaved, colonized, used, and abused Black person into a new linguistic, intellectual, and cultural slave. In addition, such Black individuals are willingly participating in their own dehumanization as well as in their own dissociation with their linguistic, intellectual, and cultural conceptualization framework. Their refusal to submit to any form of racial prejudice or any form of assimilation vividly brings to mind one of Ngũgĩ wa Thiong'o's concerns in *Decolonising the Mind*. Ngũgĩ wa Thiong'o is unrepentantly vocal on the following about colonial alienation and writes:

> Colonial alienation takes two interlinked forms: an active (or passive) distancing of oneself from the reality around; and an active (or passive) identification with that which is most external to one's environment. It starts with a deliberate dissociation of the language of conceptualization, of thinking . . . from the language of daily interaction in the home and in the community. It is like separating the mind from the body in that they are occupying two unrelated linguistic spheres in the same person. On a larger social scale it is like producing a society of bodiless heads and headless bodies. (28)

It is Zora Neale Hurston's insight into the above-mentioned interlinked forms that lays the foundation for her refusal to let Anglo-American literature swallow or steal the African American literary identity with which she desires to sow the seeds of African American memory and means to memory. Such memory and means of memory become weapons of liberating Black consciousness after which future generations of Black writers must aspire. Her capitalization on a language that breaks the norms of American Standard English (ASE) is an invitation to Blacks to reject "the prison house of European languages [value systems]" (Ngugi, *Something* 50). In effect, taking her people's story/memory and narrating it in ASE is akin to putting such in a box where it would suffocate, die, and be forgotten, as its access would be limited to the owners of the "foreign" language whose creed would surely choose out of spite to ignore Black wit.

The idea of language as a Blackman's weapon for liberating his/her French Caribbean consciousness has led Ngugi wa Thiong'o to write of Aimé Césaire, a contemporary of Zora Neale Hurston, that "Césaire did not have an African language. But he plunged into what African languages had produced in his strife 'to create a new language, one capable of communicating the African heritage… had a black character'" (52-53). Zora Neale Hurston succeeds in making of her writings instruments of practical, social, historical, and cultural life of the African American in particular and the Black man in general. Also, she achieves this by transforming her novelistic and creative universe into "… an archeological site of sentiment and spiritual power" (Arnold qtd. in Ngugi, *Something* 53). Therefore, when almost four decades after her demise, Ngugi wa Thiong'o explores these concerns in *Something Torn and New: An African Renaissance,* he is simply intoning an old song sung by Zora Neale Hurston and other Niggerati artists such as

> Alain LeRoy Locke, Bessie Smith, and Ma Rainey were among the many Harlem Renaissance headliners leading double lives in closeted homophobic America, privately affirming negated Black sexualities as they publicly affirmed negated Black artistry (Kendi 324).

In their struggle for freedom, they all understood that the first act of self-reaffirmation ought to take cognizance of the linguistic alienating status of Black folk language and refuse the status of the outcast imposed on the whole race. And Hurston takes it a step further, practicing a novel form of self-expression peculiar to the oppressed.

Moreover, Zora Neale Hurston, the undomesticated, the untamed, did all striving for the preservation of Black human dignity, Black folk memory, and Black folk memory means as well as for herself. African-American authors bid a swift retreat from Hurston's new manner of self-expression and cultural affirmation. A perplexing question is why the literary establishment, mostly in New York City, was so eager to close ranks. Such a clean break has as much to do with class as it has to do with race and gender. Zora Neale Hurston deserved praise but what she got was derision. Ellison's reluctance to be supportive was just the beginning. His behavior, and he is not alone, illustrates a different philosophy and a different way of looking at the literary world. Arnold Rampersad, in his *Ralph Ellison: A Biography*, felt, and Zora Neale Hurston rejected, that "Black writers needed now to engage their counterparts in the white world" (142). Ellison clarifies the ideas that had shaped him as an artist from his time at Tuskegee until the height of his fame. Rampersad, quoting Ellison, writes:

> Prominent among these was the habit of friendship with white people. Now he argued for the absolute necessity of such friendships for the black writer, even as that writer also respected black racial feeling. Questions about black dialect, or folk consciousness, or racial difference could be truly answered only by intellectuals who dared to cross the color line. (142)

With the above lines, the boundary line Zora Neale Hurston draws between her writing and those of most of her Black contemporaries stands out distinct as the confluence line separating one ocean from another. Even James Baldwin, a younger contemporary of Zora Neale Hurston, in his memoir, *No Name in the Street,* seems to ground the fact that Hurston was far ahead of her time when he writes, "I was also a member of the American colony, and we were, in general, slow to pick up on what was going on around us" (37). How did she accomplish this feat, being far ahead of her time?

Before delving into the analysis of her writings proper in order to elucidate the above question, it is worthwhile spending some time examining her own words as well as those of some of her earlier critics. What did she, as well as they have to say? By her own testimony, Zora Neale Hurston said, "I am not materialistic… If I happen to die without money somebody will bury me, though I do not wish it to be that way" (qtd. in Abbott 177). As simplistic as this prophetic statement may sound, she is overtly rejecting any idea of a

Faustian bargain in which she would have to cave in to the whims and caprices of Anglo-America only to enjoy the perks that come with such short-term gratification. In her life, she resisted the temptation of pecuniary attraction against the thrills of her soul. Besides, when she died, she did so in dignity, though poor but never impoverished by the forfeiture of the value of Black folk life onto which she held firmly as if to tell the future generation of Blacks that worldly material is inadequate to replace Black folk dignity, memory, and means of memory. McIver captures this succinctly, stating that [s]he took delight in the rich culture of black people and in no way wished it to be and in no way wished it to be integrated with the whites' way of doing things. Zora Neale Hurston spoke out against the 1954 Supreme Court desegregation decision that energized the civil-rights movement ("Triumphs and Tragedy of Zora Neale Hurston." in *Sun Sentinel* Jan 21 1990). Her community stood with and by her in death as Abbott writes, "Money was collected from the community for her funeral. She was buried in an unmarked grave in the Garden of Heavenly Rest, Fort Pierce, Florida" (177).

In addition, as poet, essayist, teacher, and activist June Jordan would have it, Zora Neale Hurston's locale was "a supportive, nourishing environment" for her as a writer (qtd. *in* Abbot 175). Furthermore, all of Hurston's works, said Jordan, "as novelist, as anthropologist/diligent collector and preserver of Black folktale and myth — reflect this early and late, all-Black universe which was her actual and her creative world" (qtd. *in* Abbott 176). The decision to make of her own world her creative universe underscores Zora Neale Hurston's resistance to having her world of blackness fall victim to the oedipal tragic fate, a tragedy against which Hurston guards Black people. A majority of literary scholars would agree that Oedipus is not punished in the Sophoclean tragic universe for any other reason but that of ignoring his personal, family and cultural history. Black spaces, cultures, and ways must be flown full mast in the arena of representation. Thus, this is Zora Neale Hurston's endeavor to answer the proverbial and rhetorical question to all Blacks: Who will toot your horn if you do not do it yourself? Abbott captures this vividly in talking about Alice Walker's dedication to Zora Neal Hurston in her piece *I love Myself When I'm Laughing* in which she writes:

> Alice Walker, in her dedication "On Refusing to Be Humbled by Second Place in a Contest You Did Not Design: A Tradition by Now," wrote: "We love Zora Neale Hurston for her work, first, and then again (as she and all Eatonville would say), we love her for herself. For the humor and courage with which she encountered a life she infrequently designed, for her absolute disinterest in becoming either white or bourgeois, and for her devoted appreciation of her own culture, which is an inspiration to us all." (180)

From the foregoing, it is worth looking at the works which propel Zora Neale Hurston to the apogee of her much lauded achievement. Among her celebrated works are *Jonah's Gourd Vine*, *Mules and Men*, *Their Eyes Were Watching God*, *Dust Tracks on a Road*, *Every Tongue Got to Confess*, *Moses, Man of the Mountain*, *Seraph on the Suwanee*, *Tell My Horse: Voodoo and Life in Haiti and Jamaica*, and her short stories. Heretofore, the kernel of the various works pertain to language, freedom, and the writer as a revolutionary visionary whose stake and strife draw the attention of her kind to the need for tapping from recorded memory to redeem a people whose culture and civilization have suffered the humiliation of being plundered and are on the verge of being erased. Zora Neale Hurston's effort, here highlighted, invites William Hazlitt into this conversation. Hazlitt famously said, "The highest efforts of genius in every walk of art can never be properly understood by mankind in general: there are numberless beauties and truths which lie far beyond their comprehension" (qtd. in Kinnaird 132-133). As such, it is worth spending some time overviewing Zora Neale Hurston's works addressing the genius of her efforts and concerns.

Jonah's Gourd Vine, Zora Neale Hurston's first novel, originally published in 1934, follows John Buddy Pearson in his journey as a preacher on Sundays and a "nachtel man" the remaining days of the week. He is trapped between physical and spiritual forces pulling him in opposite directions. This is akin to the dilemma in which the Blackman is caught and yet hoping that his faith, tolerance and kindness and maybe his willingness to submit to the external forces— the dominant oppressive ones—deliver him from such entrapment. Christianity seems not to yield happiness for the Blackman. John Buddy Pearson's experience of religion emphasizes the Blackman's. His retreats to the African-American folk space and lingo constitute an act of resistance. That is to say, the constant sudden flip from his Sunday preaching fervor to his uncontrollable lascivious impulses is tantamount to a rebellious revolutionary act. This accounts for Beliso-De Jesus' assertion that Zora Neale Hurston is "[d]iligent about capturing folklore, music, songs, and folktales with precision, Hurstonian hieroglyphics does not dwell on rationalities of practice" (293).

The very existence of Zora Neale Hurston's language points out and calls attention to a myriad of failures. The nation has been morally and spiritually lacking and in 1934, in *Jonah's Gourd Vine*, her first novel, we hear the words of someone who has been left out.

No sich uh thing, Ned Crittenden. Fust place us ain't had nothing but meal and sow-belly tuh eat. You mealy-moufin' round cause you skeered tuh talk back tuh Rush Beasley. What us needs tuh do is git offa dis place. Us been heah too long. Ah b'longs on de other side de Big Creek anyhow. Never did lak it over heah. When us gather de crops dis year less move. (6)

She is a fighter. She is rough, loud, and always hard to handle. When it comes to the African-American people in Harlem who developed new or experimental concepts in literature, she is not shy. Claudia Roth Pierpont presents her as an almost bar brawling personality who staunchly defends the use of an energetic, unified African American language. Hurston's energetic defense was a serious and complicated business, not merely because of the idea of black unity, but precisely because of what to unite around. Should a black woman work, keeping her money for herself? Should she be married? Should she speak "black" and in so doing use the vocabulary, grammar, and pronunciation of a region hardly any middle class African-American was interested in? Should she embrace folklore and be bold in a crowd not ready for someone so ahead of her time? When she came up with radical answers to all of these rhetorical questions and presented a written message of how a woman of color could truly be free, few were ready for her unsurpassed energy.

When Ralph Ellison got wind of Zora Neale Hurston, he found someone whose style could not have been further from his own. Ellison studied Ernest Hemingway and T.S Eliot in what might be termed a classical (and whiter) form of education. He quoted and referred to Charles Dickens and Mark Twain. Ellison, if not accommodating, was polite. Zora Neale Hurston exuded confidence and power. He had an interest in entering a larger society whereas Zora Neale Hurston either did not care or could not be bothered. Look carefully; this is what Ellison has to say at about America:

> At best Americans give but a limited attention to history. Too much happens too rapidly, and before we can evaluate it, or exhaust its meaning or pleasure, there is something new to concern us. Ours is the tempo of the motion picture, not that of the still camera, and we waste experience as we wasted the forest. (Callahan 239)

It is nearly impossible to imagine Zora Neale Hurston referring to a film camera in her writing. It is not even certain that one of her characters even had the opportunity to see a film, a camera or even to take pictures unless they were taken with their own imagination. Furthermore, Ellison was but one of many in the black community who was not particularly interested in Zora Neale Hurston's use of language and this break, divide, or separation continues to be a problem all these years later.

One of the big problems was a desire for eloquence by other

Black writers. For instance, Ellison's language, like that of F. Scott Fitzgerald, is so well sculpted and well-polished that it threatens to float off the page. If Ellison had once known the street and the people who tried to survive on it, he seemed less comfortable with them (at this point in his life). He was in New York, far from Florida cities like Miami and Orlando, and even further from Eatonville, the United States' oldest black community. Zora Neale Hurston, some would argue, never lost her connection. There was less distance between herself and the people she wanted to reach. In Chapter Twelve of *Jonah's Gourd Vine*, two men meet near what is now Chehaw State Park in Alabama.

"Where you goin'?"

"Tuh uh town called Sanford. Got uh sister dere. She keepin' uh boarding house," he looked John over, "she's a fine lookin' portly 'oman; you better come 'long" (105).

Ralph Ellison would not write like this. What's more, neither would people like Richard Wright and W.E.B. Du Bois. The fractioned words, the transposed spelling, would surely have displeased them. The sexual topic, from the first African-American female author to make such a venture, would have embarrassed them even though such an exchange today would scarcely raise an eyebrow.

To Zora Neale Hurston's credit, none of these obstacles seemed to bother her or even slow her down. Her impressions became part of the story over, and perhaps because of, other people's objections. Zora Neale Hurston does not apologize. She doesn't seem to give the impression that she is even humbled. Someone with this degree of confidence has no dilemmas.

"Ned Crittenden, you raise dat wood at mah boy, and you gointer make uh bad nigger outa me."

"Dat's right," Ned sneered, Ah feeds 'im and clothes 'imbut Ah ain't tuh do nothin' tuh dat li'l yaller gad cep'n wash 'im up."

"Dat's uh big ole resurrection lie, Ned. Uh slew-foot, drag-leg lie at that, and Ah dare yuh tuh hit me too. You know Ahn uh fightin' dog and mah hide is worth money. Hit me if you dare! Ah'll wash *yo'*

167

tub uh 'gator guts and 'dat quick." (*Jonah's Gourd Vine* 3)

Is there any woman of any color in the United States in October of 1933 who spoke like this? She has a whim of iron. John Buddy Pearson's mother, Amy, takes her tone from her literary mother who was not used to settling conditions by mutual consent. When you factor in the emotional climate of the nation, it is exactly four years after the stock market crash and the height (or depth) of the Great Depression, it is all the more remarkable. This kind of bruising, punishing exchange exacts a toll from whoever is unfortunate enough to be on the other side. In short, this type of literature would wear out a man or a woman. Zora Neal Hurston uses her words like weapons.

In the light of her use of words as weapons, in *Mules and Men* Zora Neale Hurston makes a statement aimed at taking Black folktale or oral literature, oral history, Black folks' sermons, and songs from the time of slavery as well as those from her childhood years away from the margins and placing them in the center. It is in this endeavor that Zora Neale Hurston comes to terms with her own soul-searching identity crisis of which she makes an integral part of the ethnographic scholarship and the dominant narrative that have long striven to exclude Black history, language, or all the metaphorical richness of Black folktales. This is Zora Neale Hurston's clear refusal to allow mainstream ethnography to cannibalize her own. Beliso-De Jesus points out this aspect of Hurston's scholastic work, writing, "Western attenuation, she argued, was brought about by a lack of connection to the spirit and natural worlds, a connection that she saw as more accessible or powerful in Africana practices" (291). There is no doubt that it is because of these century-long Africana practices that feminist critic Stephanie Newell, in her exploration of West African literature, writes, "for centuries, oral genres have been used by ordinary people, or 'commoners' in West Africa to express protests and complaints against people in position of power" (62). Thus, Zora Neale Hurston speaks truth to power in following the footsteps of those who came before her in West Africa and seeks to restore the harmony the powerful had disrupted.

Again, *Their Eyes Were Watching God*, by far the most widely read and highly acclaimed of Zora Neale Hurston's novels, takes the reader into an epic journey aimed at restoring harmony. It is one based upon the quest for identity during which the protagonist, Janie Crawford learns to fully appreciate love, experiences life's joys and sorrows, and peacefully comes to terms with herself. This identity trait of Black women writers, Newell contends, represents "one dimension of the violence which closes down people's shared humanity" (194). The narrative in *Their Eyes Were Watching God* operates in a space challenging codes of established discourse and opposes her contemporaneous racial difference often "articulated through a pseudoscience of gender and sexuality where a display of Africanness focused on women's genitalia, monstrosity, abnormality, or sexual excess..." (Beliso-De Jesus 294). This novel brings to the forefront Zora Neale Hurston's consciousness of Black oral rhetorical and literary extravagance and underscores her understanding that failure of self-knowledge is self-defeating.

In 1942, Zora Neale Hurston published *Dust Tracks on a Road*, at the height of her popularity. It is an imaginative and lively autobiographical account—along the lines of Booker T. Washington's *Up From Slavery*—of her rise from poverty in the rural South to a place of importance among the Harlem Renaissance Movement. Through her self-portraiture, Zora Neale Hurston is careful to reveal herself as a champion of the black experience in America and, needless to say that it is through her example that she wishes Blacks worldwide to emulate her and raise themselves from grass to grace, pulling themselves up by their bootstraps. It is an "evolutionary logic [that] emerged as part of a specific set of anthropological and philosophical questions embedded in colonial and imperial technologies of westernized experience" (Beliso-De Jesus 294). This certainly accounts for the line in the editorial blurb which reads: "*Dust Tracks on a Road* is a rare treasure from one of literature's most cherished voices." Hurston has found her identity in

169

the writing of this autobiographical narrative as she "breaks free from grammatical and linguistic codes challenging social divisions and destabilizing the boundaries" (194).

Another avant-garde publication of Zora Neale Hurston's is *Every Tongue Got to Confess*. It is a treasure trove of folktales collected in the late 1920s. The tales themselves constitute a vital, independent, and creative inspirational collection of these treasures of memory handed down from generation to generation and inspired by the very community and people among whom the author had her start. The tales touch on every aspect of African-American folk life: slavery, faith, race relations, family, romance, etc. The folk tales capture Black attitudes, language, joys, sorrows, and resolve to redeem oneself in the face of existential challenges. These folktales also preserve their historical, linguistic, social, spiritual, economic, and literary context so it is never lost to generations yet unborn. She captures the preservation in a way that dichotomizes black and white ways of thinking which according to Beliso-De Jesus makes clear that "[t]he white man thinks in the written language and the Negro thinks in hieroglyphics" (292). The book title itself is a statement to insinuate that no other tongue can confess in lieu of another. The choice of the word *tongue* plays on the anatomical organ and the metaphor for language and points to the linguistic dichotomy between the written language of the white man and the hieroglyphic language of the black man. Furthermore, the imperative mood summoning every tongue to confess stresses that only the tongues with the lived experiences must do so. In a way, the Black experience cannot be confessed in a foreign tongue. This could explicate Zora Neale Hurston's refusal to tell the tales of her folks in the language of the oppressor. Therefore the Black tongue must be heard. Zora Neale Hurston, in her essay, "Characteristics of Negro Expression" clearly states:

> We may go directly to the Negro and let him speak for himself. Few Negroes, educated or not, use a clear clipped 'I.' It verges more or less upon 'Ah.' I think the lip form is responsible for this to a great extent.

By experiment the reader will find a sharp 'I' is very much easier with a thin taut lip than with a full soft lip. (31)

Moses, Man of the Mountain, published in 1939, is based on the familiar story of the Exodus. The story is told in a blend of languages in contact and highlights the transformational process of a heroic rebel leader, making it an example for all who wish to emancipate themselves from the shackles of bondage. It is not surprising that the publisher underscores -"the hallmarks of Hurston as a writer and champion of black culture." This position is further amplified by Beliso-De Jesus who emphasizes that "[i]ndeed, Hurston does not shy away from writing those spirits, deities, zombies, and other fleshy energies—or *copresences*, ... —into her ethnographies" (291). The narrative technique of telling her story in a blend of languages in contact is Zora Neale Hurston's take on the language of African Americans, a language which is born out of multiple encounters of Blacks who had been shackled, forced, and enslaved for centuries. On the same token, they have been denied every possible contribution they might have made to humanity. In a space so alien and so oppressive, Zora Neale Hurston captures the Black man's travails in this space in her writings and with the Black voice too. This is to help the reader have a firsthand experience.

In *Tell My Horse*, there is nothing more than having a firsthand experience to hone one's intellectual ability and agility. Moreover, there is nothing more corrosive to one's intellect as dependence on hearsay or half-truths. Zora Neale Hurston would rather have and recount her firsthand account of the mysteries and horrors—if horrors they are—of voodoo. *Tell My Horse* is based on Zora Neale Hurston's personal experiences of her participation as an initiate of voodoo practices during her visits to Haiti and Jamaica in the 1930s. The account vividly captures ceremonies, customs, and religious practices of great importance to Black spiritual liberation. Zora Neale Hurston's choices—conscious or unconscious—to revolutionize ethnographic narrative techniques is clearly race leaning and culturally assertive in which context *Tell My Horse* operates a narrative shift in time and space warranted as a spiritual productive essence for the Black man. Traditional prejudice of philosophy had to be experimentally tested and she understood this very well. It is in this regards that Beliso-De Jesus, talking of Zora Neale Hurston's style, has this to say:

> ... Hurston's poetic ethnographies were subversive to traditional norms in folklore, anthropology, and literature. Ahead of her time, Hurston's prose-like style, criticized early on by her contemporaries as either not being objective enough or romanticizing her subjects, foreshadowed debates over a politics of representation that would transform anthropological research nearly five decades later. However, much of what informs Hurston's research and writing on Black religious experience in the Americas is her awareness of spiritual possibilities. Yet there has been little engagement with how Hurston embraced spiritual potentiality as she navigated liberal secularisms' inability to understand divergent voices. (291)

Yet again, in *Seraph on the Suwanee*, Zora Neale Hurston explores the evolution of a love-filled marriage with very little communication. The young woman at the center of this loving marriage is in search of herself and her place in the world. Most critics seem to read this novel to be one at odds with Zora Neale Hurston's desirous attention to Black culture, yet nothing can be farther from the truth. *Seraph on the Suwanee* rather seems to echo and reflect her love relationship with the Black world which in turn loves her. However, it is a Black world that has been displaced in time and space and is at odds with this new environment and time. Zora Neale Hurston seems to ponder through this loving marriage whether people can find true love and happiness in a place they love unconditionally and where they cannot defend themselves against civil, economic, political, and other forms of violence. The civil, economic, and political violence of her novelistic time and space become the unwanted suitors about whom she writes.

172

She thus strikes a balance between the passionate love for and understanding of Black folk culture and makes this the central concern in *Seraph on the Suwanee*. This novel is highly marked by characteristics that would leave any post-modernist reader enthralled at the centrality of her perspective to the dominant culture which, situated in time and space, is to a greater extent radical and revolutionary in perspective. It is Zora Neale Hurston's sugar coated bitter pills through a human love story that parallels the black and white race relations, or African Americans' relation, to their country, the USA. This could explain why Beliso-De Jesus says her writings comprise "an undisclosed spiritist to insert a politics of purpose where racialized spirituality bleeds into the process of ethnographic capturing" (291). In short, Zora Neale Hurston is a mind whose insights and judgments still and will always have an exemplary value for post-modernist criticism. The corpus makes sense of not only her place within history but also the black man's.

Barracoon is based on a series of interviews that Zora Neale Hurston conducted in the 1920s with the last Black human cargo who was brought to the US long after the abolition of the ignominious trade that reduced Africans to chattels. Recording this firsthand account of experience with captivity, bondage, and enslavement is a laudable effort to salvage the experience of millions of men, women, and children forcibly transported in shackles from Africa to America. At the center of this narrative is Cudjo Lewis, aka Kossola. It chronicles his past memories from when he was a child to his captivity and shipment into slavery. The narrative is rendered in a style that the book editor hails as one that has "made her [Zora Neale Hurston] one of the preeminent American authors of the twentieth-century." (qtd. in *Barracoon*) To this observation should be added Beliso-De Jesus's who, talking of Zora Neale Hurston's language use, writes: "Exploiting the evolutionary language of the times, Hurston's spyglass focused on rendering a devolution of Western metaphysics—it had attenuated, she argued, lost its rhythmic center from so-called primitive drumbeats" (292). This stance of

Hurston's is re-echoed by Ousmane Sembène who emphasizes that "the artist is here to reveal a certain number of historical facts that others would like to keep hidden" (qtd. *in* Newell 166). In consequence, Zora Neale Hurston in writing *Barracoon* salvages the ignominy that the world would have been buried with Kossola—like millions of other enslaved people before him—had she not interviewed him to record his memories of enslavement.

By writing in dialect, Zora Neale Hurston makes a strident attempt to hold on to what is in danger of being lost. Her reluctance to cross the color line, her refusal to change, is as vivid a story as anything she put down on paper. She appears to be interested in history and the language that conveys it, but others, for a myriad of reasons, simply don't feel comfortable with such a task. The African-American experience, when broached by intellectuals, is not "real" enough or lacks texture and completely drawn characters. Hurston eludes these nets and does something new that will last in the long run. Cheryl A. Wall rightly observes that "Hurston was not the first African-American woman to publish a novel, but she was the first to create language and imagery that reflected the reality of black women's lives" (qtd. *in* Gates and Appiah 76). When Cheryl A. Wall creates these words, she presents a scholar's approach that contradicts and contrasts the tightly held beliefs of authors such as W.E.B. Du Bois and Richard Wright. Are these figures encouraging the African-American woman to really and genuinely be creative, or are they ill at ease with what she might reveal? Richard Wright, instead of encouraging Zora Neale Hurston to soar as a literary talent, seems far more insistent on clipping her wings. In *The New Masses* magazine he argues: "Miss Hurston seems to have no desire whatever to move in the direction of serious fiction" (qtd. *in* Gates and Appiah 16). Imagine what she could have accomplished with a bit of encouragement. Zora Neale Hurston is trying to say something in her novels and stories that is very important and one does not have to be a feminist to see it. She is clever and writes in an anecdotal style that celebrates women who can feel good about themselves and enjoy their lives. She is not overly concerned about "crossing over" to appeal to white audiences as blues musicians such as Muddy Waters, Sonny Boy Williamson, and B.B. King did towards the end of her life. Moreover, where is it written that she had to? From her own people she had to overcome incendiary attacks such as this one from Richard Wright regarding her famous novel *Their Eyes Were Watching God.* "The sensory sweep of her novel carries no theme, no message, no thought (qtd. *in* Gates and Appiah 17). Her close associates proved more adversarial than her opponents did.

Beyond her commonly anthologized short stories such as "Sweat," "Spunk," and "The Gilded Six Bits," most people may not know that Zora Neale Hurston wrote over 50 short stories. The majority of these stories, set in her home state of Florida, in or near her hometown of Eatonville, focus on the lives and culture of ordinary black people living in the southern United States. At a time when other writers of the Harlem Renaissance were using their artistic talents to decry racism in America, some were highly critical of her writing which not only focused on blacks in the rural south, but also captured their dialect culture. As she notes in an interview with a reporter, to lose the "folklore and folk music" of the rural folk would be not just a "tremendous loss to the Negro race" but also to American culture as a whole (qtd. in McClaurin 62). In fact, she considers black dialect as their greatest contribution to American language, specifically in these three areas: (1) the use of metaphor and simile; (2) the use of the double descriptive; (3) the use of verbal noun" ("Characteristics" 67). Not surprising, Hurston calls the use of language that has been modified to "[re-interpret] for his [the black man's] own use" his interaction with white civilization "original" ("Characteristics" 58).

Hurston's story, "John Redding Goes to Sea," her first published story, appeared in Howard University's literary magazine, *Stylus*, in May 1921. Like his creator, John Redding is an "imaginative child," one who finds living with the "simple folk" in the Florida woods stifling. He uses metaphors to compare himself with "a lump of dirt," "soil," "earth." The first time he uses this metaphor is in his passionate plea to his mamma explaining why he wants to leave:

> [I]t hurts me to see you so troubled over my going away; but I feel I must go. I am stagnating here. This indolent atmosphere will stifle every bit of ambition that's in me. Let me go mamma, please. What is here for me? Why, sometimes I get to feeling just like a lump of dirt turned over by the plow—just where it falls there's where it lies—no thought or movement or nothing. I wanter make myself something—not just stay where I was born." (4)

The second time, John is talking to his father and uses a combination of these to describe his limited environment and to see himself as "just earth, soil lying helplessly to move [himself]. . . just soil, *feeling* but not able to take part in it all" (9).

What a summary of his life as a poor black boy growing up in a lethargic area void of activity and progress. For black people with imaginative minds like John and her creator, living like this in rural communities -kills the desire to expand and experiment with new things. Thus, he takes to daydreaming, as he throws dry twigs downstream to "Jacksonville, the sea, the wide world" (1). He cries when the twigs, which he calls his ships, get tangled in weeds, for the ships are metaphors for his aspirations to go beyond his impoverished life and diminished hopes to experience the world: "Pa, when Ah gets as big as you Ah'm goin' farther than them ships. Ah'm goin' to where the sky touches the ground" (2). Even the trees near his house, like the tall pine tree, seem to be part of the forces working against him and his desires, scaring and mocking him. A young black pre-teen, he imagines himself as "a prince, riding away in a gorgeous carriage" or as a "knight bestride a fiery charger prancing down the white shell road that led to distant lands" or captain of a steamboat (4). His dad, Alfred Redding agrees with his son. He had similar dreams as a boy, but his mother Marty attributes his desire to a spell cast on him by the village conjurer at birth. The desire to take a journey, to her, is "foolishness."

To the surprise of John's parents and neighbors, he married the beautiful Stella Kanty, the daughter of their neighbor. With this marriage, mamma thinks John will abandon his quest to "stray down river to Jacksonville, the sea, the wide world," but the alleged "raptures" of marriage do not settle the "poor home-tied John" (6). He tries to hang on to both desires—to marry and to go on his quest, but Stella will have none of that. She will not allow him to "sneak off" and leave her. John thinks joining the Navy will satisfy his mother and wife, but she refuses to accept that option, pronouncing curses on John that to leave without her approval means he will never return, not even when she is on her deathbed. Again, the two women in his life seem to be obstacles to his attaining his dream, carrying on an "effective war" against him (6).

The quest or journey motif to self-discovery or maturity is used frequently in literature. From *The Epic of Gilgamesh*, Homer's *The Odyssey,* and more recent ones like Mark Twain's *The Adventures of Huckleberry Finn,* Joseph Conrad's *Heart of Darkness,* Camara Laye's *The African Child,* readers have been acquainted with and men who take a journey. Usually these journeys are on the sea or a body of water, considered as men's territory as it is untamed. In fact, Alf tells his distraught wife that it "jes' comes natcheral fuh er man tuh travel" (3). But women like Hurston and her character Janie in *Their Eyes Were Watching God,* also have the wanderlust. Critic Gordon Thompson has a different interpretation of travel in the works of Hurston:

> Travel, for instance, appears to be closely linked with sexual promiscuity, as when Hurston identifies her father by his "meanderings" from Alabama to Florida and also with his possible infidelities, as suggested in her comment: "looking back, I take it that Papa and Mama, in spite of his meanderings, were really in love." (DTOAR, 18) (751)

He notes that men are granted more sexual liberties than women, and so to prevent him from traveling, as his mother and wife try to do, presents a "considerable burden" on these women (751). John's focus throughout the story seems to be on experiencing more of what life has to offer, and is more passionate about seeing the world than being with women. In fact, he chastises himself for his "rashness in marrying" when he was not ready. F Russel Redman strikes a reasonable balance when he writes:

> Travel, for John Redding as it eventually did for Hurston, also becomes a metaphor for a sort of intellectual and philosophical freedom from the traditional Southern ways of thinking, a freedom that Hurston enjoyed and engaged while completing her formal education in the North. (25)

John gets his wish to go to sea, but not in the way he has anticipated. On a fateful stormy night, Mr. Hill, the white bridge builder, looking for extra hands to save his five-month, quarter of a million dollar project, comes to recruit John to help save the bridge. It takes a white man coming in the middle of the night to recruit black people to work on his quarter of a million dollar project. With opportunities hard to come by, John does not have to be persuaded to go out on a bad-weather night, especially since he does not want his father to go on this dangerous mission. With gusty winds blowing and a portentous owl screeching a "doleful cry" (11) in the thunderstorm, the construction workers are under Hill suffer a devastating blow as two die on the spot, three drown, several are injured. John is the only one not accounted for and labeled missing. With his family on the scene and Fred Mims, a supervisor narrating the accident to Alf, John's dad sees a "man floating on a piece of timber. . . The man was John Redding" (12). As Matty screams, Alf, with a single tear on his lashes, is sad because John's dreams are never fulfilled, he thinks. Matty wants his son so she can bury him, but in a moment of illumination, Alf realizes that John's dreams actually come true and he tells the rescue party: "You all stop! Leave my boy go on. Doan stop 'im. . . Ah'm happy 'cause dis mawnin' mah boy is goin' tuh sea, *he's going to sea*." The third-person narrator concludes the story with the following: "Out on the bosom of the river, bobbing up and down as if waving goodbye, piloting his little craft on the shining river road, John Redding floated away toward Jacksonville, the sea, the wide world—at last" (14).

Did John get his dream fulfilled or squashed with his death? Is John's dad correct to see his death by drowning as a fulfillment of his desire to travel to see the world, or was his death a warning to young black men not to aspire beyond their environments? Again Hurston's use of language at the end brings out ambiguities as John seems to be on the "shining river road" ultimately to freedom at last and not just dead.

Hurston's female characters have received much attention for the various ways their creator empowers them to survive in male-dominated African American communities. Delia, the wife of Sykes in "Sweat," written in 1926, endures Sykes' infidelity and abusive ways. He does not want his wife to wash white folks' clothing, but that is the way she makes money to support an indolent husband who parades with another woman in town and seeks to drive Delia, the breadwinner, from her house to bring the second woman to replace her. Knowing Delia is scared of snakes, he brings one into the house to throw on her laundry. But Delia has the last laugh as she watches from a distance the snake kill Sykes.

Another cunning Hurston female character is an unnamed woman in her story "Monkey Junk," a parody of a biblical story or parable, using numbered verses and King James English. The opening phrase, "And it came to pass in those days," reminds us of Luke's narration of the birth of the Christ Child (Luke 2:1) and attempts to feign a tone of seriousness in looking at the story.

Her unnamed husband describes himself as a "wise guy" who "[knows] all that there is about females" (570) and is therefore cautious about marrying one of them. Unfortunately, his certainty is short-lived as a gold digger flatters him and he marries within the year, just after declaring he will not marry. In words close to the

Pharisee who felt so superior to the tax collector, he praises the Lord: "I thank thee that I am not as other men—stupid and blind and imposed upon by every female that listeth" ((Luke 18: 11; 570)

The marriage is good so long as he keeps writing checks, but when money stops flowing, the unnamed woman starts to run after other men. The cuckolded husband refuses to support her further, citing that he knows "ALL the law and the profits thereof" (572). In preparing for the legal case against her, the woman buys fine clothing, lingerie, hosiery and hires a young lawyer, Miles Page. The husband, certain he is the injured party and has a solid case against her, does not hire a lawyer in the divorce hearing.

Using her female weapons of alluring clothing, moving tears and playing victim of evil deeds, she is able to manipulate both the judge and the jury in the courtroom to look at her husband as the evil one. In the end, the judge orders the ex-husband to pay an alimony of hundred shekels. When the angry husband talks of striking her on the nose, she pulls the race card: "Thou shalt surely go to the cooler if thou stick thy rusty fist in my face, for I shall holler like a pretty white woman" (575). In this last sentence by the unnamed woman, she alludes to the unequal white legal system that will sentence a black man to prison not on the accuracy of the facts, but on the emotional state of the victim. The irony of this reference is that the unnamed black woman has just used a version of this, feminine guile, to deny her ex-husband justice. Beaten by the urban court system and an ex-wife who shows this man that he is indeed ignorant about women and justice, the poor and defeated man returns to Alabama to pick cotton.

Though the stories are short, and therefore the plots are straightforward, Hurston still focuses on issues she deals with in the other works and ends up creating memorable characters who have to navigate the day-to-day living in a society full of inequalities, whether with race, gender, or economic issues. Readers remember Missy May and Joe Banks in the most anthologized of her stories, "The Gilded Six-Bits," written in 1933. The young married couple's happy

180

marriage is almost destroyed by economic reasons as Missy May wants to get what she thinks is a gold coin from the owner of the ice cream parlor owner, a newcomer from Chicago, to give to Joe. The cheated husband, seriously hurt by Missy May's betrayal, is able to forgive and restore the relationship close to what they had at the beginning. The irony in the story occurs at the end when the white store clerk in the candy store "[wisht [he] could be like these darkies. Laughin' all the time. Nothin' worries 'em" (628)!

Zora Neale Hurston's success, and ultimately her triumph and rediscovery, can be attributed to the fact that she never forgets what is real and important. Her language, often a torrent of energy and disorder, unleashes the climate of her childhood. She is at liberty to assert her will as an author without seeking or accepting the approval of any other entity. Her reluctance to lose heart or fight back, her ability to turn and smile and competently go about her business, displays the incalculable power of a single, creative African-American woman with a keen sense of a cause for which she is ready to give up vain praises.

From all that which precedes, it is evident that Zora Neale Hurston embraced her cultural heritage while other African-Americans ran from it. This assessment may appear simplistic, but anyone who reads her can ascertain the authenticity of her fiction through her use of language. It is unchanged, unchallenged, and unpolished. This veracity gives it power. Zora Neale Hurston's works have been hailed for their representation of Black folk speech. Her writings exhibit, through dialogue and character interaction, features of resistance that allow for an appraisal highlighting her agency as a revolutionary visionary who was, " perhaps because of [her] cultural position, sensitive to the plight of African [Americans cum Blacks] and opposed to [assimilation] textually in ways that ... [others] could not" (Kadish and Massardier-Kenney 6). Her narratives bring into play such complex poetic issues of gender, race, place, speech and speaker, sexuality, social issues and nationality, all foregrounded here. These writings refuse to mimic the language, style, words, and attitudes of her white oppressor. She makes subjugation her past and speaks for Black folk while rejecting the mainstream idea of Black folks' speech and culture being a symbol of woe and dreadful shame. Also, in her works, she does not shy away from expressing her sexuality.

America has never been completely comfortable expressing female sexuality in its literature or elsewhere. It certainly has never been comfortable expressing black female sexuality. The response of the literary establishment was immediate and nearly unprecedented. This is why, one could argue, that despite *Their Eyes Were Watching God, Barracoon, Dust Tracks on a Road, Mules and Men,* and *Tell My Horse: Voodoo and Life in Haiti and Jamaica,* Hurston died without any financial resources of any kind. This is the same reason Kate Chopin's literary career came to an end one generation earlier. Both authors, despite their different racial backgrounds, suffered tremendously. The nation proved to be repressed in more ways than one. Hurston violated the rules, and she had more to lose than Chopin. Ralph D. Story, in "Gender and Ambition: Zora Neale Hurston in the Harlem Renaissance" commented: "Black women, more than anything else, have wanted love whereas black men have wanted justice and power; yet neither is guaranteed" (29). One should also add that neither is interchangeable. While presenting a female-focused narrative liberated her and gave her power, simultaneously, it caused her to collide with the men of her own culture.

The blues were not dignified, notes Jones in *Blues People* (129). Zora Neale Hurston did not strive for "dignity" if that meant clever conversation. Somehow, language that was overly polished and wordplay that was too fancy produced a finished product that was considered inauthentic. Such inauthenticity may well have been considered a way of talking for city folk. An author like Zora Neale Hurston takes her ship and purposely swerves into the wind, embracing the rough spots, delighting in the fact that she is not sophisticated and daring anyone to try to change her. She did not want to integrate (although she would not have minded if her books reached a wider audience). She does not want to write like a college graduate, which she was, and this natural inclination for her to stand without compromise caused all sorts of problems. Yet, Taylor Hagood wonders whether there is such a thing as authentic Black dialect and further casts aspersions as to how it could be represented without recourse to "minstrelsy stereotypes" (44). He thinks that Zora Neale Hurston, while embodying the paradox of Black dialect, "articulates the larger issue of accessing and celebrating black folk culture while simultaneously dismantling white-defined markers of that culture" (44).

If one listens very carefully to Black folk speak, one can hear trauma and terror in the words written by Zora Neale Hurston. This seems to be intentional and liberating if one fights through it. Sanitizing the language, taking it out of the rural south, risks losing something. Smoothing out or sanding out the edges, like someone working on a woodworking project, irrevocably alters the original shape of the piece of hickory, oak, or maple. Zora Neale Hurston, like an archivist, wants no such deterioration. She wants to experience and convey a story that others are tempted not to tell. She fully understands that accepting to create universes in a language or languages that are foreign to the one(s) spoken by its inhabitants would be treasonous and a humiliating way to surrender to an adversary. Rita Dove calls this uncompromising linguistic technique "the power of utterance" (Forward to *Jonah's Gourd Vine* viii). She goes on to call this nature's music and, all too often, in a world without environmental protection and conservation, to take the form of outrage. Zora Neale Hurston's language bristles with emotion, embraces a new type of learning, and mirrors Southern black life. The dialect speaks in anger. Damn right, she is outraged and shall tell the oppressor this directly and she is going to say it hot.

Marcus Garvey, an admirer of Booker T. Washington just like Zora Neale Hurston, famously considered African American people (and black people wherever they lived) as a mighty race. This means one race without divisions, fissures, subgroups, and disparate components. Marcus Garvey founded The Universal Negro Improvement Association (U.N.I.A.), in 1914, the objective of which was to unify "… all the Negro peoples of the world into one great body and to establish a country absolutely on their own" (Hill 5) Authors like Zora Neale Hurston and others threatened this characterization of unanimity. As time went on, a big issue, perhaps the big issue, in the African-American community, was what kind of literature would present and introduce black people to the world. Hurston's novels were such that some wanted no part of them nor her. The motto of the U.N.I.A. was "One God! One Aim! One Destiny" (Hill 5). The language of Eatonville, Florida, written phonetically and spelled uniquely, was not what they had in mind. Zora was not bending either. The first item on her official website quotes her as saying, "I have the nerve to walk my own way, however hard, in my search for reality, rather than climb upon the rattling wheel of wishful illusions" (John T. Wills, *Thought Provoking Perspectives*). Writing precisely what she heard in her all-black town in northern Florida gave her strength and stated (to other black people) that her experiences were not going to be censored.

Zora Neale Hurston's writings by their very nature are anti-assimilationist and reflect the instincts of one who having or not birthed a child, knows and feels the labor of childbirth. As such, protecting and defending her young from predators becomes her number one preoccupation. Her awareness is a shot in the arm to bolster her narrative technique and thus "alter specific cultural power structures" (Kadish and Massardier-Kenney 5). Her writings lay a foundation stone of socio-political opposition that expresses itself as one against the nauseous historical record that has hitherto been aimed at denying Blacks their humanity though slavery, colonialism, racism, police brutality, and assimilation. Her works thus shed a revolutionary light on Black struggle to make a place in the sun. It is in this regard that Zora Neale Hurston succeeds in expressing the power of Black imagination and resolve. The works restitute the most fundamental proceeds of having a memory, means of memory, identity, and culture of one's own.

Zora Neale Hurston's training in anthropology and folklore seems to reveal that a figure who jumps through hoops is rewarded with more and progressively narrower hoops. In other words, contrary to the American Dream, life becomes more difficult not less difficult. A careful study of everyday life reveals that people do not have a sense of who they are. This fear, anxiety, and shakiness seeps into the vernacular. The sound, the emotional pain, and the cries that can be heard within a language have more to do with the condition of the individual than with anything that appears in ink on the printed page. Simply put, the question of who defines the African American cannot be encapsulated in a book, it cannot be pictured in a photograph, and it cannot be culled from statistics in a survey by the Pew Research Center. Such an exploration must be answered with a song—a blues song—which offers a faint hope of freedom in a world mired in discord, violence, and sadness.

Much ink has been spilled writing about the language Zora Neale Hurston uses in writing and any writing about her language seems to rehash the same old story. However, the interest and/or question raised here is how she uses language not only as a founding member of the "Niggerati" movement but as a guide for the oppressed and formerly enslaved Black people to reclaim the only thing they have with which to make sense of and give meaning to their problems of existence. While the Samuel Becketts of the world might sum humankind's search for meaning as inexhaustibly absurd, the works of Zora Neale Hurston embrace the idea that for black people to find meaning and have a sense of purpose in life, they must reclaim their language after everything else has been taken from them forcibly. Zora Neale Hurston refuses, in her works, as would Ngugi some decades later, to be actively or passively complicit in any form of distanciation from the used and abused Black self. Zora Neale Hurston thus makes a case that misery has never held dominion over poets' perceptions and insights into the bright light that there is to pursue in a transient world. The material indigence in which the poet

185

lives and dies can never blind forever to the richness of the poets' musings. Their own generation, or the ones immediately after, might ignore the treasures that their poverty has slaved to conceal, but the generation yet unborn will in their treasure hunt, unearth, polish, cherish and care for the beautiful lines their imagination has laid on the pages. Such treasures cannot be obliterated by people's material sense-values which pit otherness against a specific dominant power structure.

Works Cited

Abbott, Dorothy. *Frontiers: A Journal of Women Studies*, vol. 12, no. 1, 1991, pp. 174-181.

Beliso-De Jesus, Aisha Mahina. "A Hieroglyphics of Zora Neale Hurston." *Journal of Africana Religions*, vol. 4, no. 2, 2016, pp. 290-303.

Callahan, John F. Ed. *The Collected Essays of Ralph Ellison: Revised and Updated,* Modern Library, 2003.

Gates, Henry Louis., and Anthony Appiah. *Zora Neale Hurston: Critical Perspectives Past and Present.* Amistad, 1993.

Hagood, Taylor, *Secrecy, Magic, and the One Act Plays of Harlem Renaissance Women Writers.* Ohio State UP, 2010.

Hill, Robert A. *The Garvey and UNIA Papers,* U. of Cal. P. 1983

Hurston, Zora N. "Characteristics of Negro Expression." In *Negro: An Anthology,* ed. Nancy Cunard, pp. 24–31., Continuum, 1996.

_____ *Jonah's Gourd Vine: a Novel.* HarperPerennial, 2008.

_____ *Mules and Men* 1935. Reprint, Harper and Row, 1990.

_____ *Their Eyes Were Watching God,* 1937. Reprint, HarperPerennial, 2006.

_____ *Dust Tracks on a Road* 1942. Reprint, HarperPerennial, 2006.

_____ *Every Tongue Got to Confess*

_____ "The Gilded Six-Bits." *The Story and Its Writer: An Introduction to Short Fiction*, edited by Ann Charters, Bedford/St. Martin's, 1995, pp. 620-628.

_____ John Redding Goes to Sea." *Narrative Magazine* Story of the Week, 2016-2017

_____ "Monkey Junk." *American Studies*, vol. 55, no. 4, 2010. African American Literary Studies: New Texts, New Approaches, New Challenges, pp. 570-575.

_____ *Moses, Man of the Mountain*

_____ *Seraph on the Suwanee*

_____ "Sweat."

_____ *Tell My Horse: Voodoo and Life in Haiti and Jamaica* 1938. Reprint, Harper and Row, 1990.

_____ *Barracoon*, Amistad, 2018.

Jones, LeRoi. *Blues People: The Negro Experience in White America and the Music That Developed From It*. William Morrow 1963.

Kadish, Doris Y. and Françoise Massardier-Kenney. Vol. 1 *Translating Slavery: Gender and Race in French Abolitionist Writing 1780-1830,* The Kent State UP, 2009.

Kendi, Ibram X. *Stamped from the Beginning*. Bold Type, 2016.

Kinnaird, John. *William Hazlitt: The Power of Critic,* Columbia UP, 1978.

McClaurin, Irma. "Zora Neale Hurston: Enigma, Heterodox, and Progenitor of Black Studies." *Fire!!!: The Multimedia Journal of Black Studies*. vol. 1, no. 1, 2012, pp. 49-67. https://www.jstor.org/stable/10.5323/fire.1.1.0049

McIver, Stuart. "Triumphs and Tragedy of Zora Neale Hurston." *Sun-Sentinel,* Jan. 21, 1990. https://www.sun-sentinel.com/news/fl-xpm-1990-01-21 9001200361-story.html

Newell, Stephanie. *West African Literature: Ways of Reading,* Oxford UP, 2006.

Pierpont, Claudia. "A Society of One: Zora Neale Hurston, American Contrarian." *New Yorker*, 10 Feb. 1997.

Rampersad, Arnold. *Ralph Ellison: A Biography*. Alfred A. Knopf, 2008.

Story, Ralph D. "Gender and Ambition: Zora Neale Hurston in the Harlem Renaissance." *The Black Scholar*, vol. 20, no. 3/4, African

Culture, Summer/Fall1989, pp. 25-31,
http://www.jstor.org/stable/41067631.

Redman, F. Russell. *Nature's Place in Zora Neale Hurston's* "John Redding Goes to Sea," "Magnolia Flower," *and* "Sweat." Thesis, Florida Atlantic University, Aug. 2008.

Thompson, Gordon, E, "Projecting Gender: Personification in the Works of Zora Neale Hurston." *American Literature*, vol. 66, no. 4, Dec., 1994, pp. 737-763: www.jstor.org/stable/2927696.

wa Thiong'o, Ngũgi. *Decolonising the Mind.* James Curry/Heineman, 1986.

_____ *Something Torn and new: An African Renaissance,* Civitas, 2009.

Wills, John T. "Marcus Garvey: Rise Up You Mighty Race." *Thought Provoking Perspectives*, 7 Feb. 2017, thought provoking perspectives. wordpress. com/2017/02/09/one-god-one-aim-one-destiny/"Zora Neale Hurston." *Home Page*, 29 Mar. 2018, www.zoranealehurston.com/.

Chapter 7

Martin Delany's *Blake; or, The Huts of America* and Sutton E. Griggs' *Imperium in Imperio* : Heralds of Afrofuturism

Mark Henderson

In the introduction to her recently influential anthology *Dark Matter: A Century of Speculative Fiction form the African Diaspora*, Sheree R. Thomas explains that the science fiction theme of the alien Otherness suits the white, historical attitude towards blackness sadly well—"the specter of blackness looms large in the white imagination" (xiii). And yet, those themes and tropes of science fiction, when wielded by black authors, can counter, clarify, and undercut such highly problematic clichés. Speaking in terms of post colonialism, if the dominant narrative of history—the "truth" written by the proverbial "winners"—is western and white, then the counter-narratives written by black science fiction authors have an important chance to speak truth to power, to call out the lie in that dominant narrative. Speaking truth to power and calling out a lie are nothing short of revolutionary and visionary.

With its use of science fiction for the purpose of addressing issues pertinent to black people around the world, Afrofuturism—black science fiction, as well as the study of how black people are both affected by and make use of technology—has proven to be a useful tool for speculation. One might erroneously conclude, however, that the term "science fiction" refers only to the twentieth century and beyond. But the fact remains that what is considered "futuristic" is relative to a given time and place—that "the future" has been envisioned and subject to speculation from the vantage point of *all* periods throughout history. In passing, African-American science fiction author, Samuel R. Delany mentions two nineteenth-century novels by African-American authors, Martin Delany's *Blake; or, The Huts of America* (1859) and Sutton E. Griggs' *Imperium in Imperio* (1899), as examples of early black science fiction (383). Both works demonstrate the science fiction trope of alternative history—that is, of creatively realizing the outcomes of certain historical events had things turned out *differently*. More specifically, both works speculate upon *successful* black-nationalist insurrection and separation, making them key, fictional points of argument in the nineteenth-century portion of American civil rights history. Therefore, both works are worthy of further exploration as examples of how Afrofuturism has been key to the liberation struggle for African-American even since the middle of the nineteenth century.

In and of itself, the forty-year distance between each work's publications is testimony to the continuing importance of Afrofuturism's speculative power. Delany was writing in the thick of slavery, in the decade before the Civil War, and Griggs was writing in the postbellum world of Reconstruction, proving how, in spite of the war and the Emancipation Proclamation, disturbingly little had changed for African-Americans—so much so that it had apparently inspired, through Griggs' fiction, the necessity of revisiting Delany's alternative-history trope so many decades later. Furthermore, both works anticipate the Black Power and Pan-Africanism movements in the latter half of the twentieth century, at the height of the American Civil Rights Movement, when *still* disturbingly little has changed. Each work is therefore startling for its enduring relevance and historical prescience.

I Alternative History and the Relative Futuristic

According to Homi K. Bhabha, there lies within the colonial dynamic a "profound internal dissonance [...] between the free standing of the citizen and the segregated status of the subject—the double political destiny of the same colonized person [creating] a troubled traffic between the psychic body and the body politic" (xxi).

Therefore, there exists for the minority a less-than-second-class sham of a citizenship that leaves him no less the subject of the colonist's "subtly punishing and disabling paternalistic power" (xxiii). The subject's realization of this existential predicament coincides with a recognition of the colonizer's deceitful double-talk concerning supremacy, society, the world, life—in short, the so-called "way it is" as the subject has been led to believe it. Consequently, and consistent with Griggs' novel, an insidiously uprising *new* nation is formed within the subjugating power; as Frantz Fanon describes, a "question of truth" arises for these new nationals:

For the people, only fellow nationals are ever owed the truth. No absolute truth, no discourse on the transparency of the soul can erode this position. In answer to the lie of the colonial situation, the colonized subject responds with a lie. Behavior toward fellow nationals is open and honest but strained and indecipherable toward the colonists. (14)

And yet, for Fanon, the colonized's meeting the lie of the colonizer with the countering lie of tricksterism creates a salvational double negative—one that, in fact, preserves truth; for, as he continues: "Truth is what hastens the dislocation of the colonial regime, what fosters the emergence of the nation. Truth is what protects the 'natives' and undoes the foreigners. In the colonial context there is no truthful behavior" (14). Within Afrofuturism, alternative histories perform this very paradoxical function—of using *fiction* to reveal essential truths by giving the so-called "lie" of an alternative story to the lie-purported-as-truth of colonialism and white supremacy. Alternative history works to thaw and to reinvigorate the "petrified zone[s]" (Fanon 14) of colonialism's ghettoized spaces, caged at a distance from so-called "history" and "truth." The fictions of Delany and Griggs contribute to this important consciousness of the inherent, problematic selectiveness of the status quo's presentation of history.

It is crucial to begin with a brief summary for each work. Delany's *Blake* arrives at protagonist Henry Blake's comprehensive plan to directly inspire widespread slave insurrection by questing about the whole of the American South by way of a sadly typical feature of American slavery and trope of American slave narratives: the forcible separation of a slave family. Henry comes back from an errand for his master, Colonel Stephen Franks, to find that his wife, Maggie, has been sold away from the plantation (because Franks' wife is getting too close to her *and* because Maggie refuses Franks' sexual advances). From the moment he runs away and throughout his quest, Henry's actions acquire the dimensions of a nearly super heroic crime fighter or spy. He aids his little son Joe and two other slaves to seemingly vanish into thin air from the plantation. He also seems to effortlessly travel great distances, blend in with a variety of local cultures and political systems (from different plantations to various river steamers), narrowly escape and fend off patrols and their slave-hunting dogs— and, above all, disseminate the desire for black self-education, self-actualization, and revolt. In one notable instance, upon hearing two slave girls complain about how a black driver named Jesse abuses and takes advantage of them, Henry mysteriously makes sure that the driver is never heard from again by the next morning. Indeed, Henry often seems to appear suddenly and from out of nowhere, and his communication with other slaves is, at times, almost telepathic; and, after reuniting with the other slaves missing from the Franks plantation (including his in-laws) in Canada, he is off to Cuba to continue these super heroic exploits in retrieving his wife.

Similarly, Griggs' *Imperium in Imperio* arrives at the discovery of the titular black secret society/nation by the novel's *two* protagonists— first by the dark-skinned Belton Piedmont, who then reveals it to the light-skinned Bernard Belgrade—by way of the injustices experienced by each protagonist throughout their lives. However, whereas *Blake* ends on an ambiguously hopeful cliffhanger, *Imperium in Imperio* ends on a more tragically ironic note. Belton, having suffered longer and from more direct violence—even surviving a lynching!—than Bernard because of his darker skin (and overcoming it all in a near-super heroic fashion similar to Henry Blake), is surprisingly less violent and militant than Bernard; and his refusal to go along with Bernard and the Imperium's plan to seize Texas as an independent nation-state for black people leads to his resignation and execution by the Imperium.

The alternative history of both plots is evident, and each proposes a turn of events that runs counter to the dominant historical narrative of white supremacy and hegemonic oppression. However, these speculations are no mere delusional, fruitless flights of fancy; as Charles R. Saunders makes clear in his essay, "Why Blacks Should Read (and Write) Science Fiction." Alternative history is a staple of science fiction that allows the human imagination to manifest itself in stories, and "[t]hose stories become legends, myths, [and] the defining elements of a culture" (404). Going further on this note, Walter Mosley discusses science fiction's ability to offer "an alternative account for the way things are" (405) and how it can provide "the first step in changing the world"—an attractive possibility for "young, black readers who crave a vision that will shut down the realism imprisoning [them] behind a wall of alienating culture" (406). As a speculative fiction—one that asks the simple, powerful question of "What if?"—science fiction is ready-made to "rail against the status quo," an end which Mosley argues is especially appropriate and applicable for black writers (406). As both *Blake* and *Imperium in Imperio* demonstrate, this usefulness has been recognized and implemented by black writers for much longer than might have been originally thought; both novels were written specifically, according to Jerome McGann, "to bring about actual social change" (xiii), not merely to provide pleasant or transcendent diversion.

The "What if?" quality of Delany's novel lies not only in its superhero-like protagonist, but also in the work's very design and in one of its key conceptual signs. They are respectively, in its cliffhanger ending (which cuts the novel off right before decisive insurrectionist action is collectively taken, giving imaginative shape to a redemptive black future) as well as in its idea of "Afraka," which, according to McGann, represents "'a world elsewhere' of black actualities and black truth"—a world, more significantly still, that is produced by "reimagin[ing] the past" (xxv). The speculative strength of Griggs' novel lies in its secret black society that has existed from the days of the American Revolution. A mysterious, wealthy black scientist, working for ultimate equal rights for both freedmen and slaves, founded this secret black society. Furthermore, Belton's revelation of the secret society's history to Bernard reinforces the antebellum placement of *Blake* and its recognition of America's foundational hypocrisies regarding civil rights. The Imperium was created, according to Belton, "because of a defect in the Constitution," and, "[e]xcept in a few, but important particulars, [their] constitution was modeled after that of the United States" (132), referencing that Constitution's incompatibilities with the Declaration of Independence's promise of equal rights for "all men."

In light of *Blake*, McGann's summation of Delany as a novelist fits both Delany *and* Griggs. It highlights the importance of their respective works' speculative nature; more so than novelists, they are "polemicist[s]" and "prophet[s]" deploying the "various conventions of traditional fiction to make an argument about what black emancipation in America meant and how it was to be achieved," by presenting "a critical account of Euro-American racism and how to escape its authority" (xvi). Their respective fictions are thus grounded in historical truth; the springboards for their respective fantasies are real events and even real people from the nineteenth century. Also, the two-part structure of *Blake* marks a sharp contrast between Henry's adventures in the American South and his similar adventures in Cuba. Whereas the Underground Railroad, the *Amistad* revolt, the Trans-Atlantic slave trade, the Compromise of 1850 (and the Fugitive Slave Law), the Dred Scott decision, and slavery conditions in Cuba compose the background of the novel's first part, its second part takes off with anachronistic alternative history that, for instance, places the revolutionary Cuban poet Placido and the insurrection that he represents, for the purposes of the novel's polemic aim, roughly ten years *after* those events, which included Placido's execution.

The alternative histories presented by Delany and Griggs coexist with other, perhaps more subtle science fiction tropes—in particular, panoptic surveillance and conspiracy. The messaging system among the slaves in *Blake*, for instance, has a speed and an immediacy that suggests a technological sophistication and ingenuity countering typical white-supremacist prejudices pertaining to black intellect. The same goes for how rapidly and widely the insurrectionist conspiracy among the slaves is able to spread. Delany's titular protagonist is, in fact, the avatar of this conspiracy. Also, the very founding of Griggs' secret society was based on science, and elaborate contraptions such as the trapdoor leading to the secret room in which Belton initiates Bernard into the Imperium suggest further technological advancement. And Belton further reveals that the systems of surveillance with which, the Imperium has been tracking Bernard run counter to the more primitive forms of surveillance associated with slavery (patrols, slave-hunting dogs, and political legislation). This forms that nonetheless still pose a significant threat, given Henry's discovery of the secret slave organizations in Louisiana and the reactionary "system of restriction and espionage toward negroes and mulattoes" created by local white officials (108-109). Together, these tropes remind one of how what is "advanced" or "futuristic" is relative to a given point in history, no matter how far back in the past that point may be.

II Revolt and Separation

The speculative power of both *Blake* and *Imperium in Imperio* is centered, again, on black revolution—particularly in the forms of separation and insurrection. The potential for such a revolution is, of course, the biggest fear of the dominant white establishment, perhaps best voiced from within Delany's text by Colonel Franks, who, in the face of Henry's daring and courage, hysterically exclaims, "It's rebellion! a plot—this is but the shadow of a cloud that's fast gathering around us! I see it plainly, I see it!" (21) As Albert Memmi points out, the colonizer's acceptance of his position of power, however tacit and unconscious that acceptance might be, confesses an inherent insecurity of that very position: "If one chooses to understand the colonial system, he must admit that it is unstable and its equilibrium constantly threatened" (120). What this fear implies most significantly is the self-conscious guilt on the part of whites who unconsciously suspect that such reprisal would be justified—that they would deserve every bit of the slaves' insurrectionist violence, for which they have been prepared, according to Fanon, "from time immemorial," having been forcibly abducted or born into a "cramped world, riddled with taboos" (3). Franks' language, in fact, foreshadows the chapter titles for Henry's running away and quest across the South—respectively, "A Shadow" and "A Flying Cloud" (both of which intensify Henry's science-fiction crimefighter aura).

What most intimidates and insults Franks about Henry is his education; it is later revealed how Henry comes from a wealthy and educated West Indian background, and that his birth name is Carolus Henrico Blacus. Furthermore, by virtue of Henry's representation, as a character, of black insurrection in general, it is revealed that the "merry-making" of a number of slaves on the Franks plantation at the time of Henry's flight was, in fact, a coordinated diversion (39). In spite of their not having had the opportunity to acquire Henry's level of education, the slaves nonetheless demonstrate an ingenuity and a subtlety counter to their white masters' racist assumptions (as well as they are consistent with those same white masters' deepest fears). This revelation recalls Henry's earlier understanding of Colonel Franks' secret plan to sell him away under the auspices of giving him a freedom pass to run errands—and Henry's turning of this machination upon itself by, while on those same errands, making intricate, incremental moves toward his escape. As much as Henry is depicted to be the larger-than-life, individual hero, Delany thus stresses through his protagonist the prejudicially ignored (and, again, paradoxically feared) intelligence of black people—especially their tricksterism in the face of bitter oppression.

The changing of Henry's last name from Holland (in Part 1) to Blake (in Part 2) is not only an act of self-reclamation but also of self-actualization. "Holland" calls to mind the involvement of the Dutch in the African slave trade, and "Blake" (from "Blacus") is a play on the word *black*. Key, then, to Delany's theme of successful slave insurrection is the importance of black education. This is the key ingredient in Henry's plans to complete a revolutionary black organization in every slave state within the span of two years. For Delany, education is the first step leading to the awakening into clear-eyed practicality that leads to serious moves toward black revolution. This revolution is thus not the chaotic, savage apocalypse envisioned by the dominant whites, but an intelligent and a rational move toward independence and self-realization. As Delany states in his pivotal and best-known work of nonfiction, *The Condition, Elevation, Emigration, and Destiny of the Colored People of the United States* (1852), "It is time that we [...] had become as moral theorists, also the practical demonstrators of equal rights and self-government" (45). For Delany, self-emancipation required a clear-headed, brave, and forthright self-reliance; like his contemporary and friend Frederick Douglass's description, in his *Narrative*, of successfully defending himself against the slave-breaker Edward Covey, such emancipation entailed becoming a man by refusing be a slave. As Fanon reiterates, "The 'thing' colonized becomes a man through the very process of liberation" (2); even should this new man continue to be subjugated and brutalized for the time being, he "deep down [...] acknowledges no authority [...] is dominated but not domesticated [and is] by no means convinced of his inferiority" (16). For Douglass and for Delany both, this proactive reassertion of and rebirth into one's black humanity is one and the same with the importance of black education.

In light of his practical and pragmatic views pertaining to black education and its role in black emancipation, Delany's literary representations of his views about black Christianity can easily be misunderstood if read incompletely. Indeed, Delany does include religion with lack of education as key to why he cannot fully explain his plans to his mother-in-law; in the face of her admonishments to simply wait and pray, Henry responds: "Religion! [...] [T]hat's always the cry with black people. Tell me nothing about religion when the very man who hands you the bread at communion, has sold your daughter away from you!" (22) However, Delany goes on to make it clear that the problem is not with religion itself but with its misuse, its perversion—a perversion resulting from a misdirection of faith and worship from the divine to the man-made, leading to a combination of hypocrisy and inflexibility that is hopelessly impossible to trust:

> [T]here are no people who ever lived, love their country and obey their laws as the Americans [...] Their country is their Heaven—their Laws their Scriptures—and the decrees of their Magistrates obeyed as the fiat of God. It is the most consummate delusion and misdirected confidence to depend upon them for protection, and for a moment suppose even our children safe while walking in the streets among them. (*The Condition* 171-172)

Henry tells the slave Charles that he will be a runaway "religiously," lending Christian sanctity to his oath of "never again serv[ing] any white man living" (38); and, later, a group of slaves to "make your religion subserve your interests, as your oppressors do theirs" (43). Indeed, black appropriation of the Christian imagery of salvation through exodus has been symbolically and rhetorically crucial throughout the history of the American Civil Rights Movements. By extension, such imagery lends itself to Afrofuturism's envisioning of worlds elsewhere and long-lost homelands, cohabiting well with the black Christianity in Delany's visions for emigration. This calls to mind Fanon's reminder that the "white man's Church" in the colonies "does not call the colonized to the ways of God, but to the ways of the white man, to the ways of the master, the ways of the oppressor" (7). The black individual is thus reminded of his humanity as well as his autonomy by having his divinity reclaimed from the worldly, back to the universal.

Along with the passivity that he had associated with the purely conciliatory version of the Christian religion taught to slaves by their white masters, Delany also had little use for education with no tangible utility. Especially for black people looking to improve their condition, education had to be tempered with *practicality*—especially concerning the ultimate futility in waiting on the dominant white culture to abolish slavery and to protect equal rights. This practicality is where Delany's belief in and insistence upon black emigration comes in (a position that eventually led to his falling out with his friend Douglass, who favored integration). And the language he uses to describe black people's "true political position" in practical terms basically begs for Afrofuturistic examination: "We are politically, not of them, but aliens to the laws and political privileges of the country" (*The Condition* 173). Delany arrived at this conclusion through direct and actively-sought-out experience. From his 1839 extended tour of the South to learn about the social and political conditions there (during which he even escaped being lynched!), to his admittance to Harvard Medical School in 1850 only to have to leave after one semester because of white student protest, to actually helping white abolitionist John Brown with a secret convention in western Canada in 1858 to plan a black insurrection (leading to the unsuccessful attack on Harpers Ferry the next year), the intensity of the Otherness with which the dominant white culture viewed black people was as uncanny as it was undeniable. Particularly decisive for Delany was the fundamental lie concerning racial equality in the country's founding documents, as exposed by the 1850 Fugitive Slave Law:

> Heretofore, it ever has been denied, that the United States recognized or knew any difference between the people—that the Constitution makes no distinction, but includes in its provisions, all the people alike. This is not true, and certainly is blind absurdity in us at least, who have suffered the dread consequences of this delusion, not now to see it. (*The Condition* 170)

Such a breathtaking contradiction between the letter of the law and that same letter's application exposed a discrimination that, for Delany, called for nothing short of resistance by force and separation without compromise. Such Other-izing placed black people in America outside of their very humanity, making them aliens where they had never chosen to arrive—outside of their very American-ness in spite of their extensive part in having built it and contributed with their very bodies to its economy.

Indeed, Delany's doubling down on his belief in emigration *after* the Civil War was the result of further anger and frustration, both personal and political, in the face of continued discrimination despite the promises offered by Emancipation Proclamation and Reconstruction. Despite his temporary move toward a more integrationist approach *during* the Civil War, for which he had served as a commissioned major and a recruiter of black soldiers, he saw the writing on the wall in the disputed presidential election of Republican Rutherford B. Hayes in 1876, which led to the so-called Compromise of 1877, which effectively ended Reconstruction by removing federal troops from the South and beginning Jim Crow. More personally, Northern Republicans and South Carolina Democrats combined to thwart his plans for a mixed-representation political body in South Carolina and remove him from his office of trial justice in 1878 through false charges of fraud and theft.

It is no wonder, then, how issues and tropes so similar to those seen in *Blake* appear again in *Imperium in Imperio* decades later, on the other side of the Civil War, by Griggs—an author who, in spite of the heavily separatist undertone of his novel, actually came off as much more of an integrationist (though not without irony). But whereas black education is something to be sought out, disseminated, and organized in Delany's novel (from Henry's stressing of education as an integral part of the continual organizing necessary for successful insurrection, to the freeing of his wife Maggie in Cuba by educating her about her actual rights), Griggs' novel *begins* with black education, tracing the lives of both Belton and Bernard from the point of view of their shared, pre-college schooling. Education married with the practical, hard lessons of racial prejudice in spite of it is what leads both young men to discover and be initiated into the Imperium. The characters' relentless, hard-nosed resolve reflect Griggs' own self-actualization; he published his own works— including *Imperium in Imperio*, which Cornel West considers his most important novel—and sold them door-to-door himself (West xv-xvi), disseminating his literature in a way that was, like Delany's Henry across the South, both independent and covert.

Even beyond their rigorous early schooling, Belton and Bernard are both, as Verdelle points out, "hungry intellectuals" during a time in which the "high moral crime" of whites' "brutish claim on knowledge [for black people]" was the rule (ix). And Griggs was a significant contributor to the campaign among post-Emancipation black writers, thinkers, philosophers, pastors, and scholars "to defend, glorify, politicize, and activate the mental skills of the Race" (ix-x). Again, continuing the beliefs put forth by Delany, practical reason, for Griggs, is essential for an education's effectiveness; as Verdelle puts it, the calamity concerning race in the post-Emancipation years required black people in America to be "alive *and* thinking," given that the "reigning positions on Negroes needed constant proving wrong" (vii, italics added for emphasis). Key to the Imperium's "campaign of education" to teach "the [American] Negro as to what real freedom was" (131) is to inspire within their dreams of liberty not just the literal release from bondage, but gaining true global equality with all other races. Furthermore, crucial to that instruction is the pragmatic dismissal of expectations for the dominant white establishment to do right by black people or to significantly improve their own outlooks on race. The only helping hand for the black American was at the end of his or her own arm. The very structure of the Imperium's stronghold, Jefferson College, reflects this necessary marriage of education with practicality: it is a school whose underground and hidden-room secrets reveal it to be the "Capitol of [their] Government" (133), the secret black government roughly as old as the United States itself. Beneath the purely academic front of the college lies a tangible testament to the black American's revolutionary autonomy and power.

III America: Future Past

The means to achieve the elevation of black consciousness begun by Delany and continued by Griggs (who was an actual, Baptist minister) lie in the speculative power of their fictions; for, although practical reason was key to both men's activism, both also clearly recognized the power of giving narrative shape to hopeful imagination. As Mosley sums up this simple power of science fiction and other forms of speculative fiction, "We make up, then make real" (405). "Reality" and "the way it is" are simply fictions given the illusion of permanence and authority by laziness, ignorance, and hopelessness in the face of "history" and "tradition." Radical change has happened and can (and *will*) happen again. Those who are oppressed can only look to the future, the past being lost and the present being intolerable. It is no wonder, then, how Afrofuturistic characteristics can be found even in works from the nineteenth century, from authors negotiating the perilous landscapes consisting of the Fugitive Slave Law, the Dred Scott decision, and the ending of Reconstruction. McGann explains how, for Delany in particular, such fictional exercise provides "a vision of black redemption" that "imagines an escape" from the "long, tormented history" of American racial injustice "that did not end with the end of the Confederacy, and indeed has not ended even today" (xiii). He grants that times have changed, but contends that those same times "have also kept up with the past, as they always do" (xxvii). In this sense, the future of the past is still the future of the present, making it not only appropriate but also important to acknowledge Afrofuturism's backwards reach into the 1800s.

Furthermore, contrary to what the white hegemonic narrative might insist otherwise, black revolution is fundamentally *American*.

The black insurrectionists in both *Blake* and *Imperium in Imperio* liken their plans to those made by the Founding Fathers during the American Revolution and the Puritan settlers of New England. In Griggs' novel, Belton admits to Bernard how the Imperium has been paying "especial attention to the history of the United States during the revolutionary period" (131) before pragmatically ceding leadership of it to Bernard because it needs "a George Washington" (134). With Delany, the need for an independent black nation is expressed with language calling to mind the "city upon a hill" portion of John Winthrop's "A Model of Christian Charity" speech: "[T]he day of our Elevation is at hand—all the world now gazes at us—and Central and South America, and the West Indies, bid us come and be men and women, protected, secure, beloved and Free" (*The Condition* 207).

In spite of black involvement with and contributions to American history, both authors recognize the long-standing fundamental hypocrisy that denies racial equality despite the very words of the Declaration of Independence. According to Delany, the necessity of black revolution in the United States lies in the country's exhaustively proven tendency to be "untrue to her trust and unfaithful to her professed principles of republican equality" (*The Condition* 44). And for Griggs, this insistent hypocrisy confesses a kind of absurd winner's remorse; as Bernard states in his address to the Imperium: "[T]he monarchical trait seems not to have left their blood. They have apparently chosen our race as an empire, and each Anglo-Saxon regards himself as a petty king, and some gang or community of negroes as his subjects" (147). How ironic that a people who had claimed oppression under monarchy as reason for revolution would so quickly revert to those same oppressors' tendencies! Also, as Delany would so bitterly face later in life, and as Griggs would communicate through his postbellum protagonists, the failures of Reconstruction revealed how even the Emancipation Proclamation, as Bernard further states, "came not so much as a message of love for the slave as a message of love for the Union [...] its primary object

203

[being] to save the Union, its incident, to liberate the slave" (142).

There is thus a twist to both authors' referencing American revolutionary and pre-revolutionary history. The "forefathers" referenced by Griggs in *Imperium in Imperio* are neither the New England Puritans nor the Founding Fathers, but those who "land[ed] in America in 1619" (141)—that is, the first African slaves brought to the Americas. In stating that the members of the Imperium are looking for a war equivalent to "Valley Forge" (149), Bernard is acknowledging how the American Revolution is, in fact, unfinished work. As McGann comments on one of Delany's chief underlying themes in *Blake*, the "tormented urge to flee, the dream of 'A World Elsewhere'" among African-Americans is a "deep American preoccupation" (xix), and the "primal act of insurrection" being "an individual's first conscious commitment to independence" (xiii-xiv) is not only fundamentally American, but is also a testimony to the true humanity and intelligence (as opposed to savageness and irrationality) behind revolution.

Delany and Griggs continue to resonate. As Toyin Falola says of Delany, "Emigration lost its appeal, but not Delany's ideas of 'Africa for Africans,' Black redemption, regeneration and emancipation, and other key elements associated with the rise of Black nationalist thought and political struggles" (23). As Cornel West says of Griggs, while he obviously had the courage to write "during the age of American imperialism (Philippines, Cuba, et al.) and U.S. terrorism (Jim Crow, lynching)," his works thus "constitute[ing] a beacon of light during the night years of the nadir of modern black history" (xv), Griggs' contributions maintain their relevance in the twenty-first century—a time, according to West, "marked by imperial ventures, domestic repression, wealth inequality, and continuing racial division [...] even among a hated black people in an American empire haunted by its past and present crimes against humanity" (xvii). Beneath the privileged and comforting myths of American exceptionalism and moral irreproachability lie unsettling and problematic facts that not only haunt the country's historical psyche, but, in fact, continue to this day. Therefore, beyond the literality of black nationalism and separatism (in the forms of emigration and secret governments) stands the need for self-reliance and self-actualization and the solidarity that engenders and encourages both.

Along with their messages of pride and uplift, there is an undeniable shock value to Delany's and Griggs' narratives. Both at least hint at the need for violence. Griggs' novel in particular concludes on an almost apocalyptic note—one that is both vivid in its violent fantasy and sacrilegious towards America's sacred, self-perpetuating myths. As Berl Trout describes seeing a remorseful Bernard by Belton's grave after his execution:

> He laughed a fearful, wicked laugh like unto that of a maniac [and said] Float on proud flag, while yet you may. Rejoice, oh! ye Anglo-Saxons, yet a little while. Make my father ashamed to own me, his lawful son; call me a bastard child; look upon my pure mother as a harlot; laugh at Viola in the grave of a self-murderer; exhume Belton 's body if you like and tear your flag from around him to keep him from polluting it! Yes, stuff your vile stomachs full of all these horrors. You shall be richer food for the buzzards to whom I have solemnly vowed to give your flesh! (176)

This account calls to mind Fanon's unsparing, ultra-violent description of "decolonization" as "reek[ing] of red-hot cannonballs and bloody knives," with an ultimately "murderous and decisive confrontation" being inevitable (3). Obviously, it scares Trout into betraying the Imperium because he suddenly believed it to be "a serious menace to the peace of the world," saying that he is ready to die "for mankind, for humanity, for civilization" (176-177). Trout's fear and horror potentially reflect that of the reader, who is torn, not only between loyalties but also between the differing parts of his or her identity—for a black reader in particular, between the blackness and Americanness coexisting within the Du Bois-ian double-consciousness; for a white reader, perhaps between his/her naïve notions of American privilege and the paradoxically guilty knowledge of the country's long-standing racial problems. Either way, and all ways, the effect is certainly sobering—hopefully, in a manner that is ultimately beneficial.

IV Conclusion: The Inevitability of Revolution

As previously mentioned, outside of *Imperium in Imperio*, Griggs was ostensibly more of an integrationist and less militant than Delany. And yet, when looking more closely at the nonfiction works from which this conclusion might be surmised, one cannot help but detect both a biting sarcasm and deliberate understatement. In the preface to his *Wisdom's Call* (1911), for instance, Griggs writes about how an important lesson for the South coming out of the Civil War is "that the white South *with all its acuteness of judgment* is *not by any means infallible*, is *not beyond the possibility of making grave mistakes*" (viii, italics added for emphasis). There is perhaps a wink and a nudge behind Griggs' words here—a veneer of friendly, compromising and practical advice for southern whites thinly covering a combined insult and threat.

However, it is, in truth, not so much a threat as it is a warning of the inevitable. Griggs continues in his preface, saying that

> with all of its power, the white South is yet not able to withstand *the eternal drift of things*, is not able to fight against *the stars in their courses*, is not able to thwart the purposes of *the guiding hand of the universe* however distasteful the pathway may be [...] eternal forces, which through the years will eat away their vitals (viii, italics, mine for emphasis).

His religiously philosophical references to astrology—obviously having proven itself important since the first runaway slaves found their way north—point again towards Afrofuturism, giving black insurrection the certainty of a natural force and a universal law of physics. Here, again, Afrofuturism appears to rescue Christianity

206

from its white-supremacist perversion—into what Fanon describes as a "[f]atalism [that] relieves the oppressor of all responsibility since the cause of wrong-doing, poverty, and the inevitable can be attributed to God" (18)—and reclaim its essential righteousness as a pivotal revolutionary tool.

Further, along in *Wisdom's Call*, Griggs continues this Afrofuturistic language in a manner that turns the white-supremacist degradation of African-Americans on its head, thanks again to a use of verbal irony and rhetorical tricksterism that paradoxically elevate and dignify black people while initially seeming to minimize them. Citing the contemporary impact of Louis Pasteur's germ theory of disease, he writes:

> We are living in a day in which great importance is being attached to what was once regarded as the small, inconsequential things of the universe, a day in which the greatest and wisest among men do not consider it beneath their dignity to what such lowly beings as flies, mosquitoes and rats are doing [...] [I]t is the weakened position of the Negro, not his strength, that is to be feared. The putrid body of a dead man lying at the bottom of a reservoir can poison the water of a city and thus slay more people than if the man were alive, dashing through the streets of that city firing on the right and on the left. (11-13)

Citing the 1619 arrival of the first ship carrying African slaves into the American colonies, Griggs goes on to describe how, despite their weakness and suffering "a condition more abject is hardly conceivable," these slaves "were not without the power of doing harm," secretly and unwittingly carrying with them the "noxious poison" of the system of slavery (13).

In comparing these slaves and their descendants to vermin and germs while also acknowledging them as "the small, inconsequential things of the universe," Griggs is using the language of science to ironically lend the so-called "inferior" position of African-Americans a power that is to be respected. And such a sobering fearsomeness is metaphorically continuous with the prospect of black revolution, recalling Fanon's "question of truth" and the conflicting definitions of heroism between the colonizer and the colonized:

> In order to maintain their stamina and their revolutionary capabilities, the people also resort to retelling certain episodes in the life of their community. *The outlaw*, for example, who holds the countryside for days against the police, hot on his trail, or who succumbs after killing four or five police officers in single-handed combat or who commits suicide rather than 'give up' his accomplices, all consume for the people role models, action schemas, and 'heroes.' (30, italics, mine for emphasis)

To those who are not privileged by the dominant culture, it is, of course, pointless to refer such outlaw-heroes as criminals or degenerates; they share too much in the plight for which such brave and decisive souls could no longer stand. Delany's Blake is, obviously, the perfect example—not only for his outlaw-heroism, but also for the insidious, pathogen-like way in which he proves capable of spreading the seeds of insurrection. To continue Griggs' metaphors, if the abject slaves carry with them a poison, the target of that poison is deserving of death; and if those same slaves are pests, their privileged masters are deserving of affliction.

Griggs' references, in the same breath, call to mind both microbiology and astrology. It reminds one of Sheree Thomas' central metaphor for black people of "dark matter" that is,

> a nonluminous form of which has not been directly observed but whose existence has been deduced by its gravitational effects [with] most astronomers believ[ing] that as much as ninety percent of the material in the universe may be objects or particles that cannot be seen (x).

Like the minimized pests and germs, the substance of dark matter, though marginal and invisible, is maximally significant and consequential. Like this dark matter, African-Americans, who have been minimized, marginalized, and rendered invisible since their first presence in colonial America, are nonetheless unavoidable, indefatigable, and undeniable in their influence upon and contribution to the American identity—movers and shakers on a cosmic scale, even from a position of horrible oppression and degradation.

Griggs' choice of Texas as the sovereign black state in *Imperium in Imperio* is, after all, no accident; he was born in Chatfield, Texas, and even died in Houston. In spite of his sufferings at the hands of racism and discrimination, he loved his home state. The "one dear life," he writes in his dedication for *Wisdom's Call*, allotted to him came from "within the borders of the imperial state of Texas." And he expresses his love for Texas' soil, air, skies—and especially, continuing the astrological focus already mentioned, for "Texas stars, whose fiery orbs searched my soul, chased out the germs of slumber and bade me come to them." By extension, his dissenting stance in the face of oppression is an *ownership* of being an American, not a rejection of it. His work in civil rights and the work of his ancestors in building America gives him perhaps the greatest stake of all in the improvement and success of the country—and, by further extension, provided by the universal proportions of his astrological, Afrofuturistic metaphors, the *world*. To this day, the alternative histories provided by the texts of both Griggs and Delany contribute significantly to the reminder that the essential truth of history lies in the stories of those not part of the standard narrative of the dominant culture.

From the beginning, and contrary to its nationalistic myths, the identity of American has been, after all, *hybrid*, multi-racial—thanks to its founding, predominant blend of European, Native-American, and African cultures. And since the Declaration of Independence, the country's problems concerning race have made all so-called national "victories" fractured, partial, and incomplete. Furthermore, through the examples of *Blake* and *Imperium in Imperio*, the important

209

utility of Afrofuturism is made clear; through the application of the trope of alternative history. Delany and Griggs reveal *true* American history—not only "true" in how it dispels the whitewashing narrative of the hegemonic culture, but also "true" in how it depicts black revolution as American Revolution and how it is, in fact, the *continuance* of the American Revolution. Far from treasonous, the uncanny resemblance of American black insurrection to that of the eighteenth-century American colonists points toward the necessity of further realizing the revolution toward its completion.

Works Cited

Bhabha, Homi K. Foreward. *The Wretched of the Earth*. By Frantz Fanon Grove Press, 2004.

Delany, Martin R. *Blake; or the Huts of America*. Ed. Jerome McGann Harvard UP, 2017.

⸻. *The Condition, Elevation, Emigration, and Destiny of the Colored People of the United States* and *Official Report of the Niger Valley Exploring Party*. Humanity, 2004.

Delany, Samuel R. "Racism and Science Fiction." *Dark Matter: A Century of Speculative Fiction from the African Diaspora*. Ed. Sheree R. Thomas. Warner, 2000.

Douglass, Frederick. *Narrative of the Life of Frederick Douglass, An American Slave, Written by Himself*. Signet Classic, 1997.

Falola, Toyin. Introduction, Martin R. Delany. *The Condition, Elevation, Emigration, and Destiny of the Colored People of the United States* and *Official Report of the Niger Valley Exploring Party*. Humanity, 2004.

Fanon, Frantz. *The Wretched of the Earth*. Trans. Richard Philcox. Grove Press, 2004.

Griggs, Sutton E. *Imperium in Imperio*. The Modern Library, 2003.

⸻. *Wisdom's Call*. Griggs, 1911.

McGann, Jerome. Introduction to Martin R. Delany. Ed. Jerome McGann. *Blake; or the Huts of America*. Harvard UP, 2017.

Memmi, Albert. *The Coloniser and the Colonised.* Beacon Press, 1967.

Mosley, Walter. "Black to the Future." *Dark Matter: A Century of Speculative Fiction from the African Diaspora.* Ed. Sheree R. Thomas. Warner, 2000.

Saunders, Charles R. "Why Blacks Should Read (and Write) Science Fiction." *Dark Matter: A Century of Speculative Fiction from the African Diaspora.* Ed. Sheree R. Thomas. Warner, 2000.

Thomas, Sheree R. Introduction. *Dark Matter: A Century of Speculative Fiction from the African Diaspora.* Warner, 2000.

Verdelle, A.J. Preface to Sutton E. Griggs. *Imperium in Imperio.* The Modern Library, 2003.

West, Cornel. Introduction to Sutton E. Griggs. *Imperium in Imperio.* The Modern Library, 2003.

Chapter 8

Re-Writing Conventions and Female Resistance: Zora Neale Hurston's *Their Eyes Were Watching God* and Harriet Jacobs's *Incidents in the Life of a Slave*

Elizabeth N.M. Ayuk-Etang

Contemporary cultural studies have provided literary scholars with critical tools that have enabled them not only to make canonical literary texts relevant to a wider audience, but also to appreciate the works of marginalized writers like Black Women. The voice of the black woman has been silenced for a long time and her image has received serious shocks and dents resulting from certain stereotypes. Lloyd Brown in *Women Writers in Black Africa*, laments that the voices of black women are unheard, rarely discussed, and seldom accorded space in the repetitive anthologies and predictably male oriented studies in the field (88). This is partly because until the second half of the twentieth century, most of the images of black women presented in literary texts came from men. Deborah Gray White confirms in *Ar'n't I a Woman* that, "slave women were everywhere, yet nowhere" (23). Loucynda Jensen in "Searching the Silence: Finding Black Women's Resistance to Slavery in Antebellum U.S History" concurs when she interprets White's thoughts thus: "She meant that they were ever present in the physical world of antebellum slavery, yet their lives are nearly impossible to find in writing from the time" (135).

However, a few black women wrote autobiographies and fiction during the nineteenth and early part of the twentieth century, although most of their works were dismissed as lacking in literary merit. Among these early women writers are Harriett Jacob and Zora Neale Hurston, authors of *Incidents in the life of a Slave Girl* and *Their*

Eyes Were Watching God respectively. Jensen in her historical analysis of black women's writings to slave narratives concurs:

> Research and publications searching for an in-depth understanding of the slave experience did not become popular until the 1970s, and even then women were largely absent from the discussion. Thanks to an upsurge in black feminist scholarship on slavery... Before this time it would be safe to say that they were ignored as individuals with their own pasts. (136)

The past of systemic slavery was neither totally ignored nor was it totally documented. During the last quarter of the twentieth century and into the twenty first century, slave discourse has attracted a lot of criticisms especially in the area of the lives of black female slaves in the antebellum United States of America (USA) and post slavery era respectively. Toni Morison in *Beloved*, Angela Davis in *Women, Race and Class*, Deborah Gray White in *Ar'n't I a Woman* and Loucynda Jesen in "Searching the Silence: Finding Black Women's Resistance to Slavery in Antebellum U.S History" are amongst the voices that have presented and examined the slave woman's experience in the USA. Validates that the black slave woman used abortion and infanticide as a technique of resistance to slave breeding (136). On her part, Angela Davis "focuses on the gendered aspect of resistance, [...] and their resistance was often 'more subtle than revolts, escapes, and sabotage" (qtd. in Jensen 137). It is in this light that this study focuses more on attitudinal resistance, which is subtle and eventually leads to revolts to use Davis words. It also seeks to demonstrate the challenges encountered by/reactions of the black woman in a predominantly chauvinist, racist, and inhumane society as exhibited in Zora Neale Hurston's *Their Eyes Were Watching God* and Harriet Jacobs's *Incidents in the life of a Slave Girl*. This study posits that, the enslaved female characters during slavery and post slavery eras challenged the oppressive conventional stereotypes against their individuality from their white husbands (rapists) and slave masters as demonstrated by Janie and Linda Brent in *Their Eyes Were Watching God* and *Incidents in the Life of a Slave Girl* respectively. Based on the above argument, the study is framed around a number of questions. What dehumanizing activities characterize the lives of female characters in Zora Neale Hurston's *Their Eyes Were Watching God* and Harriet Jacobs's *Incidents in the Life of a Slave Girl*? How do they resist the status quo? And how do the authors remonstrate against the oppression mentality? The aforementioned narratives fall within the premise of resistant literature.

The concept of 'resistance' in literature and radical feminism as theoretical constructs in the analysis of the texts undergird the analysis hereafter. Resistance presents tenets such as the non-fundamentality of shared sets of attitudes, values, worldviews, or judgment about what makes good life in identifying communities, the need for community, more dynamism with permeable membranes, and negotiable boundaries. It also includes the idea that intra-communal discussions elude attempts to understand member interest and voices, the concept of epistemic injustice, by which a group of people governs another through conversations out of claims of incompetence. Phillip Ricks in "A Theory of Resistance" perceives the woman as essentially passionate, irrational and therefore incapable of ruling herself. Such narratives are said to devalue their victims. Resistance literature as a genre of theoretical concepts in literary studies portrays the writer's scuffle against dominant ideologies. It challenges socio-economic and political norms and defies hegemonic institutions, cosmologies and systems, strategies and acts of domination. It is an open expression of rebellion for the powerless spirits around the world, and a defiance of hegemony practiced on the oppressed. Resistant literature is a global phenomenon that has emerged out of the political conflict between Western imperialism and non-Western indigenes' resistance movement. Besides, the purpose of this kind of literature is to express particular sentiments against a colonizer or an aggressor either directly or indirectly.

Resistance literature equally informs readers about some of the urgent political and cultural debates taking place within the liberation movement. Ines Mzali in "Postcolonial Reading of Resistance and Negotiation in Selected Contemporary African Writing" writes that literature contests, resists, and negotiates the representation of postcolonial violence in Africa in ways that challenge official narrative and historicized representations (23). Resistance discourse changes as national elites often use it to legitimize their position and their recuperation of the power to exert violence. He further argues that a combination of the disillusionment caused by post-independence conflicts and the prominence of post-structuralism in the humanities contributed to another shift in the concept of resistance discourse (32). Barbara Harlow, in *Resistant Literature*, affirms that literary resistance is "an integral part of organized struggle" (iv). In the same light, Rosario M. de Swanson in "Literature as Resistance: The Works of Rosario Castellanos" confirms that literature can also be an act of resistance. Marginal writers (those who occupy positions at the margins of established literary canon), often do not see themselves or their people represented in what they read. They can resist this exclusion or omission simply by representing themselves in their own works. Swanson argues that these types of works as literary interventions are purposeful acts of resistance by representation that can produce change. Because these interventions can and do have a real effect upon society, disrupting long-held views of certain groups of people or individuals, and making the world more tolerant and more inclusive of diverse perspectives (2-3). To a greater extent, Harriet Jacobs and Zora Neale Hurston would be classified as inclusive writers of resistance as they represent themselves and their experiences in their own works *Incidents in the Life of a Slave Girl* and *Their Eyes were Watching God* respectively.

Also, a feminist reading of the aforementioned texts is necessary to identify and define the women's place and space in their respective societies and eras. Feminism as a compendium of movements is aimed at defining, establishing, and defending equal political, economic, and social rights and equal opportunities for women. During the pre-independent era, that is, the 19th century, women's movements began as social reform movements. Kathy Lay and James G. Daley in "A Critique of Feminist Theory" expound that feminism has evolved in different arenas rather than as one unified concept. The labels that define those arenas vary from the first to the third waves with different ideological stances. So, the underlying goal of feminist discourses is women emancipation and liberation. However, radical feminists are out to dismantle patriarchy. This study makes use of this arm of feminism because of the attribution of the oppression of women to men. They also argue that, male power calls for critical analysis, understanding, and not a mere reduction to simplistic explanations such as labor relations.

Radical feminism is a philosophical movement that emerged around the 1960s within liberal and working class feminists, emphasizing the patriarchal roots of inequality between men and women, or, more specifically, the social domination of women by men. Radical feminism views patriarchy as dividing societal rights, privileges, and power primarily along the lines of sex, and privileging men. Radical feminists tend to be skeptical of political action within the current system and instead tend to focus on cultural change that undermines patriarchy and associated hierarchical structures.

Cynthia V. Ward in "The Radical Feminist Defense of Individualism" writes that, radical feminist theory challenges not merely in imperfect realization of equal rights but the root concepts of individualism, rational liberation, and freedom through autonomy that underlie "liberal legalism". Radical theory breaks out into several problems of unequally realized rights but as a result, systematic and deliberate victimization of women by a socially constructed male hierarchy that is reinforced by liberal law. Radical feminism believes that liberal ideas of individual rights and autonomy-based justice are not merely the wrong way to end sex inequality but help to perpetuate it, since they reflect inherently male ways of being. Thus, radical feminists delineate and defend a substantive vision of women's

217

collective oppression around which they can organize political and legal reforms. To prove that liberal legalism is innately male, feminism must construct a "woman's point of view" which in the first place allows it to perceive male domination and then gives it a base from which to fight against such domination in the name of women as a group. Radical feminist theory attempts to draw clear and necessary connections between exposing the gender hierarchy, demonstrating its perpetuation under "liberal legalism" and arguing for non-liberal methods of ending it (873).

This paper assumes Jelena Vuocic's standpoint by which the main trait of this feminist attitude (radical) lies in the study and the need for reconsideration of the source of power and desire for repression, which is attributed to the complex social factors which are constructed and not innate and essential (36). According to her, they are strong advocates against the image of the woman, constructed in the language fiction and in their personal lives through institutions that favor male dominance including the church and traditional family models. Furthermore, under scrutiny are ways by which patriarchy systematically uses oppression, the objectification of the woman, discrimination, and socio-cultural stereotyping to make naturally disadvantaged people like women, to realities that characterized the eras in which the texts under study are set and were produced.

The explanation above suggests the presence of two groups in society, namely, the oppressor and the oppressed. The former perpetrates activities that should not be tolerated in a fair society, on the latter who more often than not, is in the perpetrator's power. This general trait—of overwhelming abuse and social, political, and human exploitation by the oppressor—grounds both Zora Neale Hurston's *Their Eyes Were Watching God* and Harriet Jacobs' *Incidents in the Life of a Slave Girl*. In them, the authors seem to join their characters in decrying oppression, especially, that of the woman during the respective antebellum slavery and post slavery epochs. Their language reflects this reality since according to Harlow, all resistance literature does involve everything "…as it does question the writer and background as well as issues of readership and audience" (xviii). This is exemplified in the slave narratives heretofore examined.

Slave narratives have portrayed man's inhumanity to man, the memory and pains which are irreparable. Women's experiences during slavery and post slavery eras are undesirable as they portray gender inequality and confirm the violation of women's basic human rights. It is in observance of such violations that Deborah Gray White in *Revisiting Ar'n't I a Woman?* states that:

African-American women were close to invisible in historical writing, not because there was no need or audience for black women's history. Rather, black women were invisible because few historians saw them as important contributors to America's social, economic and political development, and few publishers identified an audience for books that connected black women's thoughts and experiences to the history of other Americans (3 - 4).

Harriet Jacobs and Zora Neale Hurston are examples of these women who have succeeded in documenting their repressed pains of sexual exploitation and violation through their autobiographical fictions; *Incidents in the life of a slave Girl* and *Their Eyes were watching God* respectively. This is because most of the "slave narratives published before the civil war were written by men, and those written by black women did not touch on the verboten subject" according to Meriwether (iv). Jacobs uses the pseudonym Linda Brent to capture through characterization, the tumultuous life of bondage and sexual abuse that countless of black women have suffered an in the hands of their slave masters. Hurston's narrative captures the life of a black woman whose individuality is suppressed by her supposed protégé. Their uncompromised slyness enabled her to develop resistant tendencies towards man. In this novel, Janie is cast as a victim of circumstances. Janie's grandmother, Nanny marries her off to Logan Killicks albeit against her will and her tender age. Forced marriage is, to many, a form of gender-based violence. However, Nanny professes that it is to protect Janie from bringing unwanted pregnancy and shame to the family just as her mother did. Gender-based violence is known to be the onus practice of human rights violation (CEDAW 1979, Maputo Protocol 2005). It includes, but not limited to sexual harassment/violence, physical and domestic violence, verbal and emotional abuse, child marriage as well as female genital mutilation (Ayuk-Etang 2019). The child (Janie) is deprived of her basic right to choose a friend, a partner, or a husband in *Their Eyes Were Watching God*.

This type of arranged marriage is often based upon interest, and not love. Killicks shoves Janie to work on the farm or split wood. Under normal marital conditions, the woman's reproductive role and gender division of labour requires that she does the cleaning, cooking, and even fetches water and fuel woods. Janie's refusal to do these chores apparently stems from the relationship that existed between the slave-owners and the plantation workers. Going back to work on the plantation or farm, according to her is seemingly a retrospection of slave life. He instructs her; "If Ah kin haul de wood heah and chop it fuh yuh, look lak you oughta be able tuh tote it inside. Mah fust wife never bothered me 'bout choppin' no wood nohow. She'd grab dat a and sling chips lak uh man. Youn done been spoilt rotten" (26). As a result, the marriage bore hatred, suspicion and oppression. Janie's marriage relationship to Killings confirms White's argument that, "women's right during slavery were inhibited and 'many women's right advocates likened the husband – wife relationship to that of master and slave" (15). John Stuart Mill endorses White's argument in "The Subjugation of Women" that, the "wife is the actual bond servant of her husband…" (qtd. in White 15). Consequently, Kellick's marriage to Janie, in the context of the story is perceived, as another exhibition of female oppression during slavery.

Furthermore, Harriet Jacobs's *Incidents in the Life of a Slave Girl* also features Linda Brent who suffers untold hardship and sexual harassment from Dr Flint, her slave master. Dr Flint "had stormy terrific ways that made his victims tremble" (35). This character trait that the narrator vividly describes with words like 'stormy' and 'terrific' exemplifies attributes of a brute that resonate oppression and pain in the lives of his victims. Linda Brent, the supposed mouthpiece of Jacobs confirms; "He peopled my young mind with unclean images, such as only a vile monster could think of. I turned from him with disgust and hatred" (35). Linda's life in Dr Flint's house is characterized by episodic violence. She laments: "I cannot tell you how much I suffered in the presence of these wrongs, nor how I am still pained by the retrospect" (36). Linda's agony is irreparable. She is just one of the other female slave victims who could not voice their repression. As a result, her "heart became heavy with sad forebodings" (36).

Linda's resistance to Dr Flint pushes her to accept Mr. Sand's love proposal, though a mirage, but bore two children for him, children who by implication become Dr Flint's properties. Linda is compelled to protect her children amidst many unpleasant circumstances. There is only so much that can be taken of the displeasures that these ladies are compelled by conventions to live with. While Janie's dream to find true love is thwarted by forced marriage, Linda's liberty is tainted by Dr Flint with a variant of sexual harassment and destabilizations. These subversions of women continue in post slavery era.

Also, when Janie, in *Their Eyes Were Watching God*, observes that Killicks subjugating attitude is by design, she abandons him for Joe Starks. Joe being a persuasive and fluent orator cajoles her into a love relationship when he says she is "hardly old enough to be weaned" because he believes that she "still craves sugar-tits" (28). He continues; "You ain't got no business cuttin'up no seed p'taters neither. A pretty doll-baby lak you is made to sit on the front porch and rock and fan yo'self nd eat p'taters dat other folks plant just special for you" (29). Coming from an undesirable marriage, Janie is flattered by Joe's love confession decides to escape with Joe. Listening to Joe, "... a feeling of sudden newness and change came over her. Janie hurried out of the front gat and turned south. Even if Joe was not waiting for her, the change was bound to do her good" (32). This feeling of love that grips Janie was short-lived. Joe eventually demonstrates his chauvinistic tendencies that communicate worthlessness to her. Her opinions were always rejected and Joe explains; "Ah never married her for nothin' lak dat. She'uh woman and her place is in de home" (43). Joe relegates her to the background and limits her functions to reproductive roles. Joe further restricts Janie's interaction with the public. He threatens her thus:

> You'se Mrs. Mayor Starks, Janie. I god, Ah can't ssee what uh woman yo' stability would want tuh be treasurin'all dat gum-grease from folks dat don't even own de house dey sleep in.'Tain't no earthly use. They's jus'some puny humans playin round de toes uh Times. (54)

According to Janie, Joe's attitude is annoying and undesirable. This leaves her feeling entangled and restricted. His negative energies toward Janie exhibit repression and cruelty towards her. This is evident when Joe dissociates her from the community members and insists she ties a scarf on her hair before sitting in the store. "Her hair was NOT going to show in the store…She was there in the store for him to look at, not those others" (55). Joe's attitude should not be read as jealousy, but as oppressive. Janie suffers from psychological violence and verbal abuse when Joe insults her saying; "A woman who stay round uh store till she get old as Methuselah and still can't cut a little thing like a plug of tobacco! Don't stand dere rollin' yo' pop eyes at me wid yo'rump hangin' nearly to yo' knees". (78). As the Mayor of Eatonville, Joe's attitude is disheartening. Linda and Janie's experiences are similar though they existed in different epochs.

As such, when attention is turned to *Incidents in the life of a Slave Girl,* Linda's master, Dr Flint torments her because she is obstinate and vehemently turns down his sexual advances. She explains:

> I suffered in the presence of these wrongs, nor how I am still pained by the retrospect. My master met me at every turn, reminding me that I

222

belonged to him, and swearing by heavens and earth that he would compel me to submit to him. If I went out for a breath of fresh air, after a day of unwearied toil, his footsteps dogged me. If I knelt by my mother's grave, his dark shadow fell on me even there. The light heart which nature had given me became heavy with sad forebodings. (36)

The omnipresence of this man constitutes both a physical and a mentally traumatic anguish to this slave girl. While it is worth noting that Linda and Janie tolerate their perpetrator's excesses for a while, the recurrence in perpetuity drives these victims to resist their perpetrators in unprecedented modus of revolt and resistance.

Women have often been taken for the 'weaker vessel', and given second-class citizens status and treatment, because men constitute the repressive agents within a system and not a gender. This is evident during slavery and post slavery eras whereby the policies and practices in those communities were phallocentric. The system provoked Sojourner Truth's multi- million question and reiterated by Deborah Gray White and other critics "Ar'n't I a woman?" This question resonates the ill feeling an inferior status the back woman grapples with at the time. This is ambiguous, given that from the novels, female subjugation and oppression are structural and systemic. The oppressors epitomize the system that put the regulations in force. Thus, it calls for attention to be given female resistance while demonstrating the various forms of resistance put up by women in the texts under study as they attempt to emancipate themselves and reassert their womanhood.

Zora Neale Hurston in *Their Eyes were Watching God*, presents a pathetic picture of how black women are suppressed and dominated by men in their various societies. The narrative also focuses on the attempts made by some of these women to resist or revolt against the male dominated society. The story narrated in the form of a flashback presents Janie, whose childhood dream of finding a lover is crushed by the realities of her society. As a victim of circumstances, she struggles and revolts against the patriarchal institution in her

223

community, symbolized in the text by her husband.

As the protagonist of the novel, Janie's grandmother forces her to marry Logan Killicks after Nanny discovers that Janie has started entertaining men. This parental pressure results in Janie accepting to marry Killicks. Upon marrying her, Killicks wants Janie to work in the farm or split wood like his ex-wife. This is buttressed in the novel when he says,

> If Ah kin haul de wood heah and chop it fuh yuh, look lak you oughta be able tuh tote it inside. Mah fust wife never bothered me 'bout choppin' no wood nohow. She'd grab dat a and sling chips lak uh man. Youn done been spoilt rotten (26).

Here, Logan wants his new bride to be as hardworking as the first. However, Janie makes him understand that, though she is married to him, it is his duty to do all that he is requesting of her. This is a subtle but potent reminder that the woman must neither submit nor subject to any and every thing that her husband says. To her marriage is not tantamount to dereliction of duty by the husband. She makes her stance clear by stating that, "Ah'm just as stiff as you is stout. If you can stand not to chop and tote wood Ah reckon you can stand not to git no dinner. 'Scuse mah freezolity, Mist' Killicks, but Ah don't mean to chop de first chip" (26). Here, Janie refuses to be like other women or better still like the ex-wife of her husband who works tirelessly to project herself as a good housewife. Thus, one sees how Janie resists the domineering attitude of most black men in America by setting her own rules. She insists that if her husband wants to eat, he must split wood and bring it inside the house. It should be noted that, forced marriages are some of the vices that most women suffer from in postcolonial societies and Janie, as a voice of the author, is determined to confront and nullify this patriarchal stereotype by setting her own set of rules

As mentioned earlier, Joe's first love impression was assuring to Janie that he tells her she is "hardly old enough to be weaned" because he believes that she "still craves suger-tits" (28). You ain't got no business cuttin'up no seed p'taters neither. A pretty doll-baby lak you is made to sit on the front porch and rock and fan yo'self nd eat p'taters dat other folks plant just special for you" (29). When Janie hears this, she is convinced that Joe has some profound feelings towards her. This prompts her to run away with Joe Starks and as the narrator says "... A feeling of sudden newness and change came over her. Janie hurried out of the front gate and turned south. Even if Joe was not waiting for her, the change was bound to do her good" (32). Here, Janie's resistance against male domination stems from the fact that she abandons her first husband and goes away with the second without the consent of the first. As a Feminist advocate, she feels it is her right to determine her emotional needs and needs not consult anybody to do so. The author here emphasizes women's liberty to make choices in relation to their emotional needs.

Moreover, Janie fights against the domineering and authoritative attitude of her husband Joe. It should be noted that in most patriarchal societies, it is said that women are supposed to be seen and not heard. What this pre-supposes is that a woman is considered a subaltern whose voice is not supposed to be heard when it comes to taking decisions. She is seen serving her husband food and fulfilling some biological assignments; but in issues that concern the entire community, she is pushed to the marginal sphere of the community. When Janie marries Joe, she is made to understand that she has no right to take part in major decisions or discourse. Joe constantly hushes her down each time she tries to give an opinion. This is evident when Joe says "Ah never married her for nothin' lak dat. She'uh woman and her place is in de home" (43). Joe is projected by the author here as a typical male chauvinist who has little or no respect for the woman and this is amongst the many vices that the author of *Their Eyes were Watching God* sets out to lambast. As an elected mayor, Joe is criticized by his constituent for illtreating Janie. This is an indication that mindsets are gradually changing in relation to the role of women in decision making. Society is beginning to consider women not only as people who should be seen but as those to whom men should equally listen.

Similarly, Joe's jealousy and authoritative attitude towards Janie is further demonstrated in the novel when he orders her not to mingle with the masses. He relegates his wife to a second-class position and this is evident in the novel when he says,

> You'se Mrs. Mayor Starks, Janie. I god, Ah can't ssee what uh woman yo' stability would want tuh be treasurin'all dat gum-grease from folks dat don't even own de house dey sleep in. "Tain't no earthly use. They's jus'some puny humans playin round de toes uh Times. (54)

Joe's oppressive and authoritative attitude makes Janie feel entangled and inactive. This is because, each time she tries to mingle, she is either sent to the store or asked to get into the house. She however, does not appreciate this treatment from her husband because she wants to be useful to both herself and her community by engaging in interactive and constructive discussions. Her jealous and authoritative husband wants her to either sit around doing nothing, or be in the store where she cannot be seen. Janie's misery is further enhanced when she is asked by Joe to constantly tie a headscarf while at the store. One can see therefore that Joe's jealous, authoritative and chauvinistic lifestyle transforms his wife to a house help and this is what the author of this novel frowns at and denounces.

From the novel, one realizes that the more Joe becomes authoritative, the more resistant Janie becomes. For example, Janie starts resisting Joe's repressive rules when she tells him that "Everybody can't be lak you, Jody. Somebody is bound tuh laugh and play" (62). Here she is by implication telling her husband that she wants to feel free to mingle, laugh and do things like everybody. Her resistance and assertiveness are further demonstrated when the narrator says

226

Janie did what she had never done before, that is, thrust herself into the conversation…. Sometimes God gits familiar wid us womenfolks too and talks His inside business. He told me how surprised He was 'about y'all truning out so smart after Him makin' yuh different; and howsuprised y'all is goin' to be if you ever find out you don't know half as much 'bout us as you think you do. It's so easy to make yo'self out God Almighty when you ain't got nothin' tuh strain against but women and chickens. (75)

Joe's violent and abusive nature precipitates the constant resistance one notices in Janie.

Further still, throughout the novel, one notices a genuine attempt by Janie to emancipate herself both mentally and physically. Through her resistance, she gains the courage to tell Joe Starks the bitter truth about himself just before he dies. Her freedom is further expressed when she takes off the headscarf that her husband had forced her to wear and stands before the mirror. This is evident when the narrator says:

She thought back and forth about what had happened in the making of a voice out of a man. Then thought about herself. Years ago, she had told her girl friend to wait for her in the looking glass. It had been a long time since she remembered. Perhaps she'd better look. She went to the dresser and looked hard at her skin and features. The young girl was gone, but a handsome woman had taken her place. She tore off the kerchief from her head and let down her plentiful hair. The weight, the length, the glory was still there. She took a careful stock of herself, then combed her hair and tied it up back again. (87)

Her sense of freedom is heightened when the narrator says "Before she slept that night she burnt up every one of her head rags and went about the house next morning with her hair in one thick braid swinging well below her waist" (89). Here, one sees a woman who is not only a strong advocate of feminism but who is determined to break all the chains that impose limits on her freedom to speak and act the way she wants. Taking off the headscarf symbolizes freedom and liberty; that is, taking off a burden.

As mentioned earlier, Janie's defiance is not only against her husbands, but against the system. She has eventually become a rich woman, and is expected to marry a man of 'that' class, and not a gambler like Tea cake. According to Janie, she needs a 'room of her own', to use Virginia Woolf's words. Janie needs her love space, not a space that is determined by others. When Pheoby tells her that "Folks think you ain't payin' de right amountuh respect tuh yo'dead husband" (113), Janie tells her that the world has always told people what to do and how to dress. She says that mourning Joe in black is because Joe did not pick a color for her when he was alive that is why she had to wear "Black" as a sign of mourning. She further tells Pheoby that she is wearing it then just to please the world, but that she has decided to dress in bright colors because Tea Cake loves them. Janie's dressing in colored clothes tells her story of resistance and outright rejection of the 'supposed' norms and standards expectations. She tells Pheoby that, the only man she loves and admires is the gambler, Tea Cake. Through Tea Cake, Janie learns to be more assertive and self-confident. When she notices the side-talk about her relationship with Tea Cake especially from the womenfolk, she retorts:

> … Tell'em dat love ain't somethin' lak uh grindstone dat's de same thing everywhere and do de same thing tuh everything it touch. Love is lak de sea. It's uh movin' thing, but still and all, it takes its shape from de shore it meets, and it's different with every shore (191).

Janie's expression of love demonstrates a sense of direction and emotional peace. She sees love as a 'wing – wing' thing, it resonates differently, depending on who/what you want. Her concluding statements are reassuring to her thus "…it takes its shape from de shore it meets, and it's different with every shore (191).

Hurston's *Their Eyes Were Watching God* evolves with Janie, from confrontational character (in her relationship with Killicks and Joe) to a 'supposedly' loving woman. However, her love to Tea Cake does not make her lay down her 'arms' against chauvinism/stereotypes that hinder the evolution of the woman.

Similarly, though from a slightly different context and perspective, Harriet Jacobs' slave narrative *Incidents in the Life of a Slave* paints a gruesome and dehumanizing picture of some of the realities that women go through in male dominated societies. The writer presents the life of a slave girl Linda Brent, who suffers untold hardships in the hands of her slave master, Dr Flint. Due to the hardship and psychological trauma this lady and other black women go through in the hands of their slave masters, these women revolt in different ways. As a result of her torture and trauma, resistance becomes a condition sine qua non for her emancipation.

Linda Brent is an example of a phenomenal slave or black woman who fights against the ills of slavery meted not only on her but on her children. Unlike other female slave characters who fall under the cruel treatment of slavery, Linda speaks up by telling her master what she thinks and feels or how she thinks a human being ought to be treated. This is seen when she says: "sometimes, I so openly expressed my contempt for him that he would become violently enraged, and I wonder why he did not strike me...In desperation I told him that I must and would apply to my grandmother for protection" (40). Linda makes this statement after Dr Flint starts making sexual advances towards her and threatening to kill her. Jensen believes that black female slaves resistance on reproductive decisions, were not only against slaveholders, but also against the system of slavery and oppression itself (136).

Linda's attitude against Dr Flint's sexual advances confirms Jensen's argument when she tells Dr Flint; "I would rather be sold to anybody than to lead such a life as I did" (44). Linda is an assertive and resistant female slave who is very courageous. She is just one of the numerous black female slaves whose attitude towards her master

229

is not indifferent, and her resistance is in-depth. Her responses to Dr Flint, the master are apparently not in conformity with his thoughts. This is evident when the narrator says; "he has reasons of his own for screening her from punishment, and that the course he pursued made her mistress hate her and persecute her" (44). Linda's attitude portrays that resistance could be verbal, confrontational or physical.

When Linda's attitude becomes confrontational, Dr Flint, on his part, becomes furious and aggressive, and strikes her for loving someone else. This can be interpreted as resistance/resistance principle (my coinage) which pushes both parties at the end of 'rope'. Linda finally retorts: "You have struck me for answering you honestly. How I despise you" (50). Linda is not ready to become a slave breeder unlike other female slaves whose children look very much like their masters. Wilma King, in "Suffer with them till Death: Slave Women and their Children in Nineteenth Century America reveals that:

> American slaveholders viewed motherhood as an asset, and they encourage reproduction for pecuniary reasons… 'the slave women and their children were considered chattel instead of persons',… slaves women were 'unable to control their fertility or make necessary decisions about their own bodies. (qtd. in Jensen 144)

As mentioned earlier, Linda is able to control her fertility and her body. She refuses to make her progeny chattel, and this spurs a lot of antagonism between her and her master. She voluntarily falls in love with Mr Sands and bore three children for him. Her actions traumatize Dr Flint and affect his relationship with Aunt Martha, Linda's grandmother negatively. As a result, Linda escapes from the master and hid herself in a cubicle in her grandmother's house for about seven years just to resist Dr Flint's advances and brutality.

Linda does not only revolt against Dr Flint, but also against the norms of the system especially in relation to education. She learns to read and write from her mistress. There was always a search team of whites going around looting black homes. Mr. Litch led this search/looting team. In a conversation with Linda, Litch becomes when he notices that Linda could read. (84). Her (in)formal education is unacceptable by the norms governing slaves seems to be rebellious, coupled with the fact that she sends her children to school. Linda is by implication saying education can no longer be considered a privilege for women. Education thus becomes a means through which she empowers herself, re-asserts her womanhood and redefines her identity.

The pivot of Linda's revolt and resistance against male domination is noticed when she escapes from the Flint's household in quest for freedom. According to her, she is ready to either gain liberty or face death. This is evident when she says "when I started upon this hazardous undertaking, I had resolved that come what would, there should be no turning back. Give me liberty or give me death" (124). In her quest for freedom, she gets help from several black women like Betty, Aunty Nancy, Aunt Martha, her grandmother. These women's assistance to Linda is important and worth mentioning, because they directly or indirect rejects the dehumanizing system of slavery. Linda's eventual status as a fugitive slave could not be achieved without their support. Women solidarity and sisterhood are put together to send Linda forth, from the antebellum slave South to freedom in the North of America where she rejoins her children and lives in harmony.

Having set out to examine the challenges that characterized the lives of women in two societies specifically in the slavery and post slavery epochs, the unpleasant realities that characterized the lives of these women as projected in the two slave narratives have been brought to the fore as underlying revolt and resistance. The above analyses reveal that there are many insurmountable challenges faced by ladies in their respective societies due to the nature of the standards set for women as represented in texts. The permanence with which the burdens of insult, abuse, intimidation and insults and exploitations recur in the texts towards the different characters pushes them to resist and fight back. While it can be seen that the

Nanny and Aunt Martha, Linda's grandmother, are of the old generation who might not be comfortable with the system, and the black woman's space. They could negotiate their survival and that of their children diplomatically. On the other hand, the children (next generation), resist their oppressors verbally, and physically emerge as firebrand characters whose actions are capable of causing a change in the law through their actions. Going by the tenet in Rick's Theory of Resistance, Harriet Jacob's *Incidents in the Life of a Slave Girl* and Zora Neale Hurston's *Their Eyes Were Watching God* use their texts to bare private and secret sufferings and torture of the oppressed to seek redress in new laws and in life. Resistance as seen in the above analysis becomes an unavoidable ideology towards deconstructing and delegitimizing gender and cultural stereotypes that stands as a barrier to the emancipation of the woman. It thus becomes a means of reasserting the image and identities of the postcolonial woman.

Works Cited

Zora Neale Hurston: *Their Eyes Were Watching God*. HarperCollins Publishers 1937.

Harriet Jacobs. *Incidents in the life of a Slave Girl*. Washington Square Press.

Secondary Sources

Abowitz Kathleen K. "A Pragmatist Revisioning of Resistance Theory" *American Educational Research Journal* 2000 Vol 37. No. 4. 877-907

Atkinson, Ti-Grace. *Radical Feminism*. Feminist, 1969.

Ayuk-Etang, Elisabeth N.M. "Gender-Based Violence and Victims' Access to Justice in Selected Cameroonian Literary Works". In African Humanities Review: A Multidisciplinary Journal. 5. (2). 2019, 98 – 114.

Davis, Angela. *Women, Race and Class*. Random House,1981.

DeShazer, Mary K. *A Poetics of Resistance: Women Writing in El Salvador, South Africa, and the United State*. U of M Press, 1994.

Finkleman, Paul. "Slavery in the United states Persons or Property". In *The Legal Understanding of Slavery: From the Historical to the Contemporary*. Ed

Jean Allain, 2012, 105 -134.

Harlow, Barbara. *Resistance Literature*. Routledge, 1987.

Henry, Akem. "Migration and the Politics of Comfort in Priscilia Manjo's *Snare* and Noviolet Bulawayo's *We Need New Names*" *Academia.Edu/ Afribrary.com* June 2019

Hinshelwood, Brad. "The Carolinian Context of John Locke's theory on slavery" in *Journal of Political Theory*. 41. (4), 2013, 562-590.

Jensen, Loucynda. "Searching the Silence: Finding Black Women's Resistance to slavery in Antebellum U.S History" PSU McNair Scholars Online Journal. 2 (1) 2006, 135 – 161.

Lay, Kathy and James G. Daley. "A Critique of Feminist Theory" in *Advances in Social Work*. 8 (1), 2007

Mackinnon, A. Catherine. *Towards a Feminist Theory of Law and State* Harvard UP, 1989.

Mzali, Ines. Postcolonial Reading of Resistance and Negotiation in Selected Contemporary African Writing." University of Montreal (thesis). 2011.

Nayyer, Abbas Nasir. Resistance in Literature. Nov. 26, 2007 access, Dec. 2, 2020 from
(https://www.thenews.com.pk/tns/details/564447-resistance-literature).

Ricks, Philip. *A Theory of Resistance. Doctoral Thesis,* University of Iowa, 2017.

Robinson, Jeffery. "Five Truths about Black History" *ACLU* Accessed 31 October 2020.

Swanson, de Rosario. *Literature as Resistance: The Works of Rosario Castellanos. Emerson College*, The Public Humanist. 2019.

The Characteristics of Resistance Literature In African American

Literature.   www.123helpme.com>essay>the-characteristics-0f-
resistance-literature-in-african-american-literature: accessed, Dec.
2 2020.

Ward, Cynthia V. "The Radical Feminist Defense of Individualism".
William and Mary Law School: Faculty Publication, 89 (3) 1995,
879 – 892.

Walker, Margaret Urban. *Moral Understandings: A Feminist Study in
Ethics.* Routledge, 2007.

White, Deborah Gray. *Ar'n't I a Woman? Female Slaves in the Plantation
South.* W.W. Norton, 1985.

Woodbridge, Linda. "Resistance Theory Meets Drama: Tudor Seneca"
Renaissance Drama, New Series Vol 38. 115-139.

Chapter 9

Dr. Walter Rodney:
Historian and Voice for the Black Working Class

John Tilghman

Introduction

Walter Rodney championed the liberation of working-class people in the African Diaspora for much of his shortened life. Trevor Campbell described Rodney best with the following statements: "He came from the masses, and he remained among them." The plight of poor and working-class African descendant people and the ill effects of the global capitalist economy shaped Rodney's worldview of creating a progressive society for the black masses. In a 1974 taped interview, with a scholarly journal titled the *Black Scholar*, Rodney identified his involvement in political activism as part of his "commitment to the working-class people." His reasons for this commitment, Rodney added, pertained to the working class's vulnerability to being exploited by capitalism. To advance the lives of the black masses in the world, he searched for solutions in history by studying slavery and colonialism in Africa and the Caribbean as well as its relationship to the global capitalist economy in order to explain how working-class people live. Rodney concluded that for the poor black working class to obtain liberation, they must mobilize people around issues concerning race, class, and adopt socialism as an alternative to capitalism in terms of governing a society. Rodney used speeches and published books to make such arguments.

Many scholars have successfully highlighted how Pan Africanism and a class analysis influenced Rodney's political and intellectual thoughts. Rodney's political thoughts on race and class shaped his philosophy of African and Caribbean independence and movements for Black Power and the working class. His political activism to working-class movements in the African world included forming coalitions with working-class Indians in the Caribbean. This chapter seeks to add to the previous scholar's work by illustrating how Rodney used historical research on slavery and colonialism as social activism to communicate with working-class movements on how to offset their conditions. The first section will highlight Rodney's philosophy on Black Power regarding mobilizing the black masses in Jamaica and the rest of the Caribbean. In his book titled, *The Grounding With My Brothers* (1969), Rodney theorized Black Power to the black masses in Jamaica to mount pressures on the elites in the Jamaican government. The second section will discuss Rodney's argument of how the global capitalism system played a major role in the underdevelopment of African countries after gaining independence. Using the book titled, *How Europe Underdeveloped Africa* (1972), Rodney illustrated how the political and economic relationship between colonial Africa with Western Europe had set a path for neocolonialism and continued exploiting African resources and fostering the underdevelopment of a continent. The underdevelopment of independent nations in African and the Caribbean had its roots in European colonialism. Rodney also uses *How Europe Underdeveloped Africa* to converse with the black working class, and show them how exacerbated their social-economic problems are, and finally he uses it to advocate for African nations to practice socialism. The chapter will end with Rodney's participation in the Workers People's Alliance (WPA) in Guyana during the last years of his life. Using his posthumous book, *A History of the Working Class Guyanese People, 1881-1905* (1981), Rodney created a guide for the future of how working-class Afro-Guyanese and Indian Guyanese could form and maintain interracial coalitions. The books mentioned in this chapter all highlight Rodney's argument that slavery and colonialism had offset how neocolonialism and global capitalism would negatively affect the lives of working-class people of African descent. A first look will be cast on *The Grounding with My Brothers.*

236

The Grounding with My Brothers and Black Power

The Grounding with My Brothers were a series of speeches on Black Power lectured by Rodney during his brief tenure as an instructor at UWI Mona campus at University of West Indies (UWI Mona campus) in 1968. Rodney talked to college students and professors on Black Power politics. He also toured Jamaica's urban and rural areas to visit the "sufferers," a term used to describe Jamaica's poor and working-class people. His lectures helped to foster conversations with the country's grassroots Black Nationalists and sufferers on black liberation. He touched on neocolonialism to describe the cause of the plight of poor and working-class Jamaicans in a nation that gained its independence from colonialism. After the Jamaican Parliament banned Rodney from the country and, after he lost his teaching job at UWI Mona campus, the Bogle-L'Ouverture Publications published his Black Power speeches into a book titled, *The Grounding With My Brothers*. The book established Rodney as a Black Power theoretician and a scholar-activist. Equally important, it allowed Rodney to articulate black liberation's meaning to the black masses by addressing white imperialism and class issues in the Caribbean.

Rodney's travels through Jamaica gave him access to Jamaica's class issues and multinational corporations in the country. Although Jamaica had gained its independence in 1962, the Jamaican elite, mostly the brown-skinned leadership class, worked with the U.S. and multinational corporations to have a stranglehold on the country's social and economic resources. U.S. and Canadian corporations also gained access to land to build hotels and resorts, which opened the island to tourists from the U.S. and Western Europe. Other multinational corporations such as Alcoa, Kaiser Bauxite, and Reynolds dominated the island's bauxite industry. The Jamaican Parliament granted land to the Royal Bank of Canada, the Canadian Imperial Bank of Commerce, the Bank of London and Montreal, and Woolworth department stores. To make way for these corporations, the Jamaican government forced the working class and poor people to move into the downtown area of Trench Town. The sufferers lived in shanty towns with no access to clean drinking water, employment, and proper education. Young Jamaicans were segregated from jobs in foreign banks and hotels in the tourist district. They were also restricted from public accommodations in shopping in department stores. In addition, they were denied patronage in the vacation and tourist sites—the socio-economic problems suffered by the Jamaican working classes and the poor after independence were much the same.

The socio-economic problems affecting Jamaica's masses helped Rodney to define Black Power, particularly for the Afro-Caribbeans. In his lecture titled, "Black Power- Its Relevance to the West Indies," Rodney explained Black Power as freedom from white imperialism, the empowerment of the black masses, and the reconstruction of society that benefits the black masses. By centering the poor black class and working class within the definition for Black Power, Rodney successfully articulated to the black masses to question the legitimacy of independence in the Caribbean. By using Black Power, Rodney justified the concept that independence in the Caribbean did not bring about a fundamental change in the daily lives of most Afro-Caribbeans even though the national independence from colonialism should have indeed brought about these changes to the black masses.

Along with centering the black masses at the Black Power movement, Rodney lectured on the importance of class-consciousness. He further opposed capitalism as an effective strategy for the black working-class. For Rodney, advocacy for socialism as an alternative for capitalism was essential to Black Power philosophy throughout the globe. When Rodney spoke that black people must separate from white imperialism, it also included the international capitalist economy. In the lecture, "African History in the Service of Black Revolution," he emphasized *Socialism and Rural Development*, an African socialist policy created by Tanzanian president Julius Nyerere, as an illustration of how the African continent could restore their traditional way of life as an alternative to participating in the international capitalist economy. Here, Rodney added that socialism would provide a more communal life for black people.

Rodney used history to illustrate that the black working class's exploitation and working poor had a history often associated with British capitalism. To demonstrate how the Caribbean's participation in the international capitalist economy had led to the exploitation of the black working class, Rodney used the history of slavery and colonialization in the British Caribbean and drew parallels on racism and exploitation of Afro-Caribbean people's labor with contemporary neocolonialism in Jamaica. In his lecture titled, "Black Power-Its Relevance to the West Indies," Rodney highlighted various major aspects of racial oppression and exploitation of labor in Caribbean history, slavery, and emancipation, the reinserting of British colonial rule after Paul Bogle's rebellion on Morant Bay in 1865, and Indian indentured servitude. He talked about these aspects of history to educate the black masses that neocolonialism in the Caribbean was a derivative of Great Britain's persistence to maintain colonial rule over the Caribbean. He told the audience that, "slavery, colonialism, and neocolonialism has always been a part of white capitalist society." Rodney illustrated to the black working class and poor an understanding of what had caused their socio-economic decline.

Rodney lectured on another aspect of Black Power to Jamaica's poor and working class; criticizing the Jamaican leadership class and politicians. Once again, Rodney used the history of Jamaica to describe the relationship between Jamaica's working-class people with the elites. Rodney referred to Caribbean elites as an extension of White Imperialism. In "Statement of the Jamaican Situation," Rodney claimed that Jamaica's ruling class was the "representation of the metropolitan-imperialist interests who would only identify with the black masses to suit their interest"; he asserted that the elite ruling class had "fallen to bribes of white imperialism."

In one of his lectures titled, "Statement of the Jamaica Situation," he demonstrated how the 1938 Jamaica worker's revolt on sugar plantations paved the way for the rise of the brown leadership class in the Jamaican Labour Party (JLP) and the People's National Party (PNP). The unemployed and poor Jamaicans had accepted the Jamaican elites as spokespeople for Jamaican independence, and in return, the brown elite class motivated the people of all complexions to unify around the motto "Out Of Many, One People." All the while, the Jamaican elite pretended to care about the plight of the working masses and aligned themselves with the comprador class who held ties to their counterparts in England and other Western European countries. Rodney explained, "But, paradoxical as it may appear, they [the comprador class] have been forced to create a psychological prop to their system of domination the myth of a harmonious, multiracial national society – "Out of Many, One People," as the National Motto pretends." He added, "In this way, they are hoping that the black masses will never organize independently in their own interests." Rodney's critique of Jamaican elites intended to identify class issues in Jamaican society among the poor and working classes, and the Jamaican elite, and to influence the black masses to obtain power. Moreover, Jamaican elites' criticisms allowed Rodney to equate Black Power with the liberation of the working class, instead of having leaders attempting to define Black Power as an independent nation with black leadership in the office while the masses of black people live in poverty. Jamaican Prime Minister Hugh Shearer attempted to persuade the Jamaican masses that the country had an all-black Parliament and claimed no skin discrimination had existed. They were the symbols of progress.

The Jamaican government did not share Rodney's views of Black Power. Those in power felt that Black Power as an ideology threatened black leadership and threatened their relationships with the United States and multinational corporations. More important, Rodney had mobilized the black working class in Jamaica. Then, Hugh Shearer referred to Black Power groups as racist and claimed that the term Black Power was a "threat to Jamaica's national security and the tourist attraction." Rodney and many other Black Power advocates in Jamaica were under an international counter-surveillance program initiated by the Jamaican and Guyanese Parliament, the British, and the U.S. embassy. Prime Minister Hugh Shearer took a hardline initiative to repress Black Power by banning readings of the Nation of Islam, Malcolm X, and Stokely Carmichael in Jamaica. On October 15, 1968, when Rodney returned to Jamaica, the Jamaican government refused to let him step off the plane and banned him from the country altogether. The Rodney ban led to protest in downtown Trench Town by at least 2,000 people, including the UWI professor and students, the sufferers, and the Rastafarians. The protest quickly turned into an uprising, and protesters destroyed Western banks and local businesses. Other Jamaican politicians dealt differently with Rodney's influence over the black working class. In 1972, Michael Manley, by earning the black masses' admiration once mobilized by Rodney, won the election and became Prime Minister of Jamaica. Manley's election muted any criticism of Jamaican elites, and he upheld Rodney's ban from Jamaica. Although Manley stated Rodney could apply for a visa to stay in Jamaica, there was no guarantee any politician would eliminate the ban or allow him to re-enter the island as a resident.

Yet, Rodney's speeches on Black Power had a major influence on the Caribbean's black masses. In Guyana, Rodney's hometown, Cheddi, Jagan and Eusi Kwayana (formerly Sydney King), an Afro-Guyanese Black Power leader of the African Society for Cultural Relations with Africa (ASCRIA), mobilized college students and faculty members of the University of Guyana to march in support for Rodney's reentry into Jamaica. The protest march was to challenge the Prime Minister, Forbes Burnham's neglect of the Guyanese poor and to demand the nationalization of national resources, banks, and industries. Rodney would also attempt to influence the black masses to oppose capitalism, the topic for discussion in the next section.

Opposing Global Capitalism

After his ban from Jamaica, Rodney continued to use his scholarship to make a case for black working-class people and independent nations in the African world to separate themselves from the global capitalist system and adopt socialism as an alternative to governing their society. Since gaining independence, many African and Caribbean leaders and nations worked with Western nations and global corporations to bring industry and technology to their nations to improve the living conditions of people and raise profits from their natural resources. The participation of African and Caribbean leaders with Western nations in the global economy resulted in the exploitation of land and natural resources in the African world by U.S. and multinational corporations. Moreover, the living conditions of the poor black class and the working class declined. Rodney articulated such thoughts during the Black Power movement. He gave a speech entitled, "African History in the Service of Black Revolution," Rodney argued that neocolonialism created the conditions for the unevenness of social-economic development between Africa and Western nations. Rodney noted that, "The contemporary situation facing the African continent was the consequences of the neocolonial forces imposed on African society, just as colonialism in its mercantile and imperialist phases had earlier deformed traditional Africa." He contended that the international capitalist economy was historically complicit with black oppression because slavery, colonialism, and the restructuring of economies forced independent nations in Africa and the Caribbean to be financially dependent on the United States, former European colonial powers, and international businesses controlled by white westerners.

Africa and the Caribbean's dependency on the West were the consequences of restructuring the global economy. Following a monetary and fiscal conference held by the United Nations in Bretton Woods, New Hampshire, 44 diplomats approved the Bretton

Woods Agreement and created the International Monetary Fund (IMF) and the World Bank (WB). These institutions, along with multinational banks and corporations, transformed capitalism into an international system. Moreover, the General Agreement on Tariffs and Trade (GATT) made non-Western countries even more dependent on the U.S. and multinational corporations as they were beholden to international trade rules and regulations. Kwame Nkrumah, prime minister of Ghana, wrote *Neo-colonialism: The last stage of Imperialism* in 1965 and argued that global corporations and IMF/WB practices used their monetary policies to control the continent of Africa.

By 1972, Rodney's ideas of Africa's financial dependency on multinational corporations had crystallized to help him write the book, *How Europe Underdeveloped Africa*. Although Rodney focused on colonial Africa, he illustrates that Africa's dependency and underdevelopment after independence was a variant of European colonialism. Rodney argued that the exploitation of natural resources in African by European colonists led to Africa's underdevelopment and impoverishment. Rodney underscored that European banks and companies in colonial Africa did very little, or nothing, to offer credit to funds created by national resources. His description of the colonial relationship between European banks and the African people demonstrated how profoundly affected were the African poor and working classes. Rodney revealed that many Africans lived in towns with little to no "sanitation [or] electricity, and the medical services and schools were all under the control of European colonizers." Rodney drew parallels between colonialism and neocolonialism to allow the poor black and the working-class to understand their current conditions. He stated the following,

Today, in many African countries, the foreign ownership is still present. So long as foreigners own land, mines, factories, banks, insurance companies, means of transportation, newspapers, power stations, then for so long will the wealth of Africa flow outwards into the hands of those elements.

Under the control of multinational banks and corporations, the African continent and the Caribbean suffered from declining agriculture and a lack of technological advances, and the working-class and poor class suffered from high unemployment and displacement from their homes. Rodney's work helped the black working class to make the argument to govern society under socialism.

Rodney deployed a Marxist approach in *How Europe Underdeveloped Africa*, criticizing globalized capitalism as it kept Africa underdeveloped and dependent upon multinational corporations. By doing so, he openly advocated for the use of socialism as an alternative to capitalism. Rodney stated that capitalism hindered human social development on purpose. For an independent nation to develop, the working class must overthrow capitalism. Rodney used socialist practices in Asia and Eastern Europe as examples of how the working class should identify how socialism had changed people's living conditions in non-Western nations. He highlighted that socialist governments in Asia and Eastern Europe attempted to create policies that focused on the human needs of their citizens and eradicate unemployment instead of making profits for people in the ruling class. In addition, Rodney illustrated the differences between capitalistic and socialist nations. He pointed out that private corporations were only interested in gaining capital and would partially intervene in a country's affairs if it involved its inability to achieve profits. However, a nation governed under socialism takes control of the economy for the benefit of the working classes.

Rodney was not the first scholar-activist to advocate against the Caribbean participation in the global capitalist system; he had many inspirations. During his childhood in British Guiana, Edward and Pauline Rodney, Walter's parents, first exposed him to socialism and modeled what socialism activism would look like with their participation in the People's Progressive Party (PPP). Rodney had other examples of governing a society under socialism, including Prime Minister of British Guiana Cheddi Jagan, the Indian-Guyanese dentist and Marxist-Leninist. Walter Rodney viewed Jagan as the only Caribbean leader who "practiced a truly democratic system to benefit the poor and working-class people."

Rodney had many inspirations for adopting socialism other than his parents'. He became more involved in radical politics as an undergraduate student at Mona Campus of The University of the West Indies from 1960 to 1963. Rodney traveled to the Soviet Union and Cuba, and he joined the Young Socialist's Group on campus and was associated with the Student of Democratic Party. After Rodney graduated from UWI in 1963, he enrolled in the doctoral program in the School of African and Oriental Studies at the University of London. Rodney expanded more on his anti-capitalist ideals while attending books sessions with C.R.L. and Selma James, and while going to Marxist lectures at Hyde Park.

Another inspiration to Rodney was a group of Caribbean intellectuals who formed an organization called the New World Group, with the purpose of discussing strategies to develop the Caribbean and to curb the effects of dependency on multinational corporations and banks. Dr. Clive Thomas, a neo-Marxist scholar, argued that the international economic system created disparities between Western nations and the Caribbean; moreover, the legacy of exploitation through slavery and colonialism contributed to the Caribbean's dependency on U.S. and multinational corporations

Andre Gunder Frank's *Capitalism and Underdevelopment in Latin America* also inspired Rodney's conceptualization of the underdevelopment of the African world by the global capitalist economy. As Rupert Lewis asserted, "Rodney tried to do for Africa what the dependency theorists, especially Andre Gunder Frank, had done for Latin America." (Lewis, 1998, 69). In 1967, Frank argued that Western capitalist exploitation led to the underdevelopment of Latin American nations, and that centuries of economic development at the hands of the Spanish and Portugal elites and

European investors led to wealth in the urban centers of Brazil and Chile while non-elite and rural workers lacked social and financial stability. Frank's *Capitalism and Underdevelopment of Latin America* was a Marxist approach to the dependency theory concept. British economist Hans Wolfgang Schyler and Argentinian economist Raul Prebisch first created the dependency theory concept in 1949. Schyler and Prebisch argued that non-Western nations in need of financial aid and development were too impoverished to purchase sufficient goods from Western industrialized countries. Non-Western nations were forced to export their national resources to Western nations; in return, Western governments exported manufactured goods to non-Western societies, but exporting national resources was not enough to change the social and economic conditions of many non-Western nations. However, Frank's book became a model of how Rodney used his scholarship to convey, to the black working class, the damning effects of capitalism and the continued economic exploitation of black people as having their legacy in slavery and colonialism. *How Europe Underdeveloped Africa* educated the masses that neo-colonialism represented a continuum in the exploitation of independent nations in Africa and the Caribbean. Upon returning to his hometown in Georgetown, Guyana, Rodney would also advocate for the black working class to work together with working-class Indians to solve the poverty issue, the object of the next section.

Working Class Coalitions in Guyana

Upon his return to Guyana in 1974, Rodney and other working-class Afro -Guyanese people formed alliances with other working-class Indian Guyanese groups along class lines and formed an organization called the Working People's Alliance (WPA). This alliance as its name indicates was not founded along racial lines. The aim of the alliance was to improve the living conditions of the poor and working class people, both black and Indian. The WPA looked beyond their racial and ethnic differences to challenge the all-black

Guyanese Parliament led by Dictator Forbes Burnham.

Rodney's participation in the WPA inspired him to write the book titled, *A History of Guyanese Working Class People, 1881-1905*, a book published posthumously in 1981, and one year after Rodney's death. The book chronicled the history of black and Indian working-class people in nineteenth-century British Guiana. He argued that British colonial rule successfully maintained racial and economic control over the country by pitting black workers and Indian immigrants against each other through stereotypes and labor exploitation. Working class blacks and Indians in British Guiana were unable to form a coalition to address class issues and racial exploitation committed by British colonists. The relations between the two groups grew worse over time. Rodney used Indian immigration by British plantation owners to replace African workers to make his point. In the 1890s, when black plantation workers walked off the plantations and sugar factories to protest their low wages and working conditions, the British plantation owners supported the country immigrating workers from India to suppress the black workers' strike. Not only did the Indian immigration to British Guiana suppress the African labor strike but created racial divisions among black workers and newly arrived Indian immigrants.

Rodney attempted to use *A History of Guyanese Working People* to explain the contemporary racial tensions of blacks and Indians in Guyana as an offshoot from British colonialism and economic exploitation since nineteenth century British Guiana. Well into the twentieth century, aluminum companies, such as Reynolds, Aluminum Company of Canada, and Demerara (DEMBA), controlled land rights to extract bauxite. Also, the Booker McConnell Corporation controlled sugar plantations. As these corporations thrived in colonial British Guiana while working-class and poor blacks and Indians suffered from unemployment and low wages, especially in the sugar industry where racial tensions between blacks and Indians were high, and making it a *sine qua non* condition that unless one belonged to the elite class, there was little to no access to technology.

Such racial tensions had declined with the formation of the WPA, well before Rodney returned to Guyana. From 1974 up to his death in 1980, Rodney joined the WPA that consisted of the African Society for Cultural Relations with Independent Africa, the Indian Political Revolutionary Association, the Marxist-Leninist group called Working People Vanguard Party, and the Ratoun group, made up of radical intellectuals from the University of Guyana The WPA mobilized poor Guyanese of all races to challenge the dictatorship of President Forbes Burnham and his authoritarian political party, the People's National Congress (PNC). In an interview with Colin Prescord, Rodney stated that the Afro-Guyanese and Indian Guyanese founded the WPA to advocate for the Guyanese government to redistribute land and resources to poor blacks and Indians. He added that the WPA also raised the idea to educate the masses on socialism as a political strategy to the Guyanese masses to challenge Burnham's authoritarian regime. To Rodney, focusing on class issues instead of racial issues among Guyanese was to better Black and Indian relations. By forming a coalition on class, the working class could avoid racial divisions imposed by the Burnham dictatorship to maintain political influence and control.

While writing *A History of Guyana's Working Class*, Rodney wanted to inform both Black and Indian masses how to avoid the pitfalls of racial strife in working-class movements. He illustrated how the British colonial rule used labor issues, and racial differences to escalate racial conflicts between Blacks and Indians in nineteenth-century British Guiana. Rodney indicated that, "Africans opposed Indian indentured immigration in defense of their self-interest." African workers drafted a petition to halt Indian immigration because it would reduce employment among black workers, lower the wages of black workers, and increase their cost of living. Both black and Indian workers had engaged in smaller clashes on colonial plantations and near villages in Guyana. Yet, without organizing against British colonial rule, both black and Indian workers in Guyana suffered from poverty, inadequate health facilities, and labor exploitation throughout the late nineteenth century.

Rodney's inspiration for his analysis of how British colonialists sowed the seeds of racial divisions among black and Indian laborers came from his participation in the WPA and his more profound commitment to working-class movements, advocating for black working-class people to form alliances with Indians in Guyana. Rodney suggested to working-class Black and Indian Guyanese to find mutual interests in developing a working-class movement by using history. For example, in *A History of The Guyanese Working Class People, 1881-1905*, Rodney highlighted how Afro-Guyanese and Indian Guyanese could create a viable society through shared cultural practices. Black and Indian workers shared cultural traditions, including Indian immigrants adopting funeral rites and customs from black people. Black people adopted dietary habits such as rice and curry in their food, and blacks participating in the "Tadjah" ceremonies. Rodney uses such examples to show Afro-Guyanese that racial and class solidarity with Indian Guyanese was possible in the past and could be possible in their present situations. Such solidarity was present in 1953 when blacks and Indians in British Guyana alike supported Cheddi Jagan, an Indian-Guyanese dentist and Marxist-Leninist, in his election as prime minister of British Guyana and elected PPP politicians to 18 seats within British Guiana's Legislative Council. Despite the level of racial competitiveness between Afro Guyanese and Indian Guyanese to become middle class, mutual political solidarity between these two groups in Guyana did exist.

As a theoretician of Black Power and Marxist Pan-Africanism, Rodney was committed to working-class struggle and always extended it to Indians in the Caribbean. In his Black Power lectures in *The Grounding With My Brothers*, Rodney included Indians within the meaning of Black Power for the Caribbean to dismantle the notion that Black Power would work against their interests as many Caribbean Indians had feared. In his lecture titled "Black Power- Its Relevance to the West Indies," Rodney stated that Black Power in the

Caribbean referred primarily to Afro-Caribbeans and Indian Caribbeans. Moreover, Rodney described in detail the history of labor exploitation of Indians in the Caribbean in the 19th century for Afro-Caribbeans to understand the social-political climate of Indians in the contemporary Caribbean of the late 1960s. Rodney stated that British colonial rule wanted to continue to exploit labor upon the plantations in the islands in the British Caribbean after many blacks have left the plantations by immigrating people from India to work as indentured servants. Rodney illustrated that Indians were not problems to the black masses, only to white colonialism and capitalism. Indian immigrants only served white society's interest with whites bent on maintaining political and economic control over the Caribbean. Rodney continued to state that Indians viewed indentured servitude as a form of bondage and that British colonial rule and policies destroyed the "life and culture in 19th century India." He added that although many Indians and Africans have joined the white power structure in the Caribbean, the underlying reality is that poverty resides among Africans and Indians in the West Indies and that they are denied power.

By forming a working-class coalition among blacks and Indians in Guyana, the WPA attempted to mount a challenge to Forbes Burnham, the dictator President of Guyana, and his corrupt PNC political party. Challenging Burnham became a challenge in the beginning. Outside of Guyana, the African world viewed Forbes Burnham as a Black Nationalist leader, a socialist practitioner, and viewed Guyana as an example of Black Power with an all-black government. In reality, the C.I.A. and Great Britain propped up Burnham as British Guiana's premier and prime minister after the nation gained its independence. After nationalizing the foreign companies in Guyana, Burnham continued his intent to work with Western economic interests and evolved into a dictator, suppressing civil liberties and freedom of the press. Moreover, he escalated racial tensions between Afro- Guyanese and Indian Guyanese. When Walter Rodney reentered Guyana in 1974 to accept a faculty position at the University of Guyana, the Guyanese Parliament controlled the University's Board of Governors and rejected his appointment. Unable to earn a living in Guyana, Rodney used his voice as a member of the WPA to exposing the Burnham dictatorship to global media. For example, Rodney stated that Burnham's dictatorship nationalized all multinational corporations and banks in Guyana but never operated the economy through a joint partnership among the government and citizens. Instead, the Guyanese elites and the PNC denied the people the right to participate in these ventures when the Guyanese people challenged Burnham's policies.

By 1979, the WPA formed a political party and avoided racial conflicts by exposing Guyana's government corruption, and sought more equitable healthcare, public utilities, employment, and infrastructure. In his 1979 lecture, "People Power, No Dictator," he attempted to unite Guyana's working-class and challenge Forbes Burnham and the PNC for political power over the country. Rodney lectured for the national unity of all Guyanese people through empowering the working class. He stated, "Guyanese are no longer divided in their struggle for bread and justice. Indian sugar workers and African bauxite workers are making common cause. African lawyers and Indian lawyers both see the need for unity to restore the rule of law. Upon completing *A History of the Guyanese Working People*, the WPA suffered from political repression and its members were put in jail for protesting the Burnham dictatorship.

Conclusion

In 1980, Walter Rodney was assassinated in Guyana. Although his assassination cut his life short, he had made a significant contribution to the field of Africana history and activism on behalf of the working-class black people. Rodney used Black Power, socialism, and solidarity among the masses to advance people's living conditions in the African Diaspora. He did so while encouraging the Africans of the Diaspora to collaborate with other working-class people of non-

African descent. Using historical scholarship, Rodney successfully made historical connections between neocolonialism in independent nations in Africa and the Caribbean, with the historical legacy of slavery and colonialism. Rodney identified the role capitalism played in these situations. Rodney's books used history to express his strategy for working-class movements to improve upon their conditions. Over and above, Rodney provided knowledge of what liberation would mean and what it could be in the future for the Black man.

Bibliography
Books

Campbell, Horace, *Rasta, and Resistance, From Marcus Garvey To Walter Rodney*. Trenton, N.J.: African World Press, 1987.

Gunder, Frank Andre, *Capitalism and Underdevelopment in Latin America: Historical Studies of Chile and Brazil*. New York and London: Monthly Review Press, 1969.

Gibbons, Arnold, *The Legacy of Walter Rodney in Guyana and the Caribbean*. Lanham, Maryland: University Press of America, 2011.

Horne, Gerald, *Cold War in the Hot Zone: The United States Confronts Labor, and Independence Struggles in the British West Indies*. Philadelphia: Temple University Press, 2007.

Lewis, Rupert, *Walter Rodney's Intellectual And Political Thought*. (Detroit: Wayne State University, 1988).

Nkrumah, Kwame, *Neo-colonialism: The Last Stage of Imperialism*. London: Panaf Books, 1965.

Lavelle, Kathryn C. *Legislating International Organization: The U.S. Congress, the IMF, and the World Bank*. New York and Oxford: Oxford University Press, 2011.

Rodney, Walter, *The Grounding of My Brothers*. United Kingdom: Bogle-L'Ouverture Publications, 1969, reprinted in 1996.

_____, *How Europe Underdeveloped Africa*. Washington D.C.: Howard

University Press, 1972.

_____, *A History of The Guyanese Working People, 1881-1905*. Baltimore and London: John Hopkins University Press, 1981.

_____, Walter Rodney Speaks. Trenton, N.J., Africa World Press, 1990.

Rose, Euclid A. *Dependency and Socialism in the Modern Caribbean* (Oxford: Lexington Books, 2004.

Tignor, Robert L., *W. Arthur Lewis and the Birth of Development Economics* Trenton and London: Princeton University Press, 2006.

Articles and Book Chapters

Campbell, Trevor, "The Making of an Organic Intellectual: Walter Rodney (1942-1980), *Latin American Perspectives* 1(8) (1981): 49-63.

Lewis, Rupert, "Black Power in Jamaica in the 1960s," in *Black Power in the Caribbean*, Kate Quinn Ed., 53-75. Gainesville: University of Florida Press, 2012.

Marshall, Dan, "The New World Group of Dependency Scholars: Reflection of the Caribbean Avant-Garde Movement," in *The Companion of Development Studies*, 3rd edition, Vandana Desai and Robert B. Potter Eds., 114-128. New York City, NY: Routledge, 2014.

Palmer, Colin A., "Identity, Race, and Black Power in Independent Jamaica," in *The Modern Caribbean*, Franklin W. Knight and Colin Palmer eds., 111-128 (Chapel Hill and London: The University Press of North Carolina, 1989).

Rodney, Walter, "The Black Scholar Interviews: Walter Rodney," *The Black Scholar* 6(3) (November 1974): 38-47.

Quinn Kate, "Sitting on A Volcano: Black Power in Burnham's Guyana," in *Black Power in the Caribbean*, Kate Quinn Ed., 136-158. Gainesville: University of Florida Press, 2012.

West, Michael O., "Seeing Darkly: Guyana, Black Power, and Walter Rodney's Expulsion From Jamaica," *Small Axe* 25, (February 2008): 93-104.

_____, Walter Rodney and Black Power: Jamaican Intelligence and US Diplomacy," *African Journal of Criminology and Justice Studies* 1, (2) (November 2005), 1-50.

Government Reports and Online Sources

Blood and Fire: Jamaica's Political History, BBC Documentary, aired August 4, 2002, Accessed Online. Available at https://www.youtube.com/watch?v=ZO5lTRMg-Js.

Prebisch, Raul, *The Economic Development of Latin America and Its Principal Problems: Economic Commission for Latin America.* Lake Success, New York: United Nations Department of Economic Affairs, 1950, 1-59.

Rodney, Walter, "People's Power, No Dictator," (speech) 1979. Accessed Online, Available at https://www.marxists.org/subject/africa/rodneywalter/works/peoplespowernodictator.htm

Chapter 10

Youth Responses to Discriminatory Practices: College of The Virgin Islands' Black Cultural Organization, 1968-1974

Derick A. Hendricks

The young adult population of the U.S. Virgin Islands played a major role in dispersing ideas about Black Nationalism throughout the Virgin Islands. The Black Cultural Organization, a group composed mainly of young college students on the St. Thomas campus of the College of the Virgin Islands, was instrumental in conveying ideas about the self-help philosophical concept of Black Nationalism throughout the American territory. From 1968 to 1974, the body organized public activities, sponsored historical and cultural programs, which emphasized the achievements of African peoples, and published a newsletter called *The Black Revolutionary* to educate the Virgin Islanders and to develop greater community awareness of racism and its ramifications. Although they faced opposition from some residents in the community and faculty and staff on the campus, members of the organization, whose gender make up included both males and females, sought support from college instructors who could identify with students who were the descendants of Africans. In this chapter, I will discuss race relations at the College of the Virgin Islands during its early years and the significance and impact of the Black Cultural Organization as well as its repercussions within the wider U.S. Virgin Islands community.

The College of The Virgin Islands

The College of the Virgin Islands was established on March 16, 1962, by the Virgin Islands Legislature during the administration of

Governor Ralph Paiewonsky. A publicly funded, coeducational, liberal arts institution, its first campus was opened on St. Thomas in July 1963, on 175 acres donated by the U.S. government. In 1964, a second campus was established on St. Croix, on 130 acres also donated by the federal government. The St. Thomas institution began with eleven faculty and staff members and a class of forty-five full-time students studying for the Associate in Arts degrees. Later, Bachelor of Arts, Master's of Arts, Bachelor of Science, and the Associate in Science degrees were added. The college introduced the Associate in Science degree in 1967, and the Bachelor of Arts and the Bachelor of Science degrees were added in 1968. The Virgin Islands College commenced the Master's of Arts degree in 1973. (See Table 4.1)

On July 1, 1963, the Virgin Islands institution began as a two-year college with a full-time equivalency enrollment of one hundred twenty-seven. There were forty-five full-time and two hundred eighty-three part-time students. The next year, full-time enrollment had nearly doubled to eighty-two students, part-time enrollment was five hundred students (an increase of 77% from the previous year), and full-time equivalency had reached two hundred twenty-eight (an increase of 80% from the previous year). In 1965, the Board of Trustees authorized its expansion into a four-year college offering programs in liberal arts and teacher education. Five years later, in 1970, the college awarded its first baccalaureate degrees, and part-time enrollment was one thousand thirty. In 1975, there were one thousand four hundred fifty part-time students enrolled in the Virgin Islands College. The statistical information in Table 4.1 suggests that the general public had confidence in the institution and that the college fulfilled the needs of Virgin Islanders.

Table 4.1. Growth Indices of the College of the Virgin Islands 1963-78

Year	Full-Time Enrollment St. Thomas	Full-Time Enrollment St. Croix	Part-Time Enrollment (Head Count)	Graduate Enrollment	Full-Time Equivalency Enrollment	Graduates	Faculty and Staff
1963	45	-	283	-	127	-	11
1964	82	-	500	-	228	-	26
1965	128	-	600	-	310	11	34
1966	229	-	700	-	450	34	38
1967	275	-	1061	-	577	38	59
1968	332	-	800	-	637	60	70
1969	420	-	1005	-	746	57	87
1970	416	-	1030	-	820	74	94
1971	471	-	1173	-	913	106	100
1972	551	25	1200	-	976	108	88
1973	491	78	1094	35	1059	130	97
1974	467	72	1295	84	1150	109	105
1975	472	86	1450	71	1341	114	109
1976	491	87	1502	42	1212	113	104
1977	541	75	1445	58	1244	104	109

Note: (1) Enrollment statistics are for the fall semesters only. (2) Part-time, full-time equivalency, and graduate enrollments are for both the St. Thomas and St. Croix Campuses from 1964-65.

Source: Isaac Dookhan, "The Expansion of Higher Educational Opportunities in the United States Virgin Islands," *Journal of Negro Education* 50, No. 1 (Winter 1981): 22.

Very early in his administration, Governor Ralph Paiewonsky expressed his intention to establish a college in the U.S. Virgin Islands. In his inaugural address on April 5, 1961, he declared that one of the proposed college's major goals was to meet the need for higher education in the Virgin Islands. Paiewonsky and the institution's Board of Trustees anticipated that with the assistance of the federal government, the college would make higher education available to the people of the Virgin Islands and also to the residents of the entire Caribbean basin. Lawrence Wanlass, a white political scientist from Utah, was selected to be the college's first president. Prior to his appointment to the college's presidency, he had been serving as Assistant to the President at Sacramento State College in California. He remained in the St. Thomas position from January 1963 to November 1978. In the opinion of Historian Marilyn Krigger, Wanlass ' 15 year tenure at the institution was an important factor in shaping the destiny of the college. Krigger does not explain the reason for her position, nor does she cite any sources as evidence to corroborate her judgment of Wanlass. However, Paiewonsky, in his memoirs, stated that Wanlass was very influential in determining the character of the college because of the president's leadership, vision, and introduction of most of the instructional, research, and community-service functions at the college, which continued for several decades after the institution was established.

Even though there was overwhelming support for the idea of creating a college in the USVI, some individuals' opinions on the subject matter varied. This became evident in a 1961 survey that was taken two years before the institution opened its doors. Some respondents to the questionnaire regarding the need for a college displayed happiness and optimism to the notion of a college in the islands. Other respondents exhibited hostility and cynicism. The opinion questionnaire revealed that 85% of adult respondents and 96% of students were in favor of the institution's establishment. Supporters of the formation of a college in the territory felt that its existence would benefit residents who could not afford to obtain an education overseas. With the existence of a Virgin Islands college, the government anticipated that potential students would have an opportunity to remain in the territory and receive a quality college education.

During the 1920s and 1930s, a few of the more privileged families sent their children to colleges and universities in Puerto Rico and on the U.S. mainland. By the 1950s, approximately 20% of V.I. high school graduates attended these colleges and universities. (See Table 4.2)

Table 4.2. Virgin Islands High School Graduates Attending Institutions of Higher Education, 1955-60

Year	High School Graduates			Number of Enrolled in Colleges and Universities			Percent
	Males	Females	Total	Male	Females	Total	
1955	64	61	125	17	12	29	23.2
1956	75	78	153	17	12	29	19.0
1957	69	78	147	17	13	30	20.4
1958	96	81	177	15	14	29	16.4
1959	63	69	132	20	14	34	25.8
1960	62	52	114	17	11	28	24.6
Total	429	419	848	103	76	179	21.1

Source: Isaac Dookhan, "The Expansion of Higher Educational Opportunities in the United States Virgin Islands," *Journal of Negro Education* 50, No. 1 (Winter 1981): 20

Many islanders attended Historically Black Colleges and Universities (HBCUs), including Hampton Institute, Howard University, and Morgan State College. In order to increase the qualifications and proficiency of Virgin Islands teachers, in the late 1940s the local government began providing or securing funds from the U.S. federal government and the Ford Foundation to conduct on and off island courses by the Polytechnic Institute of Puerto Rico, by New York University in 1950 and 1951, by Hampton Institute from 1953 to 1959, and by the Catholic University of Puerto Rico from 1959 to 1961. The government-sponsored programs made it possible for Virgin Islanders who successfully completed the course work to obtain college credits. However, from 1953-1958, only 212 persons earned college credit hours from this program. Interestingly, while these students had the opportunity to enroll at the institution of their choice, they all attended Hampton Institute.

While some individuals may have been impressed by this academic achievement and used the small number of students who had earned college credits at Hampton to support the case against the need for establishing a college in the Virgin Islands, proponents continued to argue that a territorial institution was still needed because many Virgin Islanders who attended colleges and universities on the U.S. mainland did not return. Additionally, in order to enroll in a Puerto Rican post secondary school, potential students either had to know or be prepared to learn Spanish. Consequently, it was extremely difficult for a large percentage of Virgin Islanders to attend college.

Contrary to the overwhelming feeling or sentiments among Virgin Islanders that higher education was needed in the territory, individuals, such as Allen Grammar, a white man from the United States, expressed doubts about and held negative views on the idea. In a letter to the Virgin Islands *Daily News* on August 2, 1961, he wrote that the public school system and its facilities should first be improved before introducing higher education to the islands. Grammar argued that the timing was not right for a territorial college; it would cause inbreeding because the islands' public schools would provide most of the college bound students. He argued that there was the need to first of all establish a good trade school. In the newspaper opinion column, Grammar does not provide the reasons why he supported the trade school idea. However, his background makes his intentions suspicious and, therefore, it is reasonable to speculate that he may not have wanted a Virgin Islands college because black people could benefit from it. It should be noted that the Virgin Islands Government suspended Grammar's business license in the 1950s because of his alleged discriminatory practices.

Marilyn Krigger noted the views expressed by residents writing letters to the *Daily News*. They felt that the opponents of higher education in the territory were demonstrating the same racist and class prejudices of those who had historically rejected any institutions, which had the potential of benefiting the majority of the people. Nonetheless, the College of the Virgin Islands' founding marked a milestone in the history of the islands. It was an important achievement in expanding educational opportunities to Virgin Islanders. Finally, a public institution offered Virgin Islanders, especially those of African descent, affordable access to a college education.

According to Krigger, race was not a paramount concern during the first few years of the college's history. For the most part, the institution in its early years was not characterized by racial turmoil. However, by the late 1960s, tensions between blacks and whites intensified, and radical events began to take place at the college.

Several factors led to the amplification of tense race relations at the college. At the suggestion of Governor Paiewonsky, the institution entered into a contract with New York University in 1966, whereby Education majors would attend the college for two years, spend their junior year at New York University, and then return to the College of the Virgin Islands for their senior year. Many of the students who spent the 1966-1967 and 1967-1968 academic school years in New York were stunned by what they believed was blatant racism against black people there and were deeply affected by it.

Upon their return to the College of the Virgin Islands, they shared their experiences with their classmates and displayed their new race consciousness on the campus by wearing dashikis, Afros, referring to each other as "brother," and displaying other Black Power symbols and slogans.

In the meantime, the College of the Virgin Islands offered athletic scholarships in an effort to assemble a good basketball team. Krigger noted that many of these awards went to black students from the U.S. mainland, several of whom were adept at identifying the intricacies of racism. Once at the College of the Virgin Islands, they brought to the attention of their classmates certain issues concerning race, which, because of provincialism or lack of exposure, many black islanders were insensitive to, overlooked, or excused. In the opinion of Darwin Newton, who attended the College of the Virgin Islands from 1969 to 1973 and was Vice President of the Student Council in 1972, the Black Power oratory of the U.S. mainland students spread rapidly among the college's student body, and the black Americans' presence on the campus was pivotal in increasing the race awareness of many of the black islanders.

Another reason for the increased racial awareness at the college after the mid-1960s was the composition of the institution's faculty. The College of the Virgin Islands' hiring policy was to recruit and retain faculty members with the most impressive educational background, work experience, and commitment to teaching. The institution's guiding principle was also to give employment preference to "native" Virgin Islanders, or persons who had resided in the territory for a long period of time.

Although President Wanlass emphasized that he, along with the Board of Trustees, had always adhered to the college's hiring policy, the institution's recruitment guidelines resulted in a considerable majority of white Americans on the institution's faculty and professional staff. Krigger noted that in 1967, of the 39 people who comprised the faculty and staff, only 19 were black, and by 1975, of a teaching faculty of 64, only 22 were black. Meanwhile, the student body of the college was predominantly black. In addition to local blacks and whites and whites from the states, the college attracted a significant number of students from around the Caribbean, the majority of whom were black.

In May 1968, a letter to the St. Thomas *Home Journal* highlighted the issue of the college's faculty racial composition. Signed as "A Virgin Islander from CVI," the writer asked if there were black educators in the world, and if it was possible to identify at least one majority white college with a 98% black faculty. The author felt that additional black instructors were considered necessary because the vast majority of the college's teachers were insensitive and uncaring to the needs of the students of color. According to Krigger, this opinion letter marked the first public call for a change in the racial makeup of the college's faculty composition. The writer's argument that competent black educators existed and were desperately needed at the College of the Virgin Islands in order to build a rapport between students and teachers and to resolve the students of color identity crisis, suggests that ideas about black nationalism circulated at the college and attempts were being made to influence the wider Virgin Islands community. For instance, based on the testimony of Glen Davis, who graduated from the College of the Virgin Islands in 1972 and was a President of the Student Council, Professor Lezmore Emanuel taught the students to have pride in African history and Virgin Islands culture. (Lezmore Emanuel and his black consciousness activities on the college campus will be discussed in a subsequent section of this chapter).

One other alleged incident, which increased the race awareness among the college's students and concerned how the students and the teachers perceived each other was recalled by Davis. In his interview, he said that many black students felt that a particular white English professor was a racist. Davis stated that while he never received a letter grade of A on his research papers, his white classmate always did. To test his suspicions, Davis and his white cohort completed a class assignment. Prior to submitting their work,

Davis and his white classmate switched their names in the papers' headings. After the assignments were returned, Davis learned that he had received a C for his white classmate's paper, and that his white cohort was given an A for Davis' paper. He never revealed the identity of the white student. Of course, it would not be fair to judge the English professor based solely on Davis' memory. However, other factors, such as the white student's academic performance and Davis' class aptitude, would have to be seriously considered prior to making any final judgment on the instructor. However, it must be emphasized that Newton, Barbara Isaac (a College of the Virgin Islands student from 1967-1971), and others had the same feelings about a certain white Biology professor.

Additionally, many black students resented the practice of white faculty members complaining that they could not understand the accents and Creole speech of the black Caribbean students. According to Krigger, the demeanor of the instructors led to many students being reluctant to participate in class discussions. This may have led to many of the USVI and other British West Indian students receiving poor grades. The dialect barrier between the students and the teachers worsened faculty-student interpersonal relations and intensified tensions between the two groups.

In addition to the negative perception that some black students had of their white teachers and vice versa, the living arrangements for the faculty further heightened the students' alienation. The college provided on campus housing for both students and faculty. The main problem was that a fence separated the student housing and the faculty housing areas. In the opinions of Isaac and Davis, the students resented this barrier, which was referred to as the "Berlin Wall," because it was interpreted as a symbolic separation between the elite faculty and the students.

On the night of May 21, 1968, the Student Council President, Wanlass, and several students—blacks and whites—met to discuss the alleged problems at the College of the Virgin Islands, including racism, the indifferent attitude of the faculty, and the racial imbalance of the faculty. The local press reported that one hundred and fifty-five students signed a petition requesting that certain issues be addressed and reformed. One of the demands was that the college reinstate Registrar Gaylord Sprauve, a black person whose ancestry in the Virgin Islands dated back several generations. The administration refused to renew Sprauve's employment contract because of his alleged involvement in a domestic violence incident. However, many students felt that the Registrar was dismissed because he was very vocal about matters concerning race at the college. For instance, while speaking at the meeting, Sprauve declared, "What we need to emphasize is a black power structure." The following day, 22 May 1968, the local press published front page headlines and photos of the college's students tearing down the fence that separated the faculty and student housing areas. The newspaper reports were disseminated widely throughout the islands, and the community remained cognizant of the ongoing racial turmoil at the college. Shortly after the students' rebellion, President Wanlass met with the members of the Student Council and implemented administrative policies to resolve all of the student body's grievances. For instance, concerning the students' complaints about a proposed private beach for the faculty, Wanlass gave assurances that such an idea was never considered, and it would not be initiated in the future. Other minor irritants, such as the students' demands for washing machines and ironing boards, were settled. However, Registrar Gaylord Sprauve was not reinstated. Some people felt that his Black Power speech had caused Wanlass and other administration officials to become uncomfortable and apprehensive.

The Black Cultural Organization

Even though the Student Council of the College of the Virgin Islands represented the interests of the entire student body, some students believed that their grievances and views were not being adequately addressed by this campus organization. They believed that their complaints and perspectives could be represented more effectively by a Black Nationalist group. Eventually, these dissatisfied students formed the Black Cultural Organization.

It should be noted that prior to the establishment of the Black Cultural Organization, the College of the Virgin Islands Student Council helped to circulate views about Black Nationalism on and off the college's campus during the first half of 1968. For example, on the same day of the funeral of Dr. Martin Luther King Jr., Monday, April 9, 1968, St. Thomas witnessed a large student march to memorialize and celebrate the work of the American civil rights leader. The events were organized by the Student Council of the College of the Virgin Islands.

Once the college's black students began to exhibit more race consciousness, it became easier for them to identify subtle and overt forms of racism. In the opinions of former College of the Virgin Islands students Glen Davis, Darwin Newton, and Barbara Isaac, the Student Council made attempts to resolve problems the student body faced. For instance, they believed that the administration was not helpful because it was mainly white and insensitive to the needs of the majority black students. Davis, Newton, and Isaac recalled that some members of the teaching staff gave students the impression that they were not committed to teaching. Instead, they appeared to be mainly interested in only giving academic assignments and having a good time on the island's beaches. Whereas some students may have felt otherwise, perhaps, the cultural differences, which existed between the white instructors and the black students, reinforced the negative images that a considerable segment of the student body held towards the white administration. Nonetheless, what is certain is that at this time, there was no Black Nationalist organization on campus that could articulate ideas about racial empowerment among black students. However, this changed when the Black Cultural Organization was formed on the St. Thomas campus in the late spring of 1968.

According to Sele Adeyemi, there is very little written information about the organization. Even so, it was the first Black Nationalist focused organization to surface in the U.S. Virgin Islands. Isaac, one of the group's founding members, noted that its main objectives were to promote pride in the cultural heritage of blacks, to develop greater awareness of racism and its effects, and to encourage activities aimed at improving the educational, social, and economic status of African people. In recalling the early years of the organization, Isaac also discussed the goals of the group. She stated that a loosely organized group of black students, beginning in 1967, met frequently on the campus to discuss issues such as the plight of blacks in the Virgin Islands, black history, black pride, race identity, and racism. They contemplated the idea of setting aside one week in February to celebrate as Black History Week at the college. Isaac remembered that these gatherings included the call for a Black Nationalist student organization, and the meetings eventually led to the formation of the Black Cultural Organization in 1968.

The initial officers were Edwin G. Russell, Jr. (Prime Minister), Juan Garcia, Jr. (Minister of Information), Alexis Weatherhead (Minister of Communication), Andreas Tutein (Minister of Economic Affairs), Roy J. Davis (Minister of Defense), and Dianne Marshall (Minister of Education). Isaac noted that although there were only five female members of the organization, three of whom held offices, the girlfriends of the male members regularly associated with the group. Isaac also stated that she was drawn to the student organization because, based on her experiences, it did not practice gender inequality. Given that this is merely her opinion, and it is not clear why the female acquaintances of the group's male members never joined the organization, the fact that 50% of the top offices were held by women suggests that gender was not a divisive issue in the Black Cultural Organization.

Later, some members of the organization began to use Arabic names as a substitute for their given names. Krigger argued that this practice seriously restricted the ability of the organization to influence many people in the St. Thomas community, because, aside from the college campus, many of the islanders held conservative views. She asserted that the members' name policy was one of their counterproductive decisions, which made them appear to be foreign and threatening to both blacks and whites. Indeed, the Virgin Islands community was conservative and, therefore, it is not surprising that some residents would have difficulty identifying with Arabic names. However, a counter argument to Krigger's statement is that conservative islanders would have remained steadfast to their traditionalist views whether the Black Cultural Organization adopted Arabic names or not. The main concern of the organization was to increase the black consciousness of the islanders and to instill in them pride about their African/black history and culture. The group's policy of adopting titles usually associated with sovereign nations (for example "Prime Minister"), and its subsequent practice of using Arabic names was an expression of its independence. It is also likely that the students began to identify themselves with Arabic titles because of the increasing Islamic influence among African descended people at the time. During this period, elements of Islamic culture, including the activism of Malcolm X, were often integrated with various aspects of Black Nationalism. For instance, members of the United Caribbean Association – a Black Nationalist organization based in St. Croix – published an organ called, *UCA Speaks*, and this literary news instrument was modeled after the Nation of Islam's *Muhammad Speaks*. Thus, while a few decisions of the Black Cultural Organization were unpopular, as Krigger correctly noted, the organization did pique the interest of some islanders, and it made attempts to impact the social consciousness of the black residents.

In order to inform the U.S. Virgin Islands community, the Black Cultural Organization published a weekly newsletter entitled, *The Black Revolutionary*. The slogan, "The Time Has Come for All Black Students to Stop Talking and Start Acting," and a clenched fist, symbolizing Black unity and power, were displayed on its masthead. In volume 1, number 2 of the weekly newsletter, in an article entitled, "Black People Awaken!" Prime Minister Russell raised a few thought provoking questions concerning the socio-economic status quo of the islands. His message was for Virgin Islanders to stop being indifferent about racism in the islands and instead to be proactive and analytical about their surroundings. He asked:

Why do schools having 99% black students have honky principals? Why is there any argument over whether the governor should be black or white when 75% of the natives of the islands are black? Why does a black college have a 90% white administration and faculty? Why are we questioned in forming black organizations when white organizations are accepted and encouraged?

In the publication's same issue, Admed Ali, in an article entitled "Our New Breed," expressed satisfaction at observing that female students at the Charlotte Amalie High School were wearing Afro hair styles. He said that after speaking with many of the students, it was obvious to him that both the males and females were sincere about the liberation of black people and took pride in their African heritage. Admed concluded his essay by encouraging the students to continue to seek black unity and expressed optimism about the future of African people.

In the same edition of the paper, Mal'X Ali, in an article entitled, "Our Native Land," described the islands' political leaders as incompetent. Ali charged that because of their incompetence, the politicians had failed to educate the black islanders about economic self-sufficiency. As a result, blacks whose ancestry in the islands dated back several generations owned little land, and only white American settlers could afford to purchase comfortable house plots, which sold for exorbitant prices. A second point Ali discussed concerned the lack of blacks taking an active part in the islands' economy. He asserted that while many Virgin Islanders were satisfied with having a car, wearing nice clothes, and attending Milo dances, whites were gradually taking over the economy. Ali believed that whites dominated the businesses in the American territory entirely and urged blacks to start taking an active part and more interest in the economic affairs of the islands.

A third topic Ali mentioned in his article was the importance of black unity. He declared that in order to preserve the small amount of native land, which remained, it was imperative that the black islanders put aside their petty differences and unite for the common good of their community. Ali warned that only by blacks attaining solidarity in the islands could the further economic marginalization of "native" Virgin islanders by "continentals" be halted. Other themes in that issue dealt with black history, black identity, and racial discrimination.

As noted, many residents of the Virgin Islands held conservative views. Therefore, it is not hard to imagine that these islanders may have disagreed with the perspectives expressed in *The Black Revolutionary* because they may have felt that the essays were too radical. Based on this social and political climate, it is likely that the publication did not attract the favorable attention of everyone in the St. Thomas community or on the college campus. Nevertheless, *The Black Revolutionary*'s messages about the importance of blacks achieving solidarity and economic self-reliance suggest that the Black Cultural Organization made attempts to disseminate views about Black Nationalism throughout the Virgin Islands.

According to Isaac, the group's members invited individuals from the U.S. mainland to lecture during the Black History Week programs. She remembered that the presenters specialized in a variety of academic disciplines, including Music, Science, Drama, Social Science, and English. Presenters included Valerie Ward (Drama) and John Henrik Clarke (History). A large segment of the student body supported the events, and the St. Thomas community was encouraged regularly to attend the festivities. In a letter to the editor of the Virgin Islands *Daily News* on March 5, 1971, the writer expressed thanks and gratitude to the students of the College of the Virgin Islands for hosting the previous month's Black History Week activities. He stated that while the youths of the community had often been accused of immaturity and delinquency, the actions of the college students showed otherwise, and he congratulated them on their endeavor to restore dignity and respect to people of African origin. The writer also stated that he was fortunate to go to the college night after night and attend the programs, which covered various aspects of African culture, history, and their contributions to world civilization.

These events, intended to educate the masses of the people and to enhance the self-perception of the black islanders, were consistent with those held at other campuses where Virgin Islands students were in attendance. During the 1960s and the 1970s, Morgan State College and other HBCUs also held historical and cultural programs, which emphasized the achievements of African peoples. For example, in April 1968, the student newspaper of Morgan State College—*The Spokesman*—advertised that the week of Wednesday, April 24, 1968 to Wednesday, May 8, 1968, "Malcolm X's Program" would be held on the campus. The activities included lectures, panel discussions, and audio and visual presentations, regarding the legacy of Malcolm X and the Civil Rights Movement.

On other occasions the Black Cultural Organization sometimes initiated orderly street demonstrations in St. Thomas. For example, the organization led a small group of marchers in front of Government House in 1968 and demanded that the governor reject the recommendations of a government commission, which was investigating claims of racial discrimination against the Hertz Car Rental Agency. The members also led marches in opposition to the war in Vietnam. Davis, a member of the Black Cultural Organization, recalled that its members and followers carried anti-war signs and distributed literature as they demonstrated in front of the Draft Board, which was located in St. Thomas. In the opinion of Isaac, the organization's members were the organizers of most anti-Vietnam War protests in St. Thomas, and if the group was not sponsoring a lecture presentation in a particular week, then the members were marching in Main Street against the war in Vietnam or for some other social cause.

It was also common for HBCU students on the mainland to express their opposition to U.S. involvement in Vietnam. An April 1968 issue of *The Spokesman* stated that it was anticipated that on Friday, April 26, 1968, thousands of black students throughout the United States would stay out of classes as part of a one-day International Student Strike against the Vietnam War and the Draft. The following year, an issue of *The Spokesman* reported that Morgan's students actively supported the college's Vietnam Moratorium in October 1969. Virgin Islands students, who were enrolled at Morgan State, took part in both anti-war protests and communicated their experiences with the territorial residents. The students' influence helped to increase the social activism of the islanders and facilitated Virgin Islanders' participation in the international solidarity movement against the war in Vietnam.

As noted, dozens of Virgin Islanders attended Morgan State College and other HBCUs beginning in the 1940s and continuing thereafter for several decades. Lauren Larsen, who hailed from St. Croix, obtained his BA in History from Morgan State College in 1973. In 1975, he obtained an MA in History from Morgan. In an interview with this writer, Larsen recalled participating in a student demonstration against the war in Vietnam on the college campus. He noted that some of his friends attended the College of the Virgin Islands at the time, and he shared his U.S. mainland experiences with these individuals. He also remembered that many of these students were members of the United Caribbean Association and the Black Cultural Organization. Larsen is another example of a Virgin Islander who, after attending Morgan State College and sharing his experiences, influenced the black consciousness and social activism of the territorial islanders.

One Virgin Islander who was very influential in the anti-Vietnam War Movement was Valentine Penha. Following his service in the U.S. Air Force from 1960-1964, Penha attended the College of the Virgin Islands and graduated in 1968 with an Associate of Arts in Liberal

272

Arts and a Bachelor of Arts in Biology. Isaac recalled that although he was not a College of the Virgin Islands student, when the Black Cultural Organization was organized, Penha eventually became affiliated with the group and actively participated in many community activities. According to Adeyemi, Penha was a leading figure in the anti-Vietnam War Draft and Resistance Movement, and the activist gave a memorable speech at one of the territory's largest anti-Vietnam War demonstrations, which took place in St. Thomas' Roosevelt Park in 1969 on Veterans Day.

In 1969, the Virgin Islands had been a colony of the United States for little more than a half a century. Many islanders held a strong sense of patriotism and duty to the United States. Based on the social and political climate of the time, it would not be hard to imagine, then, that Penha and other Black Cultural Organization members may have faced a difficult task in publicly opposing U.S. involvement in the Vietnam War. Nonetheless, their campaigns to persuade Virgin Islanders to think progressively and in solidarity with oppressed nonwhite peoples around the world suggest that the student group made attempts to influence the political and social culture of the American territory. Perhaps, Penha developed his assertiveness and oratorical skills in response to the bigotry and discrimination that he confronted in the U.S. military. Upon his discharge from the U.S. Air Force, he apparently used his newly acquired oratorical skills in the anti-war movement and in other social matters.

As mentioned earlier, in addition to Virgin Islanders who were enrolled at Morgan and other HBCUs participating in anti-Vietnam War demonstrations, they also attended historical and cultural programs. Thereafter, they shared their experiences with their friends and family in the islands. The students' influence helped to increase the race consciousness of the insular residents. Oswin Sewer, who hailed from St. John, obtained a Bachelor of Arts degree in Sociology and Anthropology from Morgan State College in 1970. In an interview with this writer, Sewer recalled participating in an anti-Vietnam War student demonstration and in black power activities on the college campus. In the meantime, he shared his U.S. mainland experiences with his friends and family in the Virgin Islands. He noted that following his graduation from Morgan in 1970, he returned to St. John and became involved in the Independent Citizens Movement and other community activities. The Independent Citizens Movement is a political party whose members had withdrawn from the local Democratic Party. Sewer is another example of a Virgin islander who, after attending Morgan State College and sharing his experiences, influenced the black consciousness and social activism of the territorial islanders.

Back in St. Thomas in February 1972, an advertisement in the *Home Journal* announced that the annual Black History Week, sponsored by the Black Cultural Organization, would be held at the College of the Virgin Islands from Sunday, February 20, 1972, through Saturday, February 26. An invitation was extended to the entire community to participate in the week's activities. The newspaper article stated that many scholars were sought by the college to lecture on various topics for the occasion, including ideas and issues specifically pertinent to black people and various aspects of the culture and history of the Virgin Islands. The advertisement ended with the claim that the students had invested much time and effort in producing a diverse program and reassured the residents of St. Thomas that they would receive valuable information if they attended any of the sessions.

Isaac recalled that members of the Black Cultural Organization traveled to St. Croix to attend functions of the United Caribbean Association of Black People, and the affiliates of the association made the trip to St. Thomas to attend programs of the Black Cultural Organization. The organization also held meetings regularly on the campus of the College of the Virgin Islands. According to Krigger, in addition to George Applewhite, who was the group's faculty advisor, a few other members of the institution's faculty and staff who shared the students' concerns about racism and its effects in the USVI attended meetings of the organization. Nevertheless, as previously mentioned, the student organization did have its opponents. For instance, Krigger noted that Robert Moss, the manager of St. Thomas television station WBNB, used the TV station as a platform to condemn the group. Following the appearance of three Black Cultural Organization members on a television program, letters to the local press denounced their Afro hairstyle and their declaration that black people should be in command of the insular economy since they formed the majority in the Virgin Islands.

Given that members of the student group participated in community activities and academic programs, why would any person or interest group oppose them? Was the TV manager correct in his criticism of the organization's members, or was he simply expressing the views of those residents who rejected any institution of higher learning in the Virgin Islands whose student body was composed of independently thinking students, especially those of African descent? While the answers to these questions are not definitive and are debatable, the socio-political history of the islands suggests the latter.

Furthermore, what was the relevance of the letter writers' admonition of the student activists' Afro hairdo? Would the students' outward appearance have been the target of negative comments if the length of their hair was short? It is probable that a non-Afro hairdo would not have been condemned because such a hairstyle would have been considered acceptable by the mainstream. That is, it would have conformed to norms of the conservative whites and blacks in the Virgin Islands. On the contrary, the members' Afro hairstyle was a political statement, demonstrating the ideals of Black Nationalism and rejecting the values of the status quo. By advocating for the ownership of the American territory's economic operations by black Virgin Islanders, the members of the Black Cultural Organization were in reality expressing economic nationalism, which is a manifestation of Black Nationalism. Despite the actions of their detractors, the community's supportive response to the student activists' Black History Week programs, their television appearances to promote black self-sufficiency, and their active participation in civil rights demonstrations in the general public suggest that the group made attempts to influence the political, social, and economic climate of St. Thomians.

An article in the January 23, 1969 issue of *Viewpoint: the Student Publication of the College of the Virgin Islands* stated that beginning in the Fall 1969 semester, the college would offer a course in Afro-American Culture and History. This new course, then, would coincide with the existing Caribbean History course to form a partial Black Studies program. The student writer noted that for the past couple of years, there seemed to have been unrest among black and white students for more black courses to reflect the cultural reality of the Virgin Islands. The author noted that with about 90% black students, the institution was definitely a black college.

Krigger noted that one of the Black Cultural Organization's projects was a campaign for a Black Studies program to be put in place at the College of the Virgin Islands. Partly as a result of student pressure, in 1970 the college hired Lezmore Emanuel, a black person who was born on October 8, 1927 in the Bronx, New York, but whose family was from St. Thomas. In the first half of the twentieth century, it was a common practice for expecting Virgin Islands females to travel to the mainland United States, primarily New York, for natal care. Thereafter, the offspring was reared in the islands and occasionally visited relatives in the states who migrated there to live, work, and persevere. Perhaps, after being exposed to racism and social activism in the mainland United States, these young men and women shared their experiences with their acquaintances in the Virgin Islands and subsequently influenced the race consciousness of the territorial residents. One of the pioneering black consciousness influences on the campus of the College of the Virgin Islands was Lezmore Emanuel, who formulated a Black Studies program in the early 1970s.

Lezmore Emanuel and His Black Consciousness Activities in the U.S. Virgin Islands

On June 5, 1970 Emanuel became the first graduate of the interdisciplinary Ph.D. in African Studies and Research from Howard University. During the time of his studies on the Howard campus in the late 1960s, there were many Black Power activities. Student demonstrations about the need for campus reform and protests targeting a college administration perceived as autocratic and indifferent culminated in the closing of Howard in the spring of 1968 and again in the spring of 1969. As a result of the demands of these demonstrations, disciplines in African Religion, Philosophy, History, Culture, Anthropology, Genetics, and Geography were incorporated into a single approach in the study of the African experience in the New World and in Africa. Upon receiving his Ph.D., Emanuel returned to the Virgin Islands and was employed by the College of the Virgin Islands as an Associate Professor of Social Sciences teaching Sociology, African History, and African Anthropology. At the institution, he established a Black Studies program of 51 credits while adding nine new courses to the syllabus. Apparently, Emanuel's tenure as a graduate student at Howard University made him aware of the need to fill what he felt was an academic void at the College of the Virgin Islands. Consequently, the knowledge Emanuel obtained when he was enrolled in Howard University provided inspiration for his campaign to create a Black Studies program at the College of the Virgin Islands. Isaac, another former student of Emanuel, recalled that the college major was designed in a manner whereby its graduates could specialize in a variety of fields, such as Law, Health, Science, and Education.

Krigger noted that Emanuel actively participated in several social movements in the community, most of which promoted the African cultural heritage and sought the preservation of Virgin Islands culture in opposition to its destruction by the U.S. way of life. He was asked regularly to speak by diverse community groups on themes related to Virgin Islands culture and Virgin Islands English Creole, which he advocated should be used in schools to teach Standard English. Emanuel, who participated in anti-Vietnam War marches and other demonstrations in opposition to the war, was also an influential personality in the Black Cultural Organization. When he was enrolled at Howard University, this institution's students supported the college's Vietnam Moratorium in October 1969.

Besides being an educator, he was respected by Virgin Islanders as a historian, poet, calypsonian, and author. In an effort to preserve the fading Virgin Islands folklore and to present to the masses some aspects of African heritage fundamentals, Emanuel and his supporters sponsored a series of Anansi story telling sessions. The Anansi story is the traditional folklore of the U.S. Virgin Islands. The stories originated in West Africa, and enslaved Africans introduced them to the islands. Thereafter, African descended Virgin Islanders handed down the tales from one generation to the next. Anansi, who is often symbolized as a spider, is the main character of the folklore. Although Anansi is abused and exploited by stronger animals, the character eventually tricks its enemies and survives at the end of the day. Anansi is symbolic of black Virgin Islanders who have been oppressed and marginalized by the existing power structure. The stories are told to reassure the islanders of African descent that they, like Anansi, will one day be victorious in the struggle for their liberation. Davis remembered that the public gatherings were sometimes held at Brewers Bay—one of St. Thomas' most popular beaches—and that the sessions were very popular in the community.

According to an FBI document and Mario Moorhead, the founder of the United Caribbean Association, Lezmore Emanuel was the coordinator of the United People Party in St. Thomas. In early 1974, he made several television appearances on behalf of the United People Party and during these taped messages, he discussed the strength of the political party and an upcoming party convention. An FBI source reported that Emanuel announced that the political gathering would be in preparation for the Fall election, during which candidates would be selected to run on the United People Party's banner. However, the report was ambiguous. The informant stated that many persons interested in the political affairs of the Virgin Islands felt that the United People Party had greater support and appeal than it was first thought. However, the informant concluded that the party would have little chance of obtaining minimum numerical strength to qualify for the November 1974 elections. The same individual felt that Emanuel was the only person who could appear on the party ticket as a viable gubernatorial candidate, and he could generate a large following among the territory's young people, especially College of the Virgin Islands students, to vote for the party. In spite of the uncertainties and vagueness of the agency's report on Emanuel, the fact that he was being watched closely by the FBI suggests that his activities had drawn the attention of the federal agency, and his presence had increased the political consciousness of Virgin Islanders.

According to Krigger and others, Emanuel was very popular among some College of the Virgin Islands students and was named "Professor of the Year" for the 1970-71 school year. Nevertheless, he was fired from his teaching post at the college in 1973. The Chairperson of the Social Sciences Division, a white American, recommended that Emanuel should be given a terminal contract for the following school year (1973-1974). The head of the Division based his decision on Emanuel's teaching performance as perceived by some faculty members and persons in the community, poorly organized and repetitious courses, lateness in submitting book orders and grades and having given out an excessive number of above average grades. Emanuel stated publicly that the College of the Virgin Islands terminated his employment because the administration believed him to be the source of racial and academic tension while in the employ of the college. He told a news reporter for the *Home Journal* that he believed he was being harassed by the administration because of his outspokenness and activism against racism and on behalf of the recognition and preservation of Virgin

Islands culture.

Perhaps, Emanuel's allegations were reasonable because activists who were considered a threat to the status quo were repeatedly harassed by representatives of the existing power structure in other areas of the world. African American Studies Professor Farah Jasmine Griffin exposed the practice of the institutional harassment of dissenters in an essay when she mentioned that Black Power activist Angela Davis was placed on the FBI's ten most wanted list in 1970.

Newton recalled that after Emanuel had informed some students of his evaluation, the Student Council held a meeting, and its leadership invited President Wanlass to attend, but the President did not appear at the gathering. Two days later, on the morning of Monday, December 11, 1972, acting upon a decision by the Student Council, several students held a quiet sit-in demonstration at the college's library to protest the poor evaluation given to Emanuel. Newton, who participated in the occupation of the building, noted that because the end of the semester exams were rapidly approaching, the students assembled peacefully in the library; studied for their examinations; and refused to leave the building, until they had met with the President of the college. After officers of the V.I. The Police Department made a few attempts to enter the library, the students secured themselves in the basement. Several hours later, the officers removed the doors, threw tear gas into the basement, and around 9:30 pm dragged the students out of the building.

From the viewpoint of the police officers, it was inconsequential that the students were assembled peacefully and were not causing a riot. The dissenters' refusal to abide by the mandates of the college administration was reason enough for the officers to take action. The demonstration at the library was similar in nature to the student sit-ins, which had taken place at U.S. college campuses during the U.S. Civil Rights Movement. On March 23, 1968, the front page of the Baltimore *Afro American* carried a headline of a student demonstration at Howard University and included a photograph of students occupying its administration building. The students were demanding the resignation of President James Nabrit and other university officials. It is probable that Virgin Islanders who were enrolled at Howard University may have participated in the student protest and shared their experiences with residents of the Virgin Islands. The information from the Howard University Virgin Islands students may have been a factor in subsequently influencing the activism of the students of the College of the Virgin Islands.

Thirty-one College of the Virgin Islands students were suspended for their role in the library demonstration, and three were taken to the local police station. They were eventually released on bond. Subsequently, nine persons were arrested, but pursuant to the request of college, the charges were later dropped by the Department of Law. Nonetheless, the nine students who were arrested for their part in the demonstration at the library later filed suit and charged the college President, Wanlass, and Dean Arthur Richards with false arrest, false imprisonment, and deprivation of federal civil rights. The nine plaintiffs each asked for judgments of $25,000.00 in the suit against Wanlass and Richards and $50,000.00 each from the college. On July 31, 1975, Judge Warren Young ruled in favor of the college.

The response of the local police officers to the student sit-in warrants examination because the officers' response was consistent with the administration's treatment of Emanuel and the harassment of other outspoken activists. In other words, as a result of this trend of governments' alleged illegal persecution of private citizens, the police officers' action seems to have been influenced by ulterior motives. The feeling of suspicion and ambivalence surrounding the authority's reaction to the student demonstration was evident in the community. Some residents felt that the police action was needed to quickly end the standoff because final examinations had commenced during the same week of the protest, and the university could not allow students, especially graduating seniors, to have their exams delayed. However, some observers interpreted the entire incident as a racial issue and felt that the students were justified in their actions

281

because the administration was not responsive to their grievances. Although it is not definitely known how most islanders felt about the student demonstration, both sentiments were expressed in a St. Thomas *Home Journal* opinion column.

Was the reaction of the law enforcement personnel actually necessary, or was it excessive? While it was important for the scheduled final examinations to take place on time, the extended civil disobedient actions of the students could not be prolonged, but it appears that the level of police force used was both premature and excessive. Krigger and Newton noted that the Chairman of the Legislature's Committee on Education—Athniel Ottley—had been in the library trying to convince the demonstrators to leave the building. Dr. Herbert Hoover, a black American College of the Virgin Islands Education professor, had also gone to the library because he felt that the presence of a faculty member might prevent the outbreak of violence. Conversely, just as Ottley was about to persuade the students to leave, the officers fired their final round of tear gas into the building.

The students who took part in the library sit-in were symbolic of that segment of Virgin Islands society that refused to abide by the status quo. Their association with and fondness for Emanuel, a Virgin Islands cultural preservationist and a black nationalist, made them an opponent of that sector of the society, which represented conservative status quo views in the islands. It is apparent that the local police officers were used as an instrument of the school administration to restore order on the campus.

Was the termination of Emanuel's contract warranted, or was he unfairly targeted by the college administration because of his outspokenness on particular matters? Perhaps, the answer is yes to both questions. Seemingly, the head of the Social Sciences Division, a white American, presented evidence to the department's annual evaluation committee that Emanuel's performance, or lack thereof, did not meet the requisite job requirements as set forth in the college for its faculty. Additionally, the division's director had recommended that Emanuel be given a terminal contract for the following school year (1973-1974). However, his involvement in Black Nationalist activities, especially those on the campus, resulted in exactly what the Wanlass Administration attempted to prevent, a civil disobedient act orchestrated and carried out by members of the student body. While Emanuel made important contributions to the College of the Virgin Islands, he simultaneously neglected his job duties. As a result of his flawed classroom performance, the college administration was given an opportunity to end his contractual relationship with the institution.

Was Emanuel sincere in his efforts to preserve Virgin Islands culture and to educate black Virgin Islanders about their African heritage? Was he seeking political office to empower the masses of people, or did he become involved in politics solely to advance his own self-gratification? The evidence suggests that his motives were based on the former. As noted, in 1970, he became the first person to acquire an interdisciplinary Ph.D. in African Studies from Howard University. Shortly thereafter, he was employed at the College of the Virgin Islands, and he subsequently started a Black Studies program there. It seems obvious that Emanuel's return to the U.S. Virgin Islands and to a teaching position at the College of the Virgin Islands was motivated by his desire to contribute to the betterment of the Virgin Islands. Additionally, despite his efforts to re-educate the islanders, he had many detractors who felt that he and his wife (Phyllis Emanuel-a teacher at the Wayne Aspinall Junior High School who collaborated with him in many community events) were preaching hate and intensifying racial tensions in the islands.

However, the belief that the Emanuels were responsible for escalating negative race relations in the Virgin Islands was suspect. Their involvement with cultural and historical activities appears not to have been geared towards fanning the flames of an already tense situation. Instead, the Emanuels were apparently teaching their fellow black islanders to have pride in their heritage and culture. Phyllis Emanuel accurately pointed out the limitation of their critics' argument when she wrote, "It seems to be the general attitude that

283

if a black person teaches other black persons about their origins, their cultural achievements, and their destiny, that he is accused of teaching hatred." Phyllis Emanuel's feelings may have been influenced by the precedent of black consciousness advocates being accused of spreading bigotry. For instance, in April 1968, the Baltimore *Afro American* reported on the legal troubles of H. Rap Brown, former Chairman of the Civil Rights organization, The Student Nonviolent Coordinating Committee, and a Black Power advocate. As a result, perhaps, Phyllis Emanuel's claims were rational. Given the several obstacles and challenges that Emanuel and his wife faced in the territory, he could have returned to the U.S. mainland to pursue a lucrative and scholarly career. Instead, he remained in the islands and continued his agenda of educating the masses and making attempts to preserve Virgin Islands culture. Who were the critics of the Emanuels, and what did they represent? Based on the community events in which the professor and his wife were involved, it would appear that their adversaries, both blacks and whites, opposed them to maintain the interests of the existing power structure.

Reactions to Lezmore Emanuel's influence in the Virgin Islands varied greatly. On the one hand, he was popular among some students, and they commended him for his teaching performance. On the other hand, he received a poor evaluation and was given a terminal contract by the administration. Although some individuals in the community and on the college campus expressed displeasure with his teaching methodologies and the content of his instructions, Emanuel was still a well-respected figure in the territory. The reaction of the Virgin Islands Police Department to the student sit-in, and the response of the college administration and some students to Emanuel suggest that his influence had impacted the self-perception of some St. Thomians, and how students felt about the island's socio-political status quo.

Emanuel was very influential among the black students of the college. By educating them about African and Virgin Islands history and culture, he instilled in them a sense of pride in their African heritage. He helped them to reclaim their voice and to develop a sense of identity. Emanuel's formulation of the Black Studies program at the College of the Virgin Islands was an academic and cultural milestone in the islands. The academic concentration was for, by, and about African people. In addition, the 1972 occupation of the library, which was an act of black solidarity and self-determination, proposes and suggests strongly that the students were acting out the principles of black consciousness and Black Nationalism.

During the final years of the Black Cultural Organization's existence, around 1974-1975, members of the organization held study group-reading sessions on a regular basis. The literature centered primarily on issues directly related to the Black Power Movement. Barbara Isaac recalled that on Saturdays, members would travel to Estate Adrian on St. John where they would debate themes related to the history and culture of African peoples. Organization members had always looked to the United States for inspiration by reading and discussing books on Malcolm X, the Black Panther Party, Angela Davis, Elridge Cleaver, the Nation of Islam, and other themes/individuals related to the Black Power Movement in the United States.

According to Barbara Isaac, in the mid-nineteen seventies after graduation, former Black Cultural Organization members organized "The Edward Wilmoth Blyden Society" off campus and continued to educate the African people of the Virgin Islands about the importance of having pride in their own black history and culture. The members felt that by naming the organization after a St. Thomian, the black islanders' interest may have been piqued and their black consciousness elevated to the point where they would either want to join the group or learn more about African history and culture. In addition to sponsoring black consciousness lectures and programs, such as Kwanza, the organization's members read and debated books, which focused on blacks throughout the African diaspora. This included works by or about Walter Rodney, Kwame

Nkrumah, Kathleen Cleaver, Maurice Bishop, John Henrik Clarke, and Chancellor Williams.

It is not surprising that the graduate students named the organization after Edward W. Blyden. Blyden (1832-1912) was born in St. Thomas, Danish West Indies and became one of the most important Black Nationalist leaders of the nineteenth century. In 1851, he relocated to Liberia and held various positions there, including professor and president at Liberia College, Secretary of State, and Minister to England. A pioneer African nationalist and pan-Africanist, Blyden devoted his life and work to proclaiming the status and dignity of the black race and to re-establishing African dominance on the continent of Africa. Perhaps, the organization was named in Blyden's honor because he was a St. Thomian who emphasized black pride, struggled for the liberation of Africa, and worked to enhance the lives of African peoples.

Conclusion

The Black Cultural Organization was established by college students on the St. Thomas campus of the College of the Virgin Islands in 1968. The group was the first black consciousness organization to emerge in the U.S. Virgin Islands. In order to educate Virgin Islanders and to increase the society's responsiveness to racism and its effects, from 1968 to 1974, its members held public activities and sponsored educational programs, which highlighted the importance of African/black history and culture. The group's affiliates published an organ called *The Black Revolutionary* to help accomplish its program of educating the public and to addressing social issues confronting the community.

Although the Black Cultural Organization was organized on the St. Thomas campus of the College of the Virgin Islands, many of its members and supporters were residents of St. Croix. Ministers Russell, Garcia, Davis, and Tutein were from St. Croix. Notwithstanding the struggles and achievements of St. Thomians, it must be emphasized that, historically, Crucians – "natives"/residents of St. Croix-have been very outspoken and pro-active on issues related to social injustice and economic inequality. Moreover, it was very common for Crucian students who attended the St. Thomas campus of the College of the Virgin Islands to distribute copies of *UCA Speaks* on the campus and throughout St. Thomas. Isaac and Davis recalled that many of their classmates were Crucians who often circulated *UCA Speaks* on the college campus. The actions by the students suggest that they were demonstrating black solidarity and making concerted efforts to bring to fruition the ideals of Black Nationalism.

Index

117, 119, 120, 126, 148, 248, 256, 258

Gunder Frank, Andre, 279

H

Habermas, Jürgen, 235, 238, 239, 265

Habesha, 4, 6, 7, 14, 22-28

Habib Benglia, 105

Habitus, 236, 247

Hagood, Taylor, 183, 186

Hailu, Gebreyesus, xv-xvii, 1-32

Haiti, 116, 164, 171, 182, 187

Hall, Edward T., 10, 11, 32

Hampton, R., 121, 122, 130

Hanna, J. L., 111, 121, 130

Harlem, Renaissance, 77, 107, 110, 158, 161, 165, 175, 182, 186, 187

Harlow, Barbara, 216, 218, 233

Harriet, Jacobs, xxii, 213-216, 218-221, 229, 232

Hayes, Rutherford B., 200

Hazlitt, William, 164, 187

HBCU, 260, 271-273

Hemingway, Ernest, 166

Heselgrave, D., 84, 91

Homer, 177

hooks, bell, 1, 32, 114

Hoover, Herbert, 282

Houphouet-Boigny, Félix, 102

Hubert, Maga, 102

Huey, Steve, 96

Hugh Shearer, 240-241

Hughes, Langston, 159

Hurston, Zora Neale, xv, xx, xxi, xxii, 157-189, 213-216, 218, 219, 223, 229, 232

I

IMF, 243, 252

India, 43, 250

Izsidore, Sandra, 77, 84, 89, 91

J

Jagan, Cheddi, 241, 245, 249

Jamaica, xxiii, 164, 171, 182, 187, 236-242, 253, 254

Jensen, Loucynda, 213, 214, 233

Jim Crow, 200, 204

Jing, Thomas, xviii, xix, 69, 95, 121, 130

Joyce Cary, 60

Juang, R. M., 109, 112, 115, 117, 118, 130

K

Kanty, Stella, 177

www.ingramcontent.com/pod-product-compliance
Lightning Source LLC
Chambersburg PA
CBHW022137020426
42334CB00015B/939